I0823593

REALM OF THE HEART

BY JI QI

Published by
LID Publishing
An imprint of LID Business Media Ltd.
LABS House, 15–19 Bloomsbury Way,
London, WC1A 2TH, UK

info@lidpublishing.com
www.lidpublishing.com

A member of:

businesspublishersroundtable.com

Printed in China
ISBN: 978-1-918215-17-5
ISBN: 978-1-918215-18-2 (ebook)

Cover and page design: Caroline Li

REALM OF THE HEART

BY JI QI

MADRID | MEXICO CITY | LONDON
BUENOS AIRES | BOGOTA | SHANGHAI

FOREWORD

In an age of relentless scrolling and bite-sized video, the written word often feels like a fading luxury. Yet, if we are to distinguish ourselves from the animal kingdom, we must look to our unique ability to project ideas across vast distances and generations. Language and literacy allow us to bypass individual biological limits, weaving the social fabrics that drive human progress.

While images and spoken words may offer instant gratification and wider reach, they often lack the staying power of the pen. For depth, permanence and intellectual rigour, writing remains the gold standard. There is a reason the ancients paired the 'reading of ten thousand books' with 'travelling ten thousand miles.' They understood that to truly grasp the complexities of our world, intellectual exploration is just as vital as physical experience.

Throughout my entrepreneurial career, I made a habit of recording daily reflections that eventually evolved into short essays. Initially, these were just private notes – a temporal bridge for my children, intended to help them one day navigate their father's history. However, encouraged by several persuasive, kind-hearted peers, I brought these thoughts to the public. To my surprise, the feedback from H World's guests and franchisees was overwhelmingly warm.

This volume marks the work's third iteration. When Guomai Culture & Media (the Chinese publisher of the original work) proposed creating a 'definitive edition,' I met the pitch with a healthy dose of skepticism. Nevertheless, I agreed to the experiment in the spirit of 'giving it a try.' The result is a more refined collection; I have removed dated observations and integrated new essays written in recent years to ensure the content resonates with the present. It is, perhaps, a more accurate map of my current thinking.

Tradition speaks of "Three Imperishables": the cultivation of virtue, the performance of great deeds, and the preservation of words. While I harbour no illusions of literary immortality, committing these thoughts to the page serves several practical purposes. Primarily, it acts as a personal ledger; without the permanence of ink, even the sharpest insights eventually dissolve into the haze of memory.

There is also a familial motive. Should my children one day seek to understand the man behind the father, these essays offer a map of my internal journey. For the weary traveller staying at an H World hotel, I hope these pages provide more than just a distraction from boredom; perhaps a spark of shared insight will make the stay more meaningful.

And then for our partners, investors, and employees – potential and existing – the book offers a window into our corporate soul and who H World is. In the world of business, as in life, truly extraordinary feats are only possible when people move in the same direction, guided by a common set of values.

In the Confucian classic *The Great Learning*, a clear hierarchy of progress is established: one must cultivate the self to order the home, govern the state and ultimately bring peace to the world. At the root of this expansion lies a fundamental requirement – the discipline of the soul.

The title of this book, *Realm of the Heart*, reflects the conviction that our lived reality is shaped by our hearts and minds – our internal state. The opening essay serves as a summation of what I have gleaned over the years, a portrait of my 'heart' in its full resolution. What follows are shorter dispatches, snapshots of various 'realms' encountered in the thick of both commerce and quietude. This structure rests on a singular premise: that ours is a world governed by ideas first and matter second. Before we can reshape the world around us, we must first master the landscape within.

The reflections contained in these pages are personal; I seek no consensus, merely a conversation. Financial gain is not the motive, as all royalties are pledged to the H World Charity Foundation. Nor is this a play for prestige – in the vast demographic ocean, I am but a single drop. My hope is simpler: if these words offer a solitary spark of insight to a reader navigating the complexities of life or commerce, that resonance is a form of charity in its own right.

In an era of digital noise, the quiet acts of writing and reading feel like a rare, subversive bliss. This book is born of that privilege. Should you find these chapters in one of our hotels and feel a connection to them, please consider the copy a gift. It is better used in your hands than sitting idle on a shelf.

This concludes my Foreword.

August 2024

TABLE OF CONTENTS

HEART

• COSMOLOGY

REALM

• MY DECADE LONG PATH TO ENTREPRENEURSHIP

• TO BUILD A STRONG ENTERPRISE

• H WORLD PHILOSOPHY

• LIFE IS ART

• THE FINISH AND STARTING POINTS

• FROM AFAR TO HOME

• FROM DEPARTURE TO ENTRY

HEART

COSMOLOGY

This essay is a compilation of what I have learned and understood about the nature of the cosmos. Surveying the vast library of human knowledge and its myriad, siloed disciplines, one arrives at a singular, inescapable conclusion: the universe is not a collection of parts, but a coherent whole – a grand, interconnected harmony where every thread is woven into the same cloth.

SEEKING ANSWERS

Having majored in university in the science-oriented discipline of engineering mechanics, my early intellectual life was defined by the cold precision of mathematics. Yet, parallel to the lecture hall, I devoured every Western philosophy book that I could lay my hands on, tracing the intellectual lineage outlined in Bertrand Russell's *History of Western Philosophy* to find voices that resonated with my own. It was only after the age of 45 that the scales tipped eastward; the insights of Wang Yangming acted as a gateway to Buddhist explorations of wisdom and the soul. This journey has come full circle, bridging the mechanical and the metaphysical. What follows is an attempt to formalise these reflections – a summary of a lifelong ledger of discovery, offered as a roadmap for others navigating the same terrain.

ALL LIVING BEINGS POSSESS EQUAL WORTH

Let's begin with ourselves – us humans.

THE BASIC ELEMENTS THAT MAKE US HUMAN

Consider, for a moment, the stubborn solidity of a dinner table. Why can't your hand simply pass through it? The layman's answer is 'solidity,' but the physicist sees a frantic negotiation of forces. Our bodies are hierarchies of complexity: cells built of molecules, governed by DNA, which are in turn assemblages of atoms. These atoms are bound by covalent, ionic or metallic bonds – atomic 'glue' so formidable that breaking it requires immense energy. When you press against the wood, you inflict microscopic casualties on the molecular structure, but the sheer number of bonds holds the line. In liquids or gases, this structural discipline is relaxed, allowing for easy passage.

At the atomic level, the distinction between a human, a pig, or a lump of coal evaporates. We are all forged from the same limited inventory: hydrogen, oxygen, iron and calcium. The iron in a jagged rock is indistinguishable from the iron coursing through your veins. The difference lies not in the 'stuff,' but in the 'script' – the genetic information that dictates how these identical bricks are stacked.

Let us consider the chart below – within the human body, we find iron, cobalt, copper, zinc, chromium, manganese, molybdenum, fluorine, iodine, and selenium. The most abundant elements are oxygen, carbon, hydrogen and nitrogen. We are 'carbon-based lifeforms' not by divine decree, but because carbon atoms provide a particularly stable scaffolding for complex chemistry. Sometimes, it may seem that humanity is arrogant, believing we are separate from animals. Strip away the ego, and we are merely highly evolved animals. At our most fundamental level, the carbon that powers your thoughts is identical to the carbon buried in a seam of coal. We are not separate from the world; we are simply one of its more articulate arrangements.

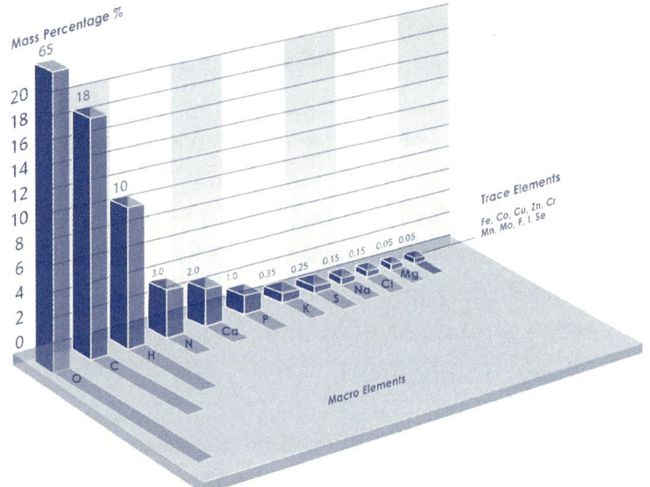

Elemental Composition in the Human Body

ELEMENTAL COMPOSITION IN THE HUMAN BODY

Structurally speaking, the human body is less a masterpiece of unique engineering and more a standard redistribution of common terrestrial stock. We are, quite literally, mostly water; it accounts for some 65% of our mass. Strip away the hydration from a 70kg adult, and you are left with a modest 25kg dry weight: a mix of 12kg of protein, 7kg of fat, and a handful of carbohydrates and mineral salts.

The deeper one digs, the more these differences dissolve into insignificance. To the casual observer, pig fat and human fat appear distinct; a biologist might point to subtle variations in cell membranes or density. Yet, break these down further, and the facade of uniqueness crumbles. Both are largely assemblages of water, calcium and protein – the latter being merely long chains of smaller, ubiquitous molecular units.

When viewed through this microscopic lens, the elements that constitute 'us' are indistinguishable from those that constitute 'everything else.' We must, therefore, discard the notion of a structural chasm between humanity and the animal kingdom, or even between life and inanimate matter. The distance is not a gulf, but a mere step.

THE SOURCE OF LIFE

To understand the origins of life, one must revisit a prehistoric act of celestial digestion. Some 1.7 billion years ago, a solitary unicellular organism engulfed a Gram-negative bacterium. In a rare stroke of biological fortune, the prey was not dissolved but recruited. This symbiotic merger birthed the mitochondrion – the cellular power plant that fuelled the leap to complexity. This 'endosymbiotic' event, thought to have occurred only once, provided the energetic capital necessary for the rise of all multicellular life, including humans, animals and plants.

Every eukaryote on the planet, from the humble yeast to the hedge-fund manager, shares this lineage. We trace our ancestry to the Last Universal Common Ancestor (LUCA), the last shared ancestor of all multicellular life on Earth, and that explains our striking genetic uniformity.

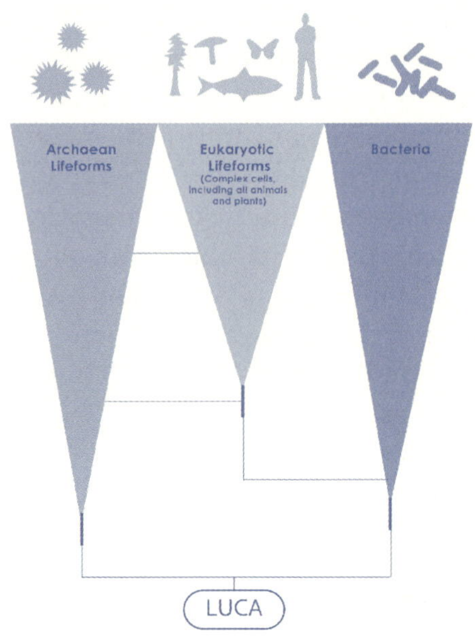

Indeed, the data suggest that the 'human' brand is less unique than we care to admit. While family members share nearly all their DNA, the gap between a human and a chimpanzee is a mere 4%, and even the gulf between a person and a banana is only 50%.

Genetic similarity:
Family members: 99.99999%
Humans and other humans: 99.99%
Humans and chimpanzees: 96%
Humans and cats: 90%
Humans and mice: 85%
Humans and chickens: 60%
Humans and bananas: 50%
Humans and yeast: 26%

Strip away the differences between the supposed racial categories like East Asian, Caucasian and African, or even between humans and other animals, and the elemental ledger remains the same. We lack any 'exclusive' ingredients – no gold plating or platinum cores distinguish us from the beasts of the field. This biological proximity is now being exploited by genetic engineering, especially with the advent of 'gene scissors' (CRISPR), which render the boundaries between species increasingly porous. In theory, splicing canine DNA could sharpen human senses, while ethnic or gender traits could be toggled like software settings. Such editing remains largely a legal and ethical taboo, yet the technical feasibility underscores our shared hardware.

As we contemplate our carbon-based heritage, a new competitor emerges: silicon-based life. While we are built on the stable bonds of carbon, the artificial intelligences of the future are etched into silicon chips. The coming era may not be a contest between different species of animal, but a fundamental rivalry between two different elemental philosophies of life.

SIMILARITIES OF DIFFERENT LIFEFORMS

Isaac Asimov, the biochemist and doyen of science fiction, once postulated that biology need not be a monoculture. He envisioned six distinct chemical architectures: from fluorosilicone-based entities and sulphur-thriving organisms to those reliant on ammonia, methane, or hydrogen. Humans, as it happens, occupy the third tier – a water-bound existence driven by oxygen-based nucleic acids and proteins. While these classifications highlight our chemical constraints, they also hint at a broader biological kinship.

This material overlap fuels what the German aesthete Friedrich Theodor von Vischer termed 'Empathy Theory.' He argued that human perception is not a passive intake of data, but an outward projection of feeling. Because our genetic hardware is so remarkably similar to that of a flower or a stray cat, beauty and suffering require no translation. We do not 'learn' that a crying child deserves sympathy; we feel it because we are, at a molecular level, made of the same script. Our empathy is the spontaneous recognition of ourselves in the 'other.'

Yet, our communion with nature is throttled by our sensory equipment. We navigate the world through the narrow keyhole of visible light and a restricted band of acoustic frequencies. Were we 'frequency-shifting' beings capable of detecting ultra-high or ultra-low vibrations, the silent stoicism of a mountain or a tree might resolve into a legible conversation. Our inability to communicate with the landscape is perhaps a failure of our antennae, not a lack of 'soul' in the scenery.

This sense of universal parity is an ancient refrain. It echoes through the Buddhist doctrine that 'all living beings possess equal worth,' and also through Zhuangzi's philosophical treaties *On the Equality of Things*. Modern cinema has caught up; with the 'Tree of Souls' and the 'Cove of the Ancestors' in *Avatar*, each race has its own tree of life and they are interconnected. We are not merely residents of this world; we are a manifestation of it. Our unity with the cosmos is a deep, structural truth we have only just begun to understand.

THE SPEED OF LIGHT CANNOT BE EXCEEDED

In the confines of the human experience, speed is a modest affair. Even the kinetic fury of a racing car or the thundering ascent of a SpaceX rocket represents little more than a crawl when measured against the universal benchmark: the speed of light. In this low-velocity theatre, the exotic paradoxes of relativity remain dormant. Instead, our daily lives are governed by the reliable, three-century-old ledger of Newtonian mechanics. Whether one is calculating the trajectory of a football or the structural integrity of a bridge, Newton's laws provide a sturdy, intuitive framework that remains perfectly 'true' for an array of activities in our everyday lives.

EINSTEIN'S REVISIONS TO NEWTONIAN MECHANICS

Newton's laws of motion are the classical ledger of the universe: objects are stubborn in their inertia, acceleration is a simple product of force and mass, and every action meets its equal and opposite ghost.

> Newton's First Law of Motion: An object at rest stays at rest, and an object in motion stays in motion at constant speed and in a straight line unless acted upon by an unbalanced force.

Newton's Second Law of Motion: The acceleration of an object is directly proportional to the net force acting on it and inversely proportional to its mass. The direction of the acceleration is in the direction of the net force. Its formula is as follows:

$$\Sigma F = ma$$

Newton's Third Law of Motion: When one body exerts a force on a second body, the second body simultaneously exerts a force equal in magnitude and opposite in direction on the first body. Its formula is as follows:

$$F = -F'$$

To Newton, the cosmos was a grand, mechanical clock – symmetrical, balanced and entirely predictable. This was the era of 'scientific fatalism.' If one knew the initial position of every atom, the future was not a mystery to be lived, but a calculation to be solved.

However, this deterministic dream faltered when confronted with the celestial and the very fast. Albert Einstein realized that Newton's rigid framework could not account for the absolute nature of the speed of light. In his Special Theory of Relativity, Einstein replaced the old Galilean transformations with those of Lorentz, revealing a universe that defies common sense. His famous equation, $E=mc^2$, implies that as an object approaches the speed of light (c), its energy becomes infinite – a cosmic speed limit that no mass-bearing particle can ever breach.

In this relativistic world, the fixed dimensions we take for granted – mass, length and time – become elastic.

As velocity increases, mass balloons and lengths contract; even the "Golden Cudgel" of Chinese myth would shorten if swung fast enough. Most provocatively, time itself dilates. We move from a three-dimensional world into a four-dimensional 'spacetime,' where a traveller on a high-speed rocket or even someone living on a fast-rotating mountaintop technically ages slower than their stationary counterparts.

Einstein proposed the Special Theory of Relativity to correct the shortcomings of Newtonian Mechanics, which can be expressed by the Mass-Energy Equivalence Formula:

$$mc^2 = E_{\mathrm{k}} + m_0 c^2$$

$$E = mc^2 = \frac{m_0 c^2}{\sqrt{1 - \frac{v^2}{c^2}}}$$

$$\Delta E = \Delta m c^2$$

According to the formula, if v (velocity) equals c (the speed of light), then the denominator is 0, making E (energy) infinite. Energy cannot be infinite; only particles with a very small mass (such as electrons) can approach the speed of light, but they can never reach it. Therefore, the speed of light cannot be exceeded.

Through Lorentz transformation[1] (Galilean Transformation was used in Newtonian systems, but was

1 Lorentz transformation: In the Special Theory of Relativity, the coordinate transformation between two inertial reference frames moving at constant relative velocity was used to reconcile the contradictions between classical electrodynamics and Newtonian Mechanics, and it became the fundamental equation set of special relativity.

not applicable to Einstein's system), many conclusions can be drawn, one of which is that the faster the speed, the greater the mass.

$$m_{\mathrm{R}} = \frac{m_0}{\sqrt{1 - \frac{v^2}{c^2}}}$$

Another conclusion is that the faster the speed, the shorter the length. If a rod moves in a certain direction, when it approaches the speed of light, the rod will contract.

$$l' = l_0 \sqrt{1 - \frac{v^2}{c^2}}$$

The third important conclusion is that the faster the speed, the slower the time.

$$\Delta t' = \frac{\Delta t}{\sqrt{1 - \frac{v^2}{c^2}}}$$

Einstein's genius lay in his bold 'metaphysical' wager: that while all other speeds are relative, the speed of light is absolute and invariant. It is the hard boundary of our reality. Intriguingly, this modern physics finds a strange echo in ancient folklore. The Chinese proverb "a celestial day equals a mortal decade" describes the very time dilation Einstein quantified. Whether through myth or mathematics, we are forced to accept that we live in a universe far more pliable – and perhaps more prophetic – than Newton ever dared to imagine.

GENERAL RELATIVITY

With the Special Theory of Relativity established, it is necessary to understand general relativity.

If special relativity suggests that space and time are the modes by which we perceive the world rather than fixed conditions of it, general relativity provides the physical architecture for that perception. The core tenet is elegantly simple: gravity is not a mysterious force acting at a distance, but the manifestation of the curvature of spacetime itself. While special relativity concerns itself with the frenetic world of light and subatomic particles, general relativity turns its gaze toward the heavyweights – stars, galaxies, and the gravitational behemoths known as black holes.

Consider the transition from an atom to a neutron star. Atoms are mostly empty space; should they collapse into a dense slurry of protons and neutrons, the resulting object becomes unimaginably heavy. Such mass warps the surrounding reality so severely that traditional three-dimensional coordinates fail. Space and time 'sink' toward the mass, creating a curved, spherical coordinate system. Even the sun exerts this influence, though its mass is too modest to create the dramatic distortions found near a black hole. In the latter, spacetime curves toward a 'singularity' – a point of infinite density where the mathematics of the known universe breaks down. Much of the late Stephen Hawking's work remains brilliant conjecture precisely because the event horizon of a black hole permits no light, and thus no data, to escape for verification.

At the heart of this theory lies the Einstein Field Equation of General Relativity. It is a second-order partial differential equation, a sophisticated mathematical tool used to describe how matter and energy dictate the geometry of spacetime. In the world of calculus, such equations require specific 'boundary conditions' or starting points to find a solution.

$$G_{\mu v} = R_{\mu v} - \frac{1}{2} g_{\mu v} R = \frac{8\pi G}{c^4} T_{\mu v}$$

Crucially, each unique solution to this equation represents an entire universe – a distinct spacetime system. If our universe is merely one solution born of specific initial conditions, the mathematics here suggests that other solutions – and thus other universes – are not only possible but likely. This is the bedrock of the 'multiverse' hypothesis. It serves as a reminder that in cosmology, one cannot discuss the grandest theories of existence without first mastering the rigorous language of mathematics.

MATHEMATICS – THE HIGHEST EXPRESSION OF HUMAN THOUGHT

Humanity possesses a sprawling toolkit for self-expression, ranging from the lyricism of language to the fluidity of dance. Yet, as the *Tao Te Ching* suggests, the 'Tao' that can be spoken is not the eternal one. Language and writing are inherently imprecise instruments; they are shadowed by nuance and cultural baggage. Mathematics, by contrast, offers an abstract precision that describes the world with far greater fidelity. Indeed, many argue that mathematics is the singular epitome of human thought – a universal ledger that transcends the limits of the vernacular.

Crucially, mathematical truths are not 'invented' in the way a patent is filed; they are 'discovered.' One might envision a vast, pre-existing corridor of locked cabinets, each housing a fundamental law of the universe. Humans do not build these cabinets; the 'smart and lucky' among us simply stumble upon them and find the keys. This perspective posits that abstract mathematical objects exist independently of our language, our minds, and even the physical world itself.

This is the essence of mathematical Platonism. Plato believed that concepts like numbers and geometric forms inhabit a realm of objective existence, untethered from time, space or human consciousness. When a mathematician solves a complex proof, they are not creating something new, but rather describing a feature of this independent reality. Truth, in this view, is objective and absolute.

It is reached not through the five senses, but through a refined 'mathematical intuition' – a mental experience that allows us to peek into a world that exists quite happily without us.

DIFFERENTIAL EQUATIONS

When discussing mathematics, we cannot avoid mentioning differential equations.

In the hierarchy of human thought, simple algebra is the nursery. An equation such as 2x=10 is a static snapshot and easy to solve: ten apples divided by two eaters yields a tidy five.

But the world does not sit still. As complexity rises, variables cease to be fixed numbers and become 'functions' – dynamic entities that change over time or space. To describe a world in flux, one requires the 'general formula' of the cosmos: the differential equation.

While simple equations find values, differential equations seek the relationships between change and state. They are the essential scaffolding for almost every rigorous discipline. Whether calculating a rocket's landing trajectory amidst shifting winds and thinning air, or modelling the swirling wake of a submarine, these equations are the only way to map reality. Even the modern electronic age owes its existence to a set of four partial differential equations: Maxwell's Equations. By linking electricity, magnetism and light, they provided the blueprint for the technological revolution.

> Maxwell's Equations are a very important example of a partial differential equation. This is a set of equations describing the relationship between electric fields, magnetic fields, charge density and current density, and consists of four equations.

$$\nabla \times \boldsymbol{H} = j + \frac{\partial \boldsymbol{D}}{\partial t}$$
$$\nabla \times \boldsymbol{E} = -\frac{\partial \boldsymbol{B}}{\partial t}$$
$$\nabla \cdot \boldsymbol{B} = 0$$
$$\nabla \cdot \boldsymbol{D} = \rho$$

From Maxwell's Equations, it is inferred that electromagnetic waves propagate at the speed of light in a vacuum, leading to the conjecture that light is an electromagnetic wave. From the related theories of these fundamental equations, modern electrical and electronic technologies have been developed.

Yet, the mathematical properties of these equations offer a humbling metaphysical lesson. First, they typically have no 'general solution' – suggesting that in our perceivable world, absolute, one-size-fits-all truths are non-existent. Second, they often yield infinite solutions. Just as Einstein's field equations allow for a multiverse, mathematics suggests there is no single path to the summit of understanding; there are, as the proverb goes, eighty-four thousand methods to reach the light.

Third, most complex differential equations cannot be solved exactly, only approximately through numerical analysis. This mirrors our own cognitive limits: our most 'certain' perceptions of the universe are, in fact, merely useful approximations. Finally, there are 'singularities' where equations have no solution at all – vast, unmapped territories that may represent the hard boundaries of human cognition, akin to the mystery of dark matter or the interior of a black hole.

Ultimately, the study of these mathematical truths should serve as an antidote to human arrogance. At an atomic level, we are barely distinguishable from the animals; at a cognitive level, our grasp of reality is hazy and relative. The self-proclaimed 'authorities' and 'pioneers' of our age would do well to study the ledger of the differential equation. To truly understand the universe is to realize how much of it remains unsolvable, demanding a profound sense of awe as we navigate our limited, subjective version of the truth.

IMAGINARY NUMBERS

Now let us talk about the problem of imaginary numbers, which is also quite interesting.

In the standard ledger of mathematics, the rules are intuitive: square a positive number and you get a positive; square a negative, and the result is the same. Yet, there exists a 'fine and wonderful recourse of the divine spirit,' as Leibniz (the inventor of calculus) put it: the imaginary number i, which is defined by its property $i^2 = -1$.

While a real number can represent a tangible asset – an egg, a car, a bowl – an imaginary number represents nothing in the physical world. It is a mathematical amphibian, suspended between being and not being.

Despite its name, the imaginary number is no mere flight of fancy. Without it, the equations of quantum mechanics would lose their predictive power; the subatomic world simply cannot be verified using real numbers alone. It is an abstract necessity for describing a reality that our senses cannot directly touch.

This brings us to two other pillars of mathematical analysis that often elude the undergraduate mind: the infinitesimal ($\delta \to 0$) and the infinite (∞). To say that $\delta \to 0$ is to suggest that the universe is infinitely divisible. No matter how small the crevice, there is a further detail within; there are 'crevices within crevices' that defy a final bottom. Our pursuit of knowledge, much like the division of a line, is an asymptotic journey toward a destination we can approach but never truly reach.

Conversely, ∞ is a concept so vast it renders the mundane tools of measurement and decision-making obsolete. It is the mathematical equivalent of unconditional altruism or a love without motive – limitless, eternal and effortless. It is the 'everything' that exists beyond the boundary of the finite. If the infinitesimal teaches us about the depth of the world's details, infinity reminds us of the scale of its totality. Together, these concepts suggest a universe that is both endlessly deep and boundless, existing far beyond the narrow spectrum of human utility.

TIME CANNOT BE REWOUND

Having audited the important and elegant architecture of mathematics, we must now confront the more visceral problem of time. Is the ticking of the cosmic clock a constant, or can the tempo be altered? More provocatively, is the 'arrow of time' fixed in one direction, or can the film be rewound? To answer these questions, one must look beyond the symmetry of equations and into the messy, irreversible reality of the Second Law of Thermodynamics.

THE LAWS OF THERMODYNAMICS

Before tackling the temporal riddles of the Second Law, let us recap the more familiar pillars of thermodynamics. The First Law is the universe's ultimate accounting principle: the conservation of energy. It dictates that energy can neither be created nor destroyed, only laundered into different forms. In any isolated system, the total remains fixed. The internal energy of a body ($\boldsymbol{\Delta U}$) increases only by the sum of heat absorbed ($\boldsymbol{Q}$) and work performed upon it ($\boldsymbol{W}$).

$$\Delta U = Q + W$$

Classical physics once held a parallel ledger for the 'indestructibility of matter,' asserting that mass remained constant in any chemical reaction. However, Einsteinian physics revealed that at high velocities, mass is as elastic as time. This led to the unification of these principles into the Law of Conservation of Mass-Energy. It serves as a reminder that the tidy certainties of Newtonian mechanics – while perfectly serviceable for many of humanity's activities such as building bridges or driving cars – are merely helpful approximations of a more complex, unified reality.

The Third Law, meanwhile, introduces a cosmic 'floor' that humanity can observe but never tread upon: absolute zero. Defined by French physicist Guillaume Amontons in 1702 at -273.15°C, this is the theoretical point where the pressure of a gas hits zero and molecular motion grinds to a halt. Because reaching a state of zero pressure is a physical impossibility, absolute zero remains an asymptotic goal – an unreachable frontier that defines the lower limit of our thermal world.

FATE OF THE UNIVERSE

Let us focus on the Second Law of Thermodynamics: the principle of entropy increase.

$$dS(\text{entropy increase}) \geq 0$$

In an isolated system, order inevitably surrenders to disorder. It is a one-way street; once things fall apart, the cosmic centre cannot hold. This is the most 'despairing' of laws, for it dictates the ultimate fate not just of steam engines, but of companies, biological life and the universe itself.

Entropy is a measure of chaos. An isolated system – be it a withering flower, a declining enterprise or the cosmos – moves toward an equilibrium of maximum disorder. People age, suns burn out and galaxies fade. This suggests that there is no eternal existence, only a slow slide toward a state where no more work can be done. Yet, within this gloom, there are 'islands' of order.

How do we reduce entropy? The first tool is information. While mass and energy are conserved, information is not; it is the 'negative entropy' that allows a manager to organize a firm or a physician to heal a body. The second is gravity, which pulls matter into the structured embrace of stars. On Earth, we are remarkably fortunate to be an 'open system.' We survive by importing low-entropy 'ordered polymers' (food) and exporting high-entropy 'disordered molecules' (waste and heat).

However, this local tidiness comes at a global cost. To keep a human body ordered, the Sun must sacrifice itself, fusing hydrogen into helium and increasing its own entropy. Every decrease in entropy here requires a larger increase elsewhere. It is a grand, interconnected chain of cosmic sacrifice. When the Sun's nuclear furnace finally reaches thermal equilibrium – its maximum entropy – it will die.

If the universe is indeed a closed system with no 'outside' to provide fresh energy, it faces an ultimate 'Heat Death' – a perfectly uniform, frozen state where all change ceases. This fate links the subatomic to the galactic; the destiny of a single cell is bound to the destiny of the stars.

I believe that on the level of the 'Tao,' modern and ancient, East and West, science, philosophy and religion are all interconnected. For instance, Lao Tzu's observation that the 'Way of Heaven' diminishes surplus to supplement deficiency describes the levelling effect of entropy. Meanwhile, the 'Way of Humans' – concentrating wealth and order – represents our brief, local struggle to decrease entropy against the universal tide (in a rapidly advancing society, the wealth gap will inevitably continue to widen). "Who has the surplus to serve the world? Only the Tao."

BREAKING THROUGH THE BOUNDARIES OF SPACE AND TIME

The Second Law of Thermodynamics serves as the universe's one-way valve. Processes are irreversible; as Heraclitus famously noted, one cannot step into the same river twice. This arrow of time dictates that the film cannot be rewound. Between the unbreachable speed of light and the irreversibility of time, humanity finds itself confined within a 'spacetime box' – a set of cosmic boundaries that define the limits of our species.

Is there an exit from this enclosure? The most likely candidate is the black hole. Under the crushing gravity of extreme density, General Relativity suggests that light is trapped and time itself collapses into a singularity. At this point, where mass density tends toward infinity and spacetime coordinates approach zero, the standard laws of physics resign. Such singularities may represent the only legitimate 'breakout' from this spacetime boundary.

Furthermore, our understanding of the cosmos remains embarrassingly parochial. We now know that the universe is composed of roughly two-thirds dark energy and one-third matter, yet a staggering 85% of that matter is 'dark' – undetectable and mysterious. Like the interior of a black hole, dark matter and dark energy represent a vast, unknowable frontier. We are effectively blind to most of the reality we inhabit.

Time is relative. It can be fast or slow, and it is irreversible. So, what exactly is time? I think it is a sophisticated illusion conjured up by the human mind. Much like space, time is a mental construct used to organize perception, yet its foundation is remarkably shaky. When we fall into a deep sleep, we experience a 'reset;' under total anaesthesia, we suffer a complete 'loss' of time. These lapses suggest that time may be less an external condition of the universe and more a subjective flicker of consciousness.

WHAT IS THE WORLD?

Since antiquity, we have found ourselves persistently posing the same fundamental questions: what, exactly, is this world we inhabit? Where did this universe come from, and toward what inevitable conclusion is it travelling?

PHILOSOPHERS' THOUGHTS

To understand the cosmos, one must first examine the ancient accounts of the philosophers, beginning with Plato.

PLATO

Plato's cosmology depicts an origin story where a divine creator imposed a rational plan upon undifferentiated chaos. The universe was formed from chaos and became organized. In Plato's ledger, the universe is a living, breathing entity – a perfect, symmetrical sphere animated by a 'world soul.' He championed circular motion as the highest form of physical expression, reflecting the perfection of its creator.

Plato was equally preoccupied with the architecture of the human heart. His concept of 'Platonic love' is far more rigorous than modern usage suggests. It posits a unity of body and soul where love eventually transcends the physical to pursue 'beauty itself.' In this idealistic framework, sex, love and marriage are independent variables. Love is an unquenchable pursuit of an 'ideal' that exists beyond the tangible world.

He illustrated this through a myth of primordial wholeness. In the beginning, there were three types of people in the world. The Sun God represented men, the Mother Earth represented women, and the Moon represented the androgynous. The androgynous had twice the functions and strength of humans. In a bid to undermine humanity, Zeus cleaved humans into two. As a result, humans became only half as strong as before, but there were twice as many of them, to better serve the gods. Thus, our lifelong yearning for 'love' is, in fact, a biological and spiritual drive to recover that lost, original completeness – our search for our 'other half.' Descendants of primeval men and women developed homosexual tendencies, and descendants of primeval androgynes developed heterosexual tendencies. There is only one path to happiness for all of mankind, which is to achieve love, by finding our partner to heal the natural state that was cleaved from us.

However, the cornerstone of Platonic thought is the distinction between the 'World of Forms' and the 'World of Appearances.' The World of Forms is the true existence, unchanging and eternal, while Plato argued that the reality we perceive through our senses is merely a faint, flickering shadow of this higher, eternal truth. This world is composed of appearances, each exhibiting temporary changes and other related traits because of factors such as time and space. This is most famously captured in Plato's 'Allegory of the Cave.' Prisoners bound in a dark cavern mistake the shadows on the wall for reality. When one escapee returns to speak of the sun and the true objects outside, he is mocked as a fool. For the prisoners, the shadow is the only truth that exists.

This duality – the unchanging essence (World of Forms) versus the shifting illusion (World of Appearances) – remains a fundamental pillar of Western thought. It finds surprising echoes in both modern physics, which identifies the hidden variables behind phenomena, and Buddhist teachings on the illusory nature of the material world. While centuries of scholars have refined these concepts, the original blueprint remains unmistakably Platonic.

KANT

Immanuel Kant's philosophical ledger is famously balanced across three 'critiques,' each examining a distinct human currency: Truth (*The Critique of Pure Reason*), Goodness (*The Critique of Practical Reason*) and Beauty (*The Critique of Judgment*). At the heart of his system lies a fundamental partition of reality. He divided the world into the 'Phenomenal' – the realm of appearances accessible to human senses – and the 'Noumenal,' the world in which supernatural entities such as God, freedom and the soul reside in an inaccessible territory, beyond the reach of reason and firmly within the province of faith. These two worlds communicate via aesthetic judgment.

Kant argued that humans do not merely observe the world; they construct it. We can never grasp the true essence of an object, only its appearance as filtered through our mental hardware. This echoes a central tenet of modern quantum mechanics: the properties of a system are inextricably linked to the act of observation. If, as Kant famously asserted, 'man is the measure of all things,' then the observer is more significant than the thing observed.

Regarding the divine, Kant was a pragmatist. Since neither experience nor logic can prove God's existence, he categorised such beliefs as 'Postulates of Practical Reason.' We must assume God and an immortal soul exist not because they are provable, but because they are necessary for a coherent moral life. In the 'unsolvable' areas of modern physics – think dark matter or the singularity of a black hole – we find the modern equivalent of Kant's void, where science ends and an assumption of God's existence is made based on the most perfect representation of this world, which is what Kant called 'morality.'

In his aesthetic theory, Kant distinguished between two types of greatness. First is 'Free Beauty,' a pure, disinterested pleasure found in form and sensation. The second is 'The Sublime,' which he split into the 'Mathematical' – the overwhelming vastness of the infinite – and the 'Dynamical' – the terrifying, irresistible power of nature. While nature bestows beauty upon humanity, art is the gift humans bequeath back to nature. Through aesthetic judgment, Kant believed, the bridge between our sensory world and the unknowable 'Noumenal' world is finally crossed.

HEGEL

G. W. F. Hegel's examination of the human mind partitions the development of consciousness into five distinct tranches. The first three – Consciousness, Self-Consciousness and Reason – constitute the 'subjective spirit.' These then evolve into 'Objective Spirit' (the social world) and finally into 'Absolute Spirit.' For Hegel, this Absolute Spirit is not merely an observer of the cosmos but the origin of the world – the foundation of all things.

The world's relentless motion and upheaval are, in this view, the 'self-development' of the Absolute Spirit as it seeks to understand itself. Crucially, Hegel insists that this Spirit does not transcend the world; it is not a distant, detached deity. Rather, nature, human society and the flicker of human thought are all manifestations of the Absolute Spirit at various stages of its maturation. The eternal churn of life and the development of history *are* the spirit itself.

The following statement is rather interesting: "The Absolute Spirit is the ground of the world, but it is not something transcending the world." It would mean we – as individuals – are not merely residents of the universe. We are the Absolute Spirit itself, caught in the act of becoming. We are not just watching the development of the cosmos;

we are the very process of that development, manifesting through time in various, evolving forms.

SCHOPENHAUER

Arthur Schopenhauer's examination of reality concludes that the world is composed of two fundamental tranches: Will and Representation. For him, the Will is the ultimate, driving force, while Representation is merely the way that Will objectifies itself for our perception. Representation and Will are one and the same, constituting the world together.

To navigate the history of Western thought, one might compare the accounts offered by the four giants of the field. Though their terminology varies, their structural maps of the universe share a striking family resemblance:

Philosopher	*The 'True' Reality*	*The Perceived World*
Plato	World of Forms	World of Appearances
Kant	Noumena	Phenomenal World
Hegel	Absolute Spirit	Subjective Spirit
Schopenhauer	Will	Representation

The mystery of the world (universe) begins to dissolve once one recognizes that these thinkers are often describing the same fundamental dualism using different conceptual currencies. Each established their own bespoke system based on their own assumptions and terminologies (concepts and names used to describe and differentiate between things). Friedrich Nietzsche, for his part, did not so much invent a new system as rebrand Schopenhauer's 'Will.' By appending a single suffix, he birthed the 'Will to Power.'

Where Schopenhauer saw a hopeless and pessimistic world of suffering, Nietzsche thought otherwise and advocated for the *Übermensch* (or Superman) concept.

He argued that through the exercise of the Will to Power, humanity could transcend its limitations. His masterpiece, *Thus Spoke Zarathustra*, serves as the manifesto for this shift from Schopenhauerian despair to heroic self-mastery. It's wonderfully written and very much worth a read.

SCIENCE AND MYTHOLOGY

Science explains the origin of the universe as follows. Some 13.7 billion years ago, the universe was a 'Singularity' – a point of nearly infinite density and heat. Triggered by a mysterious quantum fluctuation, this point exploded. In a few 'Planck times' – the smallest units of the temporal clock – it expanded from a microscopic speck to the size of an orange. This cooling, expanding debris eventually formed the cosmos we navigate today.

Just as the universe expanded from a point, complex life sprouted from a single, improbable merger: the birth of the LUCA (Last Universal Common Ancestor). Here, a simple cell recruited a bacterium to become its mitochondria, an event that proves a minuscule disturbance can yield fundamental evolution. On a cosmic scale, the energy of the Big Bang was sufficient to inflate 11 dimensions. As energy condensed into mass, these dimensions 'folded' away, leaving us with the three dimensions of space and one of time that characterize our current four-dimensional reality.

Ancient mythologies examine this process through a different lens. In Chinese lore, *Pangu opened the sky. A long, long time ago, heaven and earth had not yet separated, and the universe was in a state of chaos. A giant named Pangu slumbered in this chaotic universe for 18,000 years. One day, Pangu suddenly awoke. He saw nothing but darkness around him, and brandished his great axe, cleaving the darkness before him. With a deafening shatter, darkness began to dissipate. The elements that gradually rose became the sky, and the elements that gradually sank became the earth. After heaven and earth were separated, Pangu feared they would merge again, so he used his head to prop up the sky, and planted his feet to the earth. Each day, the sky rose ten feet, and Pangu grew taller along with it. This continued for countless years, and the sky and earth gradually took form. Pangu finally collapsed in exhaustion. After his fall, his body underwent a great transformation. His breath became the winds and clouds of the four seasons; his voice turned into rumbling thunder; his eyes became the sun and moon; his limbs became the East, West, South and North cardinal directions of the land; his skin became the boundless earth; his blood became the torrential rivers; and his sweat became the rain that nourished all living things* – a poetic transformation of energy into the physical world.

The *Book of Genesis* tells a similar story of order emerging from the void. *Before the universe, heaven and earth were formed, darkness shrouded the boundless void and chaos. The life-bearing spirit of God moved within it, coursed through it, beginning the work of His remarkable creation, establishing the world and bringing all things into being. God created the world in seven days. The wonder and mystery of this creation cannot be fully captured by words or writing. On the first day, God said, "Let there be light!" And there was light. God separated the light from the darkness, calling the light 'day,' and the darkness 'night.' Thus, there was evening, and there was morning. On the second day, God said, "Let there be a firmament between the waters to separate them." So God created air, and called it the 'sky.' On the third day, God said, "Let the water under the sky be gathered together so the dry land will appear.' And so it was. God called the dry land 'earth' and the gathered waters 'seas.' He then commanded the earth to sprout grass, seed-bearing plants and fruit-bearing trees – each according to its kind. On the fourth day, God said,*

"Let there be lights in the firmament of the heavens to divide day from night, and let them serve as signs for seasons, days and years." So God created two great lights: the greater light to govern the day and the lesser light to govern the night. He also made the stars and set them in the heavens. On the fifth day, God said, "Let the waters teem with living creatures, and let birds fly above the earth across the sky." So God created great sea creatures and every living thing that moves in the waters, each according to its kind, as well as every winged bird. Seeing that it was good, God blessed them and commanded them to multiply and fill the seas and skies. On the sixth day, God said, "Let the earth bring forth living creatures – livestock, creeping things, and wild animals, each according to its kind." And it was so. Then God said, "Let us make man in our image, after our likeness, to rule over the fish of the sea, the birds of the air, the livestock on the earth, and every creeping thing that moves on the ground." So God created man in His own image. God blessed them and said, "Be fruitful and multiply; fill the earth and subdue it. Rule over the fish of the sea, the birds of the air, and every living thing that moves on the earth." On the seventh day, the heavens and the earth and all their hosts were completed. God finished His work of creation and rested on the seventh day. He blessed it as a special day and made it holy, for on it He had completed His creation and ceased from His labour. Thus, Sunday became a day of rest for mankind.

Whether one reads the equations of physics or the couplets of the Tang poet Du Fu – who wrote of nature 'cleaving dusk from dawn' – the core message remains strikingly consistent. Strip away the specialized terminology, and the scientific theory, the Chinese myth and the biblical book of *Genesis* are all describing the same grand opening: a singular, transformative moment when the dark, dense and chaotic became the structured and the living.

TAOIST PHILOSOPHY AND CALCULUS

In the sixth century BC, Lao Tzu observed that a formless, serene perfection preceded the birth of the universe. In the *Tao Te Ching*, he names this 'mother of the universe' the Tao. "There was something formless and perfect before the universe was born" – this 'formless something' refers to chaos.

Lao Tzu also said, "All things are born of being; being is born of non-being." This finds a parallel in quantum mechanics, where the vacuum is not truly empty but a frothing sea of potential, giving rise to high-energy existence.

He further said: "The Tao that can be spoken of is not the constant Tao; the name that can be named is not the constant name. The nameless was the beginning of heaven and earth; the named was the mother of the myriad creatures." This passage defines 'Tao' and 'name' aptly. Before the Big Bang, there was no information, no 'name' and no observer; it was, quite literally, beyond description. Lao Tzu further posited a generative sequence: "The Tao begets One; One begets Two; Two begets Three; Three begets all things. All things carry Yin and embrace Yang, blending these vital breaths (Qi) to attain harmony." This is the foundational logic of Yin and Yang, which is essentially binary. It suggests that the complexity of the 'myriad creatures' is merely an expansion of simple, harmonized opposites.

In that era, Lao Tzu had already explained many of the secrets of the world. This is the same as the stories of Pangu opening the sky, the Christian creation of the world, and the Big Bang. Therefore, wisdom transcends distance, and myths are not so absurd; in fact, they carry deep meaning.

This ancient intuition found a formal mathematical foundation through Gottfried Wilhelm Leibniz in the 17th century. Leibniz did not just establish calculus – on which all differential equations and modern mathematics are built – he also invented the binary number system. Leibniz believed 1 and 0 were the 'divine source' of all numbers, a logical language that mirrored the creation of something from nothing. It is likely he was inspired by Chinese thought; records show he spent considerable time debating Yin and Yang with a Jesuit missionary recently returned from China.

Under a binary lens, Lao Tzu's sequence becomes a digital progression: 0 (Tao), 1 (One), 10 (Two), 11 (Three), and so on. Leibniz saw divine symmetry here. To him, the number seven – the days of creation – was represented in binary as 111. In this trio of 'ones,' he glimpsed the Holy Trinity!

Leibniz also sought to prove God's existence. He argued that to understand any effect, one must trace its cause; and to understand this cause, one must trace back to the cause of that cause, and so on. Since a deterministic chain cannot be explained or caused by an agent within a world, there must be a transcendent, metaphysical cause: God. This mirrors Immanuel Kant's later 'postulates,' where God is a necessary assumption to sustain a coherent moral universe.

Finally, Leibniz argued that we live in the 'best of all possible worlds.' He believed that a God of infinite goodness would, by definition, choose the most harmonious and perfect design. Here, 'goodness' is different from secular morality (with which we are more familiar); it is a value system, a state of supreme aesthetic and structural perfection. Leibniz believed that God created the world because of 'goodness,' because the world is like this.

IS THE WORLD PERFECT?

Almost all philosophers and scientists, including Plato, Einstein, Kant, Leibniz and Newton, believed that the universe is fundamentally 'good' and structurally perfect. They have spent centuries examining the cosmos for signs of symmetry, harmony and conservation. Yet, these are not merely technical requirements; they are aesthetic ones. Whether a theory must be 'simple,' 'complete' or 'consistent' is often a matter of the researcher's own taste. For giants like Kant, Einstein and Newton, beauty was not just an ornament of truth, but a reliable guide to it.

Many scientists and philosophers did indeed develop their hypotheses and theories from an aesthetic perspective. Consider Albert Einstein's lifelong obsession with the theory of unified fields. When I was in high school, I asked myself whether the structures of these two formulae could be unified since they were the same. Einstein pondered the same. Newton's Law of Universal Gravitation and Coulomb's Law of electrostatic force are, mathematically speaking, nearly identical twins:

Universal Gravitation:

$$F = G\frac{m_1 m_2}{r^2}$$

Coulomb's Law:

$$F = k\frac{q_1 q_2}{r^2} = \frac{q_1 q_2}{4\pi\varepsilon_0 r^2}$$

To Einstein, such symmetry could not be a mere coincidence of cosmic accounting. He believed that 'God does not play dice,' and that everything He does must be pure and unified. Einstein believed there should be a unified theory that was possible behind similar structures. Having revolutionized our understanding of gravity with General Relativity, Einstein spent his twilight years in a relentless pursuit of a 'Unified Field Theory' – a single, elegant set of equations that would weave gravity and electromagnetism into the same fabric.

Despite his conviction that the universe must be 'pure and unified,' the proof eluded Einstein. To this day, the quest for a 'Theory of Everything' remains the ultimate, unfinished business of physics. We are left to wonder whether the universe is truly a singular, harmonious masterpiece, or not.

THE INCOMPLETENESS THEOREMS

In the early 20th century, the respected (but less famous) mathematician David Hilbert harboured a grand ambition for the cosmos. He envisioned a 'final' mathematical edifice built upon a solid foundation of axioms, from which all the theorems of the universe could be neatly derived. In Hilbert's world, mathematics would eventually reach a state of completion, rendering further discovery obsolete.

This dream was shattered by Kurt Gödel, an Austro-American logician, mathematician and philosopher, who proposed the renowned '*Incompleteness Theorems.*' Gödel's first theorem posits that any mathematical system robust enough to handle basic arithmetic is either incomplete or inconsistent. His second theorem adds the sting: such a consistent mathematical system cannot even prove its own consistency.

To put this in the layman's terms: 'Completeness' suggests every true statement can be proven; 'Consistency' means you never prove a contradiction. Gödel's genius was in proving that you cannot have both. There are truths that are undeniably real, yet forever beyond the reach of formal proof.

While his Incompleteness Theorems are quite difficult to understand, Gödel used them as a springboard for a deeply metaphysical worldview and to derive the existence of God. The philosopher Wang Hao recorded a list of Gödel's philosophical beliefs in his book, *A Logical Journey: From Gödel to Philosophy*, which is quite interesting. Let us take a look:

1. The world is rational.
2. Human reason can, in principle, develop further (through certain techniques).
3. A systematic method to solve all problems exists (including those in art and other similar fields).
4. Other worlds and higher forms of existence exist.
5. This world which we inhabit is not the only world we will exist in or have existed in.
6. There is more innate knowledge that exists. What we currently know is negligible in comparison.
7. The intellectual development of humanity since the Renaissance is entirely comprehensible.
8. Human reason will gain development in every direction.
9. Formal rights form a true science.
10. Materialism is false.
11. Higher beings are connected to others through analogy, not composition.
12. Concepts have objective existence.

13. There exist a scientific (precise) philosophy and theology, which deal with the highest levels of abstraction; they are also the most effective for science.
14. Many religions are largely flawed, but religion (according to its definition) itself is not.

Today, Gödel's important work offers great value in contemporary debates about Artificial Intelligence. If every man-made system is inherently flawed, it follows that a creation can never spiritually or intellectually surpass its creator. AI is a prime example of a man-made creation. AI may comfortably outpace a human in processing power or data retrieval, but in the realm of wisdom and/or intellect, AI cannot exceed humanity. Human cognition and capability have obvious limitations. We have previously discussed humanity's boundaries of time and space. In most cases, differential equations have no solution. There are plenty of areas in the universe that are off-limits to us, and human cognition has its limits. This is also the case for AI.

However, humans possess a 'mathematical intuition' – a non-computational method of grasping truth that seems to bypass Gödelian constraints. We can 'see' a truth that a machine, relying solely on first-order logic, might never compute. Unless machines can replicate the messy, non-linear realms of experience and experimentation, they will remain beneath us in the hierarchy of wisdom.

Ultimately, Gödel's work suggests a universe of 'boundary layers.' Just as the Second Law of Thermodynamics and the speed of light hedge our physical movements, Incompleteness hedges our intellectual ones. There are deep, fundamental truths about our reality that may remain forever unproven – not because they are false, but because we lack the celestial tools to unlock them. It is, perhaps, another boundary set to us by the Creator.

DOES GOD EXIST?

Here, we use the term 'God' to refer to the metaphysical existence that has been humanity's perennial topic of discussion throughout the ages. While theologians have long relied on revelation, mathematicians like Leibniz and Kurt Gödel sought a more rigorous, mathematical approach. Gödel's mathematical proof treats divinity not as a person, but as a property – a logical necessity derived from a set of formal axioms.

Gödel's mathematical proof of the existence of God:

Axiom 1 (Dichotomy): A property is affirmed if, and only if, its negation is negated.

Axiom 2 (Closure): A property is affirmed if it necessarily implies an affirmative property.

Theorem 1: An affirmative property is logically consistent (special cases are possible).

Definition 1: Something is God-like if, and only if, it possesses all affirmative properties.

Axiom 3: 'Being God-like' is an affirmative property.

Axiom 4: An affirmative property is necessarily affirmed.

Definition 2: If, and only if x possesses feature P and when feature P is necessarily the most fundamental property, then feature P is the essence of x.

Theorem 2: If x is God-like, then being God-like is the essence of x.

Definition 3: x necessarily exists if the essence of x does not necessarily have some instance.

Axiom 5: 'Being necessarily existent' is affirmed.

Theorem 3: There necessarily exists some x, where x is God-like.

The logic of Gödel's proof rests on 'affirmative properties.' He defines a 'God-like' entity as one possessing all such positive attributes. By asserting that 'necessary existence' is itself an affirmative property, Gödel concludes that a God-like being must, by definition, exist. Crucially, this is not the God referred to by Christian doctrine; Gödel's 'God' is a mathematical predicate. He did not even rule out the possibility of there being multiple gods in the universe, provided multiple entities satisfy the criteria of being God-like.

To discuss the existence of God, one must also account for another philosopher – Baruch Spinoza. His 'God' is not a separate creator but the universe itself – an all-encompassing entity that merges the material and the spiritual (making God and the universe as one and the same). In Spinoza's view, nature is simply the incarnation of the divine. As a young man, I was deeply influenced by this viewpoint.

This pantheism suggests that only God has complete freedom in the world; individual humans, caught in the gears of a vast, infinite system, lack genuine free will. It is a perspective that finds a striking mirror in Buddhist thought, where the distinction between the self and the totality dissolves.

Ultimately, this 'God' remains as elusive as a singularity. Just as the interior of a black hole defies our observation and most complex differential equations remain unsolvable, the absolute truth remains beyond the human paygrade. We might summarize our understanding of God in three points:

- *Absolute Truth*: God represents the complete, infinite truth. Humanity, shackled by Gödelian incompleteness, must settle for versions that are either partial or inconsistent.
- *Omnipresence*: God is the universal constant, existing beyond the constraints of spatial dimensions.
- *Eternity*: God is the 'now' that transcends the linear arrow of time.

DOES GOD PLAY DICE?

In physics, an object has a place and a purpose; it is measurable and certain. Quantum mechanics, however, upends this stability. Albert Einstein famously resisted this volatility, grumbling that 'God does not play dice.' Yet, to understand the universe at its smallest scale, one must accept that reality is not composed of solid points, but of 'quanta' – indivisible bundles of energy, such as the photon.

At this microscopic level, Werner Heisenberg's 'uncertainty principle' reigns and is a cornerstone of quantum mechanics. It dictates a cosmic trade-off: you can know a particle's position or its momentum, but never both with total precision. The more you pin down one, the fuzzier the other becomes. This fuzziness is inherent; quanta exist in a state of 'wave-particle duality,' behaving like discrete bullets one moment and rippling waves the next.

This ambiguity is best demonstrated by the famous double-slit experiment. Fire photons at two slits, and they produce an interference pattern on a screen, acting like waves. But the moment you install a detector to 'spy' on which slit the photon enters, the pattern vanishes. The light begins to act like particles. The mere act of observation forces a 'collapse of the wave function.'

The double-slit experiment pertaining to quantum wave-particle duality and the Uncertainty Principle. In the double-slit experiment, monochromatic light is shone on an opaque barrier with two narrow slits. A detection screen is placed behind the barrier, and an interference pattern can be observed on the screen. This shows that photons behave like waves. Now, install a narrow-slit detector to track the photon's path. Of the two slits, which slit will the photon pass through? When the slit detector is turned on, the familiar interference pattern disappears and changes into a different pattern.

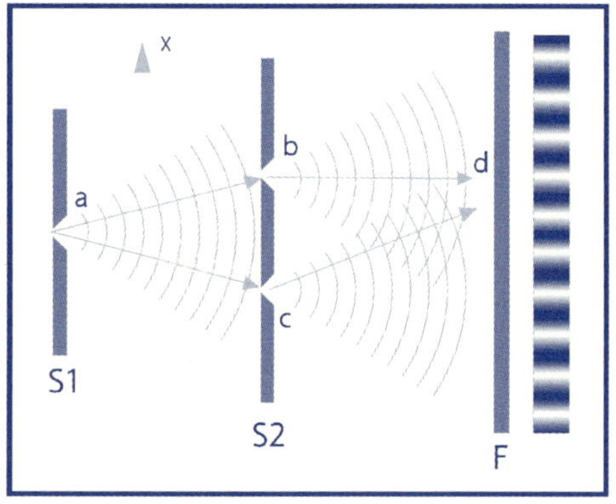

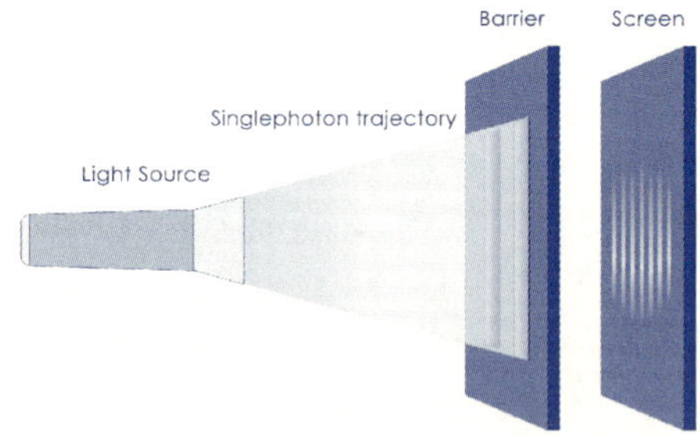

The Copenhagen Interpretation, a theory of quantum mechanics championed by Danish physicist Niels Bohr and Heisenberg, suggests a radical role for the observer. So long as we do not observe it, a particle (photon/electron) exists in a 'superposition' – a vague bundle of every possible state at once. It is only when it is observed or measured that the particle's state collapses into a definite one. It is the observer's presence and consciousness that is one of the factors that influences the state of the physical system, and this is known as the 'observer effect.' Thus, we are not merely spectators of the cosmos; we are active participants whose existence changes the outcome.

The governing rule of this strange realm is the Schrödinger equation. It holds the same structural authority in quantum mechanics as Newton's laws do in classical mechanics and Maxwell's equations in electromagnetism. Unlike simple algebra, it is a complex partial differential equation – often involving 'imaginary numbers' – that describes the probability of finding a particle in a particular state. Rather than being derived from more basic principles, the Schrödinger equation is taken as a fundamental assumption.

THE SCHRÖDINGER EQUATION

One-Dimensional Schrödinger Equation:

$$-\frac{\hbar^2}{2\mu}\frac{\partial^2\Psi(x,t)}{\partial x^2} + U(x,t)\Psi(x,t) = \mathrm{i}\hbar\frac{\partial\Psi(x,t)}{\partial t}$$

Three-Dimensional Schrödinger equation:

$$-\frac{\hbar^2}{2\mu}\left(\frac{\partial^2\Psi}{\partial x^2} + \frac{\partial^2\Psi}{\partial y^2} + \frac{\partial^2\Psi}{\partial z^2}\right) + U(x,y,z)\Psi = \mathrm{i}\hbar\frac{\partial\Psi}{\partial t}$$

Stationary Schrödinger equation:

$$-\frac{\hbar^2}{2\mu}\nabla^2\Psi + U\Psi = E\Psi$$

To illustrate the friction between quantum world of possibilities and the macroscopic world of certainties, Erwin Schrödinger proposed his famous feline paradox. A cat is placed in a sealed container with a small amount of radium and cyanide. There is a certain probability of radium decay. If the radium decays, it triggers a mechanism that shatters the bottle of cyanide, causing the cat to die. If the radium does not decay, then the cat survives. According to quantum mechanics, because the radioactive radium is in a superposition of both decayed and non-decayed states, the cat is supposed to be in a superposition of both dead and alive states – hence, the paradox of Schrödinger's Cat.

THE FUTURE IS UNKNOWN

In classical physics, the world is a clockwork mechanism. Newtonian mechanics suggests a rigid fatalism: if one knew the exact position and velocity of every particle in the universe, the future would be as readable as the past. However, Werner Heisenberg's uncertainty principle effectively bankrupts this idea. Heisenberg argued that the act of measurement itself disturbs the system; to observe a particle is to alter its trajectory. In the quantum realm, the observer is not a passive bystander but an active participant.

This aligns with a long-standing philosophical examination of reality. Immanuel Kant famously argued that it is not things that affect people, but people who affect things. People construct the world of reality, and in the process of recognizing things, humans are more important than the things themselves. We can never recognize the true nature of things, only their appearances. Across the globe, the Ming dynasty philosopher Wang Yangming reached a strikingly similar conclusion: "When you do not look at this flower, it and your mind both return to stillness; when you look at this flower, its colours suddenly become clear." Both suggest that reality is not something that exists 'out there' independently, but is crystallized by the act of perception.

While Newtonian physics implies fatalism (if the state of the universe is known at any given moment, then any event that will occur in the universe can be predicted), quantum mechanics suggests a more complex causality. Every observation forces a 'quantum collapse,' pushing the universe into a new state and initiating a 'new era.' However, predicting this future remains impossible. Heisenberg pointed out that the premise of classical predictability – "if we know the present exactly, we can calculate the future" – is fundamentally flawed. At the quantum level, details are 'pervasive' and fuzzy; we cannot audit the present with enough precision to calculate what comes next.

Information theory adds another layer of impossibility. From a computational perspective, predicting the future based on every physical variable would trigger an infinite recursion – a 'loop' that crashes the program. Furthermore, there is a problem of hardware: a computer cannot fully simulate a system more complex than itself. If our universe operates at a certain processing speed, simulating a future version of that same universe would require more 'MIPS' (Millions of Instructions Per Second)[2] than the system possesses.

---

2 This is a measurement indicator of a computer's processing speed.

We are thus caught in a peculiar paradox. While the current state of the universe is objectively 'certain,' it remains measurably elusive and it is impossible to predict accurately future events. Quanta exist as a spectrum of possibilities until they collapse into a single reality under our observation. This is the same principle powering quantum computing: by processing massive arrays of possibilities simultaneously, a 'solution' is simply the one state that collapses out of the calculation.

HARMONY AND UNITY

I am a science student who studied mathematics, physics and other sciences. Yet, a persistent curiosity for the humanities led me to the libraries of literature and philosophy, initially with a heavy lean toward Western works. It was only after reaching middle age that I returned to my own roots, seeking to learn and understand the wisdom and works of ancient Chinese masters. This journey involved not just reading, but the practical application of meditation and seeking the counsel of contemporary experts.

As I mentioned at the beginning of this section, this essay represents a compilation of that lifelong inquiry. In the vast sea of books and countless fields of knowledge, it all comes down to one conclusive sentence: Everything in our universe is deeply interconnected and profoundly harmonious.

EASTERN-WESTERN CONNECTION

In our modern analysis of global affairs, we tend to fixate on the differences between East and West – the friction of national borders, distinct culture and heritage, and the peculiarities of geography. In doing so, we overlook a deeper, underlying convergence.

This reminds me of the Zen koan regarding Huineng and Shenxiu. Despite lasting for over a thousand years, the debate between their two schools has yielded no conclusive answer.

Shenxiu's approach was one of meticulous maintenance: "The body is the Bodhi tree... wipe it ever so often, so it is not stained by dust' Huineng countered with a radical void: "The Bodhi tree is no tree in truth... since all is void from the very start, on what could dust be bound?"

Broadly speaking, the Western tradition has followed Shenxiu's path of rigorous refinement. Figures like Einstein and Gödel were the ultimate 'dusters,' using the tools of physics, mathematics and logic to clear the mirror of reality. The Chinese tradition, by contrast, has often sought Huineng's path of 'convenience' or direct intuition. This cultural split is visible even in the arts: Western painting historically relied on the strict mechanics of perspective to achieve realism, while Chinese 'freehand' brushwork prioritized the symbolic and the intuitive over the literal.

Yet, to declare one system superior is to succumb to a 'discriminating mind.' Whether one adopts the precise, incremental logic of the West or the holistic, intuitive grasp of the East, both can lead to the truth; both can attain the way. In the Buddhist tradition, there are said to be 84,000 paths to truth, each tailored to different temperaments and eras. Though the paths are different, both lead to the same mountaintop and the same view.

PHILOSOPHICAL CONNECTION

Philosophy, it turns out, is a highly interconnected business. Regardless of the school of thought, Eastern or the Western, the result is the same: the human mind can only ever grasp a fragment of absolute truth. Yet, each of these fragments remains an authentic piece of the larger puzzle. As our previous survey suggests, the great Western thinkers may have used different conceptual currencies, but they were often trading in the same fundamental ideas.

This is why I believe that our world is, first and foremost, a world of ideas; the material reality we inhabit is merely the secondary manifestation of these underlying thoughts. We do not just observe reality; we shape it. While various philosophical schools take different paths in their pursuit of the truth, they are all climbing the same mountain. In the end, their diverse perspectives do not conflict; they converge at the same peak.

RELIGIOUS CONNECTION

Many concepts across different religions are, to some extent, interconnected.

Take Chinese Taoism and Buddhism – their core principles share many similarities:

Taoism: Tranquility (静), Steadiness (定), Wisdom (慧)
Buddhism: Morality (戒), Concentration (定), Wisdom (慧).

RELIGIOUS AND PHILOSOPHICAL CONNECTION

Consider the philosophical blueprints for the 'ideal' human. Whether one looks at Friedrich Nietzsche's *Übermensch* or the 'Sage' envisioned by Wang Yangming, Lao Tzu and Confucius, the structural parallels are striking. These figures are more than mere moral archetypes; they bear a heavy resemblance to religious concepts. Indeed, philosophy and religion function as parallel pathways to the pursuit of fundamental truth.

The Buddhas, saints and sages of history were essentially those who managed to balance the cosmic books. They perceived a reality that exists beyond the reach of formal logic or traditional accounting. As we have seen previously, the boundaries between science, philosophy and religion are far more porous than modern studies suggest.

Humans possess a relentless urge to categorize, neatly filing knowledge into separate folders labelled 'Science,' 'Religion' or 'Philosophy.' Yet the pioneers of thought – the Newtons and the Lao Tzus – were often scientists, philosophers and even spiritual seekers simultaneously. They were all engaged in the same trade: seeking the 'Tao' or the 'Truth.' It was only later generations who insisted on compartmentalizing their discoveries into distinct disciplines.

Besides this, two characteristics also stand out. First, the human intellect operates within strict limits; our understanding is inherently bounded. Second, the ultimate truth is 'ineffable' – it is a value that can be felt and lived, but never fully captured in the prose of a report or the symbols of an equation.

THE LIMITATIONS OF HUMAN UNDERSTANDING

Our previous discussion of human expression reveals a sobering reality: language and writing have their limitations. Even the 'hard' sciences of chemistry and physics, and mathematics – long considered the highest form of human expression – operate within strict limits. Most differential equations used to describe our universe lack exact solutions; general solutions are rarer still. This mathematical shortfall is not merely a technical glitch, but a profound validation of the boundaries of our cognitive reach.

This represents the ultimate ceiling on human knowledge. We find ourselves in a position where we can speculate on the direction of the trend, but we can never fully comprehend the entirety of the truth.

THE INEFFABILITY OF TRUTH

Truth is notoriously difficult to express in words. Part of the problem lies in the nature of language itself: it is a symbolic system of human convention, and as such, its precision and subtlety are never guaranteed. Immanuel Kant pointed to the fundamental error at the heart of communication: things are concrete and materialized, whereas language is abstract and removed. How can these two possibly be identical?

This limitations of language are vividly captured in the *Vimalakirti Sutra*, specifically in the chapter on the "Entry into Nonduality." The layman Vimalakirti invited a gallery of bodhisattvas to explain how one might pass through the gate of nondual truth. Each offered a sophisticated verbal defence of their position. Finally, they turned to Manjushri, the personification of wisdom, who argued that to enter this gate is to be silent – to move beyond speech, cognition and the binary of questions and answers.

When Manjushri then asked Vimalakirti to offer his own definition of this sacred entry, the latter responded with a silence. He did not say a word. Manjushri was moved to praise: "Excellent! Excellent! Not a single word or letter, not a trace of verbal expression – this is true entry into the nondual Dharma!"

THE MEANING OF LIFE

How do we understand life and death? How do we understand the meaning of life?

ABOUT LIFE

Arthur Schopenhauer viewed existence as a series of reallocations rather than absolute gains or losses. In his examination, birth is merely a transition from a prior state, and death is not a return to nothingness but a shift within the world of appearances. This mirrors the religious landscape: Christianity offers salvation through belief, while Buddhism promotes 'awakening' – realizing that, as the Zen master Huineng put it, we are "inherently endowed with all".

This idea that the whole contains its parts, and the parts contain the whole is foundational. If you cut a block of wood in half, its essence remains 'wood.' Continue this division to its physical limit and you reach the quantum level, the smallest unit in physics. Gottfried Wilhelm Leibniz formalized this with his 'monads' – indivisible, extensionless points of 'thought' that serve as the fundamental building blocks of the universe. For Leibniz, all our concepts (ideas) are composed of a very small number of combined simple, 'alphabetical' thoughts. Hegel echoed this interconnectedness with his famous line, "I that is We, and We that is I."

Traditional Chinese acupuncture offers a practical application of this part-to-whole logic. By stimulating specific acupoints – a 'small universe' – information is transmitted to the 'large universe' that is your body to heal you. In the language of physics, this information acts as negative entropy, guiding a disordered system back toward order. Acupuncture is not about using needles to heal your illness. It is an information-based therapy that treats the body as an integrated network rather than a collection of isolated parts.

Mahayana Buddhism takes this further with the "Theory of Dependent Origination." It posits that all phenomena are impermanent and 'selfless,' existing only through interdependent causation. Suffering arises when we cling to the delusion of a permanent 'I.' To realize 'non-self' is to achieve Nirvana – a state of serene, unhindered freedom. The Swiss psychologist Carl Jung touched on something similar with 'individuation,' the process by which a living thing fulfils its original destiny.

The "wisdom of the Tathāgata" suggests that absolute truth is already within us, obscured only by our delusions and attachments. Lao Tzu's *Tao Te Ching* advises a return to these roots through emptiness and stillness: "All things flourish in abundance, but each returns to its root." Meditation may help reach this realm – it is worth a try.

While Confucius pragmatically avoided the question of the afterlife – remarking that one cannot know death without first knowing life – Buddhism suggests the answer lies in the 'present.' To seek answers to life and death, one must look at the here and now.

THE MEANING OF LIFE

If the mysteries of life and death remain beyond our understanding, where does that leave the 'meaning' of life? For myself, the pursuit of the meaning of life started at a very young age. And after some time, my conclusion is this:

there is no meaning to life; there is only the journey. Indeed, the very inquiry into 'meaning' is structurally flawed. There is no meaning to discussing the meaning of existence. It only applies to an object in relation to something else. In that case, where does the meaning lie, for us, as the objects?

If life must mean anything, then physics offers a candidate: frequency. In the quantum world, higher frequency correlates with greater energy. If existence has a purpose, it is likely the elevation of our own 'frequency' – increasing our spiritual energy to move closer to higher-dimensional space-time. This apex is where 'God' resides – not as a sectarian deity, but as a placeholder for absolute truth and existence. As Baruch Spinoza noted, the closest one gets to the divine is not through eternal life in Christian faith, but by recognizing the inevitability of the universe. The more we see things as inevitable, the easier it will be to attain union with God.

If God exists, then so must the soul. Therefore, we should not despair or lose hope. The probability that our world is actually a simulation – a game designed and orchestrated by higher-dimensional beings – is quite high. In such a scenario, what would be the point of the game? Is it to simulate their way of life in a simulation of their world? As characters in the game, perhaps we all have our own scripts. We are here to cultivate and 'level up' our souls, and to refine our wisdom and spirituality to attain evolution and achieve perfection.

When a character within a game begins to question its 'meaning,' it is indeed quite meaningless. Our lives may simply be the 'scripts' through which we cultivate perfection. We progress through the levels of this reality, elevating our energy to eventually transcend our current dimensions and draw closer to our creators. In this light, the goal of the game is not to find a hidden meaning, but to evolve into a version of ourselves worthy of the next dimension.

GOING HOME

In truth, all things possess a spirit. Being human holds no special privilege. To understand the 'true nature of things,' one must first let go of the 'self' and peer into the higher-dimensional logic that governs existence. In Eastern thought, this is the *Dharma* – the essential laws and principles that underpin reality. To realize this is to achieve a state of unhindered freedom, allowing the traveller to finally 'return to the Tao,' or path.

Because we came from the 'path.'

If the "Tao begets One; One begets Two; Two begets Three; and Three begets all things," then our final destination is a process of reduction, a journey of return. It is a journey where complexity yields to simplicity: all things return to the Three, the Three to the Two, the Two to the One, and the One back to the Tao. This "Path" is not a foreign destination but a homecoming – our final destination is to 'return to the path,' to 'go home.'

If music is the mathematical expression of the soul, then there is no better accompaniment for this transition than the echoes of Yo-Yo Ma's rendition of Dvořák's *Going Home*. May this beautiful melody accompany us on our journey back home.

Cosmology: Full speech delivered on 3 October, 2023
Compiled 6 September, 2024

REALM

MY DECADE LONG PATH TO ENTREPRENEURSHIP

I believe the following traits propel me forward unceasingly: the audacity to embrace risks, the courage to sacrifice, a brimming passion, keen business acumen, an open mind, unwavering tenacity, an insatiable thirst for learning and reflection.

THE FIRST JOURNEY: CTRIP

In 1999 my university classmate Wan Hui introduced me to James Liang, who at that time was working for Oracle. We often went travelling on weekends. Once, after James returned from visiting his girlfriend in America, he was very excited because internet companies were taking off like wildfire and he said we should take a shot at it, too. At the time I already had a small company which was making a bit of money, though no matter how hard I tried it wasn't growing. I was thinking about how to achieve something big and influential. All of us really clicked and decided on the spot to set up a business. We then dragged both Neil Shen, who was working in finance (and coincidently was also introduced by Wan Hui), and Fan Min, who was working in tourism, into the scheme. We were kindred spirits and worked together to build a business: Ctrip.com, an online travel agency.

At the time our motivation was mainly to take advantage of the surge of interest in the internet to make some money. Of course, there was an element of idealism in that I wanted to do something to prove myself and achieve something big. That is to say, it was an everyday business story of four impetuous young men dissatisfied with the status quo, excited by the trends of the time and, with a dash of idealism, pursued the dream of wealth.

Our business model was hardly an earth-shattering innovation; we just followed Expedia's model, by first creating content, then relying on hotel room and ticket bookings to take profit.

That was an era when a good business plan was enough to attract financing. Our plan was not as exciting as a web portal but with the impressive qualifications of the four founders we were able to get some venture capital. The first tranche came from IDG, since then they've invested in the three enterprises I have been involved in founding: Ctrip, Home Inn and Hanting Hotels. It just goes to prove that even in a crazy era there are smart people who understand what's going on.

We tried a few different profit models, starting with selling admission tickets to tourist attractions, and later grouped retail customers together and sold travel packages to them at wholesale prices. At the time, travel agencies and airline ticket offices were too proud to deal with a company like ours. We approached a number of room-booking companies. They were not large-scale enterprises and were also going through the dilemma of taking profit vs business expansion. We made use of the internet as a great concept to attract some of the best people in several fields. Later, with internet-related companies at a high price premium, we purchased the biggest room-booking company at the time. Since then, the main business model of Ctrip has been room-booking.

We company founders firmly believed from day one that the business had to actually make money, because relying only on click-rates or venture capital to support the business was not reliable. That's why, from the very beginning, we desperately strived to look for profit models. Just when the dotcom bubble burst, we stumbled across the 'mouse and mortar' model of online room booking. The last tranche of venture capital funds (from IDG and the Carlyle Group) saved our lives, enabling us to stay in business until we became profitable and then went public, achieving our dreams of glory.

Some say venture capitalists and private equity investors are greedy bloodsuckers, while others have a poor impression of investment brokers. At this juncture, allow me to express my opinion: commerce is an organic value chain, and each link has its reason for being. Profit sharing and mutual benefits are necessary, and there is no who's right and who's wrong, the key is the way of thinking. Some businessmen are always in a lather because they worry that someone is getting the better of them. When financing an operation there is no hard and fast standard for valuations. There are, of course, technicalities like cash flow rebates, PE (price-earnings ratio) or EBITDA (earnings before interest, tax, depreciation and amortization) multiples, but mostly it all depends on the feelings of both parties. Going public is the same; the fundamentals are still mutual profitability and long-term stable development.

Market bubbles attract a lot of criticism. Actually, smart people can take advantage of bubbles to do many good things, like financing, headhunting and free publicity.

When a bubble forms financial costs are never priced low because even the most brilliant investors find it difficult to avoid being caught up in the exuberance of bubble markets. They are very close to the stock markets and thus more susceptible to being influenced by market fluctuations. The ability to get financing during a bubble will determine the fate of a business; the valuations will inevitably be high in a bubble market because entrepreneurs never want to lose out.

The dotcom bubble caused many people to dive into internet businesses, some coming from foreign invested enterprises (like James Liang and Neil Shen) and some from senior positions in domestic state-owned enterprises (like Fan Min). This probably would not have happened without the lure of a huge bubble.

Bubble economies, whether the dotcom bubble or a real estate bubble, will always attract attention from the public and the media. Why not make use of the opportunity to promote oneself, increase name recognition and media exposure? During the internet bubble, Ctrip was not as much in the limelight as web portals but it was well-regarded and a centre of focus for the media.

As mentioned earlier, since the establishment of Ctrip we insisted that a commercial enterprise must make money. Hence, we took pains to find profits, first in selling tourist attraction admission tickets to selling group tours, then on to hotel room-bookings. We had our own 800 number for bookings in as early as 1999; in 2000 we bypassed the conventional hotel booking model used by travel agencies, which involved collecting payments from guests and paying the hotels while keeping their commission. Our new model was to use Ctrip.com as a room-booking platform. Guests made payments when they arrived at their hotels. The hotels paid our commission later. We became profitable in 2002.

After the bubble deflated, capital markets gradually warmed up again. Ctrip was the first one off the starting block and listed on Nasdaq in December 2003. Today, market capitalization is US$6 billion.

17 June, 2011

THE SECOND JOURNEY: HOME INN

The last tranche of financing for Ctrip was at about the time of the bursting of the dotcom bubble. We were concerned that we had insufficient cash reserves, so we sought even more financing. That's why when the company began to be profitable, we had a lot of excess cash. The company decided to forge a new direction for investment to make best use of the excess capital – the cost of this capital was extremely expensive, having come from the dilution of the founding shareholders' shares.

At the time, Ctrip's online bookings were already in the tens of thousands and we were quite familiar with hotel sales across China. Many clients pointed out that Ctrip did not have enough booking options for budget hotels. And, unlike most hotels that seemed to have limitless room supplies, the most popular budget hotel, Xinya Star Hotel, allocated us only a few rooms. The supply-demand situation told us that there was a market gap in budget hotel supply. Our company decided to test the water by investing in budget hotels and appointed me to explore. This later led to the emergence of Home Inns.

The initial business model was hotel franchising, which is common in the West. We used Ctrip's marketing power to attract three-star hotels to adopt the Home Inn brand. Though facilities, quality of service and pricing varied, we persevered with the brand.

But the hotels had different operators and many hotels displayed two brands. This profit model brought in little income because brand identity was not distinguishable enough.

Also, financing was not smooth. Neil Shen and I visited numerous venture capital companies in Beijing, but it never resulted in anything. No one was interested in this kind of small-scale hotel because most of the investors could not get a clear picture of the hotel industry in a short time.

At an IDG investment meeting we suggested that investors stop focusing only on IT and high-tech industries and try some traditional fields. IDG was sceptical; with a let's-give-it-a-try approach they again became our first investors. The key factor behind their investing in us was that they valued our personnel – the Ctrip team had been through many trials, giving IDG confidence in our ability to accomplish things.

It's almost impossible to count on venture capitalists and private equity investors to understand an industry better than entrepreneurs, especially new industries or ones that are innovative or undergoing reform. Investment houses employ a large number of analysts, but it is unrealistic to expect that recent university graduates will truly understand an industry in a short time. The best method to decide on investments is to seek the most outstanding talents of an industry to evaluate if a team is capable and possesses unique advantages.

After meeting the main players in the budget hotel arena in China we were extremely lucky to have an opportunity to work with the Beijing Travel Group (BTG). Many people were pessimistic about working with a state-owned enterprise, but the results were beyond the expectations of most observers.

The reasons for this are: firstly, the highest levels of management at the BTG were not bothered by small initial losses, because they were looking for brand investments and value investments, and they fully trusted the management team of the joint venture company. It was purely a business-oriented approach.

Secondly, we gained time by cooperating with the BTG. At the time I said we were at least two years ahead of starting from scratch on our own. Now I realize just how important those two years were.

In fact, they were a lifesaver. If we had been two years slower, the rapid rise of branded hotel chains like Motel 168 and 7 Days Inn would have eaten up the advantage Home Inn had as the first in the business.

Our experience with the four BTG hotels convinced me more than ever of the direct management model, making me determined to abandon alliances, which is why Home Inn developed so fast and quickly became profitable.

At Home Inn I brought a great deal of IT and internet business style with me, much of which was picked up from my partners who had worked with me setting up businesses.

An example is the way traditional businesses attract venture capital. It might not seem unusual from today's perspective, but in those days venture capitalists mostly looked at the Silicon Valley experience and were concentrating on high-tech investments, especially IT, and rarely invested in traditional businesses like hotels. From the beginning we decided to utilize several tranches of capitalization in order to go public and achieve our initial goal of making the greatest use possible of our excess cash.

I took the 'fast fish eat slow fish' ethos of the internet industry into the hotel business, advocating speed and efficiency, rather than simply following conventional thinking on development of a business. At the same time, I brought in modern management tools and methods, such as ERP systems and balanced scorecards to assess performance.

This was a break with the norms of the hospitality industry and marked the beginning of a new era for the hotel industry in China. However, fate does not always abide by the wishes of man. Soon after the establishment of Home Inn, the 2003 SARS epidemic broke out. Fear shrouded our vast country and affected some investors. The board decided to stop new projects, reduce staffing levels and cut costs, which was a huge hit for the entire team. It was the biggest test I have experienced since embarking into business. There were challenges inside the company and on the outside: on the inside many of the founders departed because they were unwilling to endorse some of the board's ideas; on the outside no one could say how much SARS would affect the hotel industry.

I believed that both the investors and I were correct. It was an unprecedented threat of which no one had any previous experience. If too many risks were taken, it would be the same as gambling and the business would be destroyed. Whereas the investors considered controlling the risk, I saw opportunities, which meant taking a somewhat longer-term view. But this friction over a disagreement planted the seeds for our parting of ways later.

By the end of 2004 we were moving closer to stock market listing. The board decided to hire a professional manager. We all thought Sun Jian was a good candidate – a modest and friendly man with good communication skills and franchising experience. The company had passed the initial establishment stage, and everyone thought it would be wiser for it to be managed by a professional in the field. Someone also suggested I stay in the company to ensure a smooth transition. But I decided to leave for I felt a lack of respect and trust due to the friction that had occurred earlier.

Therefore, my departure from Home Inn can be described as 'I left Home Inn,' or 'Home Inn pushed out its founder.'

To be fair, Sun Jian has been good for Home Inn. The management has been consistent, and the transition was smooth. The company has moved up one stage. In October 2006, the year following my departure, Home Inn successfully listed on Nasdaq. Its current market value is about US$ 1.4 billion.

27 June, 2011

THE THIRD JOURNEY: HANTING

I did not plan to start another business to compete with Home Inn after leaving it. Instead, I thought about opening mid-range hotels, similar to Accor's Novotel and Marriott International's Courtyard. Hanting's Ji Hotels and Home Inn's Hotels nowadays belong to this category. At the time I was also interested in commercial properties. In Shanghai I was involved in a few investments in the Creative Industry Zone. I also acquired a few properties, planning to join Home Inn's franchise program.

In hindsight, these ideas were very advanced at the time. And it was true: the idea of opening mid-range hotels was way too advanced, because entering a saturated market takes time. And worse, at the time there were not many cities and neighborhoods suitable for this type of hotel, which meant it was hard to expand the network. The operation of my first Home Inn franchise was also not smooth. Eventually, I gave up the idea of buying properties to join Home Inn's franchise program. After all, the capital I had was inadequate to purchase a large number of properties. This approach did not allow me to fully utilize the advantages of my business skills and fully leverage them for greater impact.

I struggled for two years, then returned to the budget hotel market. I must attribute this change to my friend Wu Jiong. Once he asked me: "How many budget hotel chains can China accommodate in the future?" "At least four or five,"

I answered. "Is there anyone else in China who is more familiar with the budget hotel market?" he continued. "I won't be the only one, but I am definitely one of the people who is familiar with this market," I replied. So, it was natural for me to return to this market.

My return to the budget hotel market meant setting a clear goal and taking fewer detours. We had a new, higher starting point: our products must be better; hotel locations must be more convenient for our main customers; our team must be stronger and more complementary; the shareholding structure of our company must be more stable; our goals must be higher and our vision must be more inspiring; and the development of our company must be faster than our competitors.

As for hotel designs, we did not repeat the bold and colorful décor of other hotels and opted for a calming style: stylish bathrooms with patented fixtures; a more advanced fibre optic internet connection with Wi-Fi accessible in all public areas; multi-function key cards that provide access to rooms, elevators and the main gate, and serve as membership cards; an express check out; buckwheat pillows that provide better neck positioning and spinal alignment; and tasteful impressionist oil paintings ... Hanting Express hotels are arguably an upgraded version of existing budget hotels.

Our hotel site selection strategy was different from other hotel brands. They focus on expanding their network. We focused on getting into busy central business districts of major cities, especially in the Yangtze River Delta. And from there, we expanded to cities in the Bohai Bay region and the Pearl River Delta. This strategy enabled us to connect the most economically vibrant regions on our map right from the beginning and was a convenient choice for business travellers.

During the process of catching up with our already well-established strong competitors, we laid out some strategic goals: our revenue per available room (RevPAR) should be 10% higher than theirs, our construction costs should match theirs, but our operating costs should be 10% less. After a few years of hard work, this strategy enabled us to gradually catch up with our competitors and we became one of the best performers in lean management in the hotel industry.

The founding stage of Hanting was blessed with luck. In addition to people like Jin Hui, Wang Haijun and Cheng Jun, who had been working with me right from the beginning, Zhang Tuo and Zhang Min who joined us in 2007 are also outstanding individuals. I once said the Hanting team is just as good as the original Ctrip team.

The ownership structure guaranteed the original team the largest number of shares, exceeding 50% of the total after listing. Too much dilution of equity would not help the company's long-term planning, pushing emphasis on short-term profit taking. Several years of toiling in the industry convinced me that a hotel business will develop more smoothly and stably if there is a single large shareholder. As Liu Chuanzhi, the founder of Lenovo, has said, a company must have a boss.

In the setup stage of Hanting, listing on the stock market was not the objective; rather, it was considered a means of achieving our objectives. Hanting's vision was to become a leading international hotel chain. I characterized this ideal: a group of like-minded friends happily working together to achieve something great.

We were quite lucky with initial financing because most of the investors were close friends who understood us well. That was especially true of IDG when Zhou Quan jokingly said once in Hainan, "Ji Qi, we will definitely invest in your next enterprise, even if you go into trading dog poop." That was hugely encouraging and left me deeply touched.

It sometimes felt like fate was testing us when the global financial crisis erupted not long after the company was set up. It didn't actually have a big impact on sales, but the capital markets slumped. This was not the first time something like this had happened to me and it led me to believe that crises provide great buying opportunities because prices are cheap. Real estate prices during SARS and businesses during the financial crisis were very cheap. During the financial crisis I made the biggest investment of my life – I invested a lot in Hanting together with other investors. It was my commitment to and faith in Hanting, and it proved to be a wise investment.

We took advantage of the crisis to build up inner strength: better cost control, better staff training and building IT systems, so that when the crisis was over, Hanting was one of the first businesses to emerge. In March 2010 Hanting successfully listed on Nasdaq and the market capitalization now exceeds one billion US dollars.

1 July, 2011

THE STORY OF THE FIRST HANTING HOTEL

The first Hanting Hotel was in Kunshan, just outside Shanghai.

That was in 2005 and there was a commercial site next to the Kunshan railway station that was looking for tenants. We managed to get it with the help of friends.

That was before high speed rail when the Kunshan station was tiny and the property was just across the road from the station. The building is L-shaped with about 12,000 square meters of floor space. We rented out almost all of the ground floor. One of the tenants was a Hao Xiang Lai Steak House and the best corner site was rented out to a China Unicom mobile phone service shop. This way we recouped one third of the building's rent. We kept a part of the ground floor for the hotel lobby. The second floor was for the restaurant and the rest of the building was for guest rooms. The rent in those days was cheap, allowing us to have large, comfortable guest rooms.

We hired a team from Trendzone Decoration, a famous company from Shanghai, to design and renovate the hotel. Unfortunately, the collaboration did not go well because I made many changes to their design. They said that this had never happened to them before.

In the design phase, the designer planned to use a large amount of marble, but I thought it was unnecessary for three reasons: first, expense; second, assembling and maintenance are troublesome; third, there is a radiation issue. I said that I couldn't afford this material and didn't want it.

An immaculate and stylish benchtop was good enough. Why did we have to use marble? Then the designer insisted on using wooden furniture, which I also vetoed. This would be a subject for argument nowadays but, at the time, the designer did not understand our expectations.

I later wondered if the reason behind the disagreement was that I had already listed two companies on the stock market and they wanted to show us what we 'deserved,' thinking, "Your company is rolling in money, isn't it?"

Kunshan at the time was a third- or fourth-tier city. My reasoning was that it would not be surprising if Hanting failed in Kunshan because, after all, there were not many tourist and business traveller flows. If we failed in Kunshan, we might make it work in Shanghai. But if we were successful in Kunshan, then we could make it work everywhere.

It was a bold decision at the time. I was confident of my understanding of the hotel industry. I was an IT person by training. My first reaction after entering the hotel industry was that there were huge opportunities for IT people like me to break conventions.

The common management protocol at the time was to be apprenticed to a senior person in the industry. After years of muddling along, some might be lucky enough to become a GM or a Deputy GM by the time they reached my age. Seniority was the highest principle. People who worked in five-star hotels believed they were superior to their peers in three-star hotels. In my view, this does not make sense.

Most people in the industry in those days did not know how to utilize venture capital and computer technology in management. At the time, landline phone calls were free in guest rooms but Wi-Fi connections were not. Guests who used an in-room landline service tended to be the ones with a weaker payment ability because most more affluent guests would use mobile phones to make calls. I thought: I want to shuffle things around a little. In Hanting, all Wi-Fi internet connections are free of charge.

The traditional hotel industry is filled with a sense of vanity and riddled with bureaucracy. In my view, the IT industry has none of that. Its no-nonsense style is like a young man wearing a T-shirt and sporting a crew cut; whoever is capable comes out on top. Let me do it if you can't. The entire industry is constantly being pushed forward by young people. The value of older generations depreciates fast.

This kind of belief in equality, advanced management concepts and technology was precisely what the traditional hotel industry lacked. My involvement in the hotel industry was a process of an outsider analysing, deconstructing and then reconstructing a traditional industry. I've become very confident with this process. I believe that there is not much that I can't anticipate in this industry now.

Our first hotel in Kunshan was a great success. With that confidence boost, we proceeded to open another one in Suzhou, and then one in Shanghai. By the end of 2017, Hanting had opened 2,244 hotels all over China.

28 December, 2017

WHAT THE THREE BUSINESSES HAVE IN COMMON

The three businesses – Ctrip, Home Inn and Hanting – have much common ground.

First, the actual business models were not entirely the same as those conceptualized at the time of the initial financing. Ctrip moved from an online travel agency to hotel room-bookings, while Home Inn moved from the hotel franchise model to privately owned and operated budget hotels, and Hanting moved from mid-range limited-service hotels to budget hotels.

But the key was the adaptability of the founding team which constantly explored solutions and constantly innovated. If we had stuck with our initial unrealistic ideal models, these businesses would have died in the cradle. When ideal models are tested in the light of experience, we must be able to finesse a feasible way out of a difficult situation and, by constantly expanding upon the fruits of small battles, win the war.

Also, the trust of investors is vital to give you time and space to test by trial and error and manoeuvre. For that reason, it is essential to choose investors and funds that understand the Chinese market.

Second, each of the businesses required about three years to take shape. For Ctrip it was from 1999 to 2002; Home Inn 2003 to 2005; and Hanting from 2007 to 2010.

In a similar manner to human development, the basic shape of these three businesses, their teams, structure, character and culture was formed in the first three years.

Thereafter it was just a question of continued growth. Three years is a critical time for Chinese companies to reach a certain level to be able to enable significant future growth. This is because Chinese companies grow fast and there are many imitators and followers. If a company can't stand out from the crowd within three years, it risks becoming just another contender like them and will be stuck in mediocrity.

Third, each of the three companies faced at least one major challenge. Ctrip was hit by the dotcom bubble; Home Inn was hit by SARS; and Hanting was hit by the global financial crisis.

Facing crises forced each company to mobilize all possible positive factors and put their most outstanding attributes into play, forcing every ounce of their potential into the fore. Crises became the driver of our growth. In the same way the petrel faces the storm in the Russian writer Maxim Gorky's 'Song of the Stormy Petrel': Let it break in all its fury! These crises also destroyed or weakened many similar businesses and competitors, so that the businesses with superior genes found it much easier to continue growing after the crises passed. A crisis is a test of a company's true character – whether or not it's an opportunistic player or a diligent and assiduous one. Only the latter can weather storms and grow larger, and not drown in a bubble or be destroyed by a storm.

Fourth, all three companies were the perfect marriage of entrepreneurial spirit and professional management. From the outset of initiating the setup of Ctrip I had an absolutely professional team with James Liang establishing a solid foundation, Fan Min carrying it forward, and Neil Shen dealing with the financial and legal aspects. I established a firm base for Home Inn, then Sun Jian took up the baton; I also initiated Hanting and established a solid base together with Zhang Tuo, and Zhang Min has maintained a steady pace right up to the present day.

Fifth, all three businesses were a reformation of a traditional industry. Ctrip was transformed from a traditional travel agency to a modern travel service company. Both Home Inn and Hanting were upgraded from traditional hotels to modern hotel chains. These are representative examples of 'China Service' that I often talk about.

28 December, 2017

MY MANAGEMENT EXPERIENCE AND LESSONS LEARNED

I have always thought of myself as a company executive with no formal education in management. I have never enrolled in a formal MBA program. I have never studied at Harvard. And I have never worked in a large corporation either. After graduating from university, I worked in a state-owned enterprise for less than two years, then quit. I am an open-minded person who does not like to be constrained and I used to think I may not be able to manage a large company well.

For these reasons, I started to search for a company manager as soon as H World reached a substantial scale. At the time, I thought the ideal candidate would be like our current CEO Jenny Zhang – a Harvard graduate who studied management and had work experience in a foreign invested corporation. So, I persuaded all the veterans of the company to hire an outsider to be CEO. I soon discovered I had made a huge mistake.

I thought that with a CEO the company would be just fine and I could go sightseeing with my friends while the CEO just ran the company by tracking the stock price and watching budgets. But in time, the business lost its vitality and became lifeless. This is because some managers possess skills but lack an ability to engage in long-term planning and do not understand the culture behind the company. In the end I had to return to the CEO position myself and correct the mistake I had made. It was a difficult time that cost me dearly in terms of my health.

Actually, a company like H World needs both types of people. It needs an entrepreneur like me; a founder and a disrupter, who is a leader. I'm a sensitive person and a laid-back leader with something of an artistic temperament. A company also needs a professional manager of which Jenny Zhang is an outstanding example. She has received formal training, has managerial experience in a large enterprise, is exceptionally smart, and also loves the business with genuine passion.

In this way we can find a point of convergence between the two fields of passion and idealism. She is particularly well-trained in technical skills, so we are excellent as complements to each other. If I had continued to hand over everything to a manager, the company would never have been equipped to face challenges and would have fallen behind the times, obsolete.

28 December, 2017

A SMALL NEIGHBORHOOD AND A BIG NEIGHBORHOOD

Over the years, I have been involved in site selection and final decoration design for the bulk of our hotels. For important projects I visit the sites.

Recently we've been renovating a site on Yan'an Road in Shanghai which we intend to turn into a Ji Hotel 4.0. It's an excellent location that used to be occupied by a famous old all-you-can-eat buffet restaurant chain called Golden Jaguar, probably known to everyone in Shanghai. The layout, however, was a complete mess. The internal structure was complex and there were also three domes on the roof. That's the sort of site I must examine personally to get a feeling for it.

On the eve of the Beijing Olympics, we acquired a site on Dongzhimen in Beijing that we planned to use for a Hanting Hotel. It was a vitally important project, being the only site we could get on Chang'an Boulevard in Beijing. It was only about seven or eight thousand square meters and the rent was very high, around five yuan a square metre per month, which was an exorbitant price in those days. The landlord said a competitor was ready to sign if we didn't. The rent was so high for this project that no one was able to decide, so I had to inspect it myself.

One evening I flew to Beijing, arriving on the site at dawn. I used my mobile phone torch to look around, then rushed to the airport to fly to Shanghai. While on the site, I began to think about how to lay out rooms. The rooms would have to be quite small to cover the cost of the rent.

A place as significant as Beijing's Chang'an Boulevard has very few foreign invested hotels, so when Hanting was open for business it was an instant success.

When considering hotel projects, first look at the immediate surroundings; second, examine the internal structure of the building; third, go up on the roof and look about.

Look at the immediate surroundings to gauge the price range a hotel in the neighborhood will be able to achieve in the future. Examine the structure to consider remodelling and room layout. I like large open area floors, though many buildings are not like that with numerous partitions. That will mean a lot of geometrical problems to solve. On the roof the whole environment of the hotel can be taken in. For a project in Singapore, I clambered up to the 12th floor together with designer Ray Chou for a look. That's the only way to observe traffic flows and the areas around the site. At street level we can take in the small neighborhood while on the roof we can observe the big neighborhood.

Often when we are able to reward our partners it is because our brand is strong, or our designs are good. If our style of doing things is rough and ready, we have no chance of succeeding.

28 December, 2017

MY DARKEST MOMENTS

There have been crises in my life that were my darkest moments.

The first one arrived when I was a second-year university student. I came from a poor family. I was hungry every day when I was studying in Shanghai. At night, I had to cram textbooks. It was hard. I felt like I was a living corpse – my life was being dictated by others; activities such as going to class, having meals, cramming textbooks and going to bed, were all beyond my control. I thought: What am I doing? Why should I live like this? I could not find a convincing reason.

At the time, I did not fit in with my surroundings and could not find myself. That was probably the first time I pondered the meaning of life and asked questions like, "Why do people live?"

With these perplexities in mind I eagerly read many books on philosophy and literature. In hindsight, I can see how hardship indeed inspires people to seek spiritual meaning. Religion plays the same role. Many people seek comfort in religion after suffering hardship. The conclusion I reached in my university years is that there is no such thing as 'meaning' in life; the noumenon can't define its own meaning. Life is a process and there is only experience. For the noumenon, there is no meaning. This conclusion was a great relief for me.

My second crisis was the Home Inn experience.

In late 2004, the board of Home Inn decided to approach a professional manager to run the company and, as the founder of the company, I left. At the time one board member said that my grassroots background meant I would not be able to manage the company, and that the company now needed a professional manager, someone with a Western education.

This crisis was heartbreaking. At the time, I even thought: What's the point of living? Many of my old partners and friends abandoned me right at that moment and I could not find the meaning of my existence. The departure of many people who had once been so close to me was like a total negation of my life. I did not know who to talk to and what to do.

All of my dreams were violently destroyed. No reasons given and I was powerless. It was a very dark moment in my life which I am reluctant to revisit even today.

This time, Mozart saved me.

I lived in an ordinary residential compound. One night as I was taking a stroll alone, I saw the Moon come out from behind dark clouds. I love to watch movies and often buy DVDs from a vendor, an Anhui native, in the neighborhood. I bumped into him that night.

"Mr Ji, this CD is great. Just arrived. Take it," said the vendor.

"No, I never buy CDs. Just DVDs," I replied.

"You can give it back to me if you don't like it. Try it. It's a Mozart collection," the vendor insisted.

The CD collection helped me tremendously. When I played Mozart's Symphony No. 31, I thought it was just beautiful and this beauty made me realize that the world is worth living in.

The beauty of Mozart's music is in its magical balance between harmony and being unyielding. It made me see a world that is splendid, pristine and graceful. The music has a spiritual power that transcends my world and instantly lifts me out of darkness.

At the time I had not yet left Home Inn though I knew I would soon have to leave. I vowed to establish another company and make it better than anything I had achieved to date.

The third crisis I faced was when I was working on Hanting. Its early investors were all my friends. When the global financial crisis hit, Hanting was on the second leg of financing. A close friend invited me for breakfast at the Radisson Blu Plaza Xingguo Hotel Shanghai. He told me that his fund was unable to invest further at that time. That hit me like a bolt of lightning. The investment agreement had been signed and without anything unexpected the investment would have proceeded smoothly. Of course, he had a right to not invest but it was a huge blow for me.

I have a habit of mixing sentiment and business. At a critical moment when a good friend said, "Sorry brother, I can't invest in this," I became truly despondent.

Had I been a quintessential businessman I would not have felt so much heartache and simply thought, this one doesn't want to invest, fine, I'll find another investor. But at that time, I was numb and had no idea at all what I should do, and my mind was a complete blank; I did not even have the rage to blame him.

In the end I decided to sell my Home Inn shares and invest in Hanting myself.

Routine business decision-making is something I find very simple and gives me little cause to hesitate. But I am prone to get hurt when sentiment and business are mixed together. Not because the other party did not invest but rather, that when I trust the other party, I expect them to act like a friend. In my view, one should be willing to sacrifice everything for friends.

Every single person experiences a darkest moment, but in my case, it led to the light.

"The black night gave me black eyes, I use them to seek the light," as the famous Chinese poet Gu Cheng wrote. These darkest moments did not destroy me. They led me to constantly reflect and move forward and, ultimately, became the drivers of my success.

28 December, 2017

CHINA STYLE SERVICE

In China, most high-tech uses American and European technology with little originality which, of course, is much more difficult. This is because too little is invested in Chinese technology and there is an insufficient supply of talent. It's also related to society's prioritization of short-term profitability and speedy return on investments.

That's why Chinese-style innovations tend to be inherited innovations; borrow business models from developed countries in the West and modify them according to market conditions in China. Humanity's material and spiritual needs evolve from primitive to sophisticated, from basic to complex. The hospitality industry in America and Europe started earlier than ours and has been shaped over time by guests. The hospitality industry in China will more or less follow the same trajectory. Therefore, it is particularly worthwhile to adopt the developed business models of America and European countries. And analysing their development trajectory and the reasons behind their successes and failures is beneficial to latecomers like us.

In China there are basically two successful business models: one is the low-cost 'made-in-China' model, and the other one is to reform the traditional service industry and upgrade it to an advanced service industry. E-commerce, advanced management and market-driven mechanisms are all common upgrade tools.

The main characteristics of the made-in-China model are low cost and 'good-enough quality.' From manufacturing disposable picnic utensils barely good enough for a single use, to the assembly of high-end Apple products, the quality of made-in-China products meets users' requirements, no more, no less. These products are not as durable as products made in Germany, and not as well-designed and compact as products made in Japan.

In the past, products made in China produced a cohort of wealthy factory owners, solved some employment problems for the government, and generated a huge tax revenue and foreign currency income for the country. These factories took advantage of the low cost of land, plant buildings, energy, environmental protection, and tax and labor to export a massive quantity of products in exchange for enormous amounts of foreign currency. As made-in-China products are dominating the world, they are bringing a huge trade surplus to China, widespread environmental destruction, and a large amount of assembly line workers whose living conditions are of great concern. These farmer-workers earn very little. The long hours they spend doing repetitive work on assembly lines have turned them into machine parts. The double-digit number of Foxconn suicide victims, known as 'Foxconn jumpers,' are merely representatives of farmer-workers who live a life of despair.

But the made-in-China model has reached the point of inflection of its development curve and is exposing its flaws. As consumer expectations are rising and tastes are changing, some companies maintain the status quo, while others are starting to adapt to the changes by adding value to their products, such as increasing design and technological elements.

The changes we are experiencing now will have a great impact over the next 30 years. If we say the manufacturing industry has been the engine for China's economic growth in the past 30 years, then China Style Service will replace made in China to become the engine for China's economic growth in the coming 30 years. Most entrepreneurial, investment and wealth-generating opportunities will cluster around the service industry. As the incomes of half of the 1.3 billion Chinese people are increasing, providing value-added services to this group in areas such as food, clothing, housing and travel will be a major component of the Chinese service industry in the future.

In the advanced service sector, Chinese enterprises can take advantage of the scale of the local market to attract investments, including international investments. More and more venture capital investments and private funds will enter this sector in the foreseeable future. More and more enterprises from the advanced service sector will launch their IPOs in stock markets in the US, mainland China and Hong Kong (PRC).

When we compete with our international peers, we can take advantage of our local knowledge and in-depth understanding of local consumers' tastes to overcome foreign players' leads in branding and capital.

As for services and product content, the ability to remaster and utilize traditional Chinese culture, and integrate with modern aesthetics and lifestyle elements will become a crucial part of our competitiveness.

Written on 22 December, 2006
Revised in 2010

THE CHINA DREAM

The American Dream is an ideal; in America, you will achieve a better life if you work hard. That is, people must rely on their own hard work, courage, creativity and determination to succeed, and not depend on social status or the help of others. The American Dream often brings the accumulation of wealth and the spirit of entrepreneurship.

China's rapid development also offers opportunities to the population to achieve their China Dreams, especially for the China of today; it is particularly suitable for entrepreneurship and investment and the accumulation of wealth.

The root cause is, first, that many business sectors, especially the service industry, have been shackled for a prolonged period by the system and policies of a planned economy that prevented them from developing fully and meeting the requirements of the market. What we are witnessing now is like the first day of creation – industrial integration and development have enormous potential.

Second, China's long-term rapid economic development has stimulated robust demand which, in turn, has stimulated the market and motivated businesses. Supply now exceeds demand in the manufacturing sector, but in the service sector supply cannot satisfy demand. A budget hotel like Hanting hits full occupancy as soon as it is open for business.

Third, the government offers encouragement and support. The central government pushes mercantilist policies and local governments spare no pain to support investment with tax incentives, low land costs and easy financing.

Fourth, there is a stimulatory momentum of capital markets. Every single wealth story of venture capitalism, private equity or IPOs is an archetype of Deng Xiaoping's most famous aphorism: "Let a small group of people attain wealth first." It sets everyone drooling. Fifth, is the huge population of China. It's the largest consumer market in the world. And the largest consumer market will produce the world's largest businesses.

China Mobile, the ICBC, Tencent and Alibaba are already global scale businesses. This will spread to other fields of the service sector: e-commerce, the video game industry, the online travel industry, apparel, food and beverages ... and, of course, hotels.

My rough estimate is that the key players in the future hotel industry in China will have over ten thousand hotels, of which the driving force will be budget hotels. That scale will make it a world leader in the future.

As for global expansion, Chinese companies in the service sector might enter overseas markets through purchases and mergers, instead of opening their own hotels in other countries. China's rapid development will be reflected on the capital market through high price-to-earnings (P/E) ratios. With their global scale and a continued strengthening of the Chinese currency, Chinese enterprises will find it easier to purchase businesses in the developed countries of Europe and America, and the success rate will increase.

22 December, 2006

A BRIEF SUMMARY OF MY ENTREPRENEURSHIP

In the decade from 1999 to 2010 I founded or cofounded three companies. I was the founding CEO of all three. I built a core management team and established core business models for each one. Eventually, all three listed on Nasdaq and the current market value for each exceeds a billion US dollars. This rare achievement is a world first.

Many people ask me the secret to being so fortunate, with everything turning out so smoothly. When I think about the reason, I know it's not that I'm particularly smart or capable, and it is certainly not because I'm a genius.

First of all, we should be thankful we live in an age of stability and be thankful to our motherland. This is from the heart, not just an empty platitude. Without the reform policies and the opening up of China's economy starting in 1978, China would not have today's market economy and thriving corporations. A stable country and open-minded policies are the bedrock for the survival and development of Chinese companies.

Next comes the support of venture capital, private equity and the capital markets, which facilitated rapid growth and exceptional development. They came to the table expecting to profit (and sometimes with expectations of enormous profits) but, in effect, they helped entrepreneurs like me. When we had no money, they gave us money; when we were concerned about risk, they shared the risk with us; when the company was yet to make profits, they provided capital that helped us leapfrog development; when the company reaches a significant size, they help us expand our assets on the market; they have helped many people realize their dreams of wealth. Without investors, it would have been impossible to build three companies in ten years.

Another important factor is teamwork. The teams that set up and ran the three companies were first-rate. I am a typical entrepreneur, but I am not a superman, much less am I perfect. My shortcomings and merits are in equal measure. Without these team members to complement my work and carry it forward, the three companies would not be the outstanding enterprises they are today. Without them I wouldn't have been able to do it because I don't have the ability and, even if I had the ability, I would not have had the energy.

And then there's single-mindedness. During the several crises we were always able to turn disasters into success because we were not opportunistically chasing quick profits. And we chose not to diversify, just concentrating on our own sector and our market niche. We took advantage of trends and were not influenced by them, always paying attention to business fundamentals. When Hanting was just starting, a real estate company undergoing restructuring was short of capital and offered 50% of their shares for a mere 50 million yuan, which would grow to several hundred million yuan in a few years. When the opportunity came up, we turned it down to concentrate on our own business. We decided to stick with what we knew and earn what we knew how to earn.

If I must draw some conclusions, I would say that the following character traits induced me to never stand still: willing to take risks, willing to make sacrifices, deeply passionate, good business instincts, being open-minded, and dedicated, perseverance, always learning and always reflecting on my actions. I think the ability to learn is the most important. I have always benefitted from my competitors and my partners, and from adversities and failures.

28 December, 2017

THE REWARDS FOR ME OF ENTREPRENEURSHIP

People who do not know me tend to think the most significant reward I have received from establishing the three Nasdaq listed billion-dollar enterprises must be money and fame. I will not pretend to be a virtuous person who claims to despise money and fame. Wealth indeed enables us to have financial freedom, which means we no longer have to endure hardship to make a living and can freely make choices.

But my reward is more than that.

Founding Ctrip realized my aspiration for wealth. It took away the pressure of making a living and allowed me to remain calm and composed.

Founding Home Inn put me through many tests: loyalty and betrayal, crisis in trust, deception and conspiracy, jealousy and hatred. But these trials strengthened me. They broadened my mind and taught me to become more tolerant.

Founding Hanting helped me understand what my calling is and let me see what I really want in this life. I had not arrived at this understanding when I was working on the first two companies. At the time my heart was filled with desires: desire to become rich, desire to become famous, desire to be an achiever. As an ancient Chinese saying eloquently put it: "Preserve heavenly principles and discard human desires." You will be able to better understand the intrinsic qualities of life when you ease your desires.

Once, on the edge of the Houhai lake in Beijing, I engaged in a conversation about life with Paul Dubrule, co-founder of

Accor Hotels. I asked him: "You have lived an extraordinary life. Do you have any regrets?" He replied that first, he had spent too much time on politics. (He used to serve as a member of the French Senate and mayor of Fontainebleau.) Second, though he had a successful career, he had some regret over family life.

At the time I thought, my life would be rather sad if a young person asked me the same question and I gave the same answer as a 70-year-old man sitting by the shore of the Houhai lake. Since a respected senior figure in my field has already told me about his regrets in his life journey, can I, a 44-year-old, do a little better?

Now my goals in life are very clear:

First, I want to work with my partners to make Hanting the biggest and best hotel group in the world, which is my ideal of a group of like-minded friends happily working together to achieve something great.

Second, I want to live a life I want. I will not delight in material gains and will not be burdened by fame. I want to truly live my life well by treasuring the creation of me by God, and by living a full life so that I can calmly say, "I've lived a life I wanted to live," if a young person asks me the same question when I am 70 years old. This is what I learned through founding the three enterprises, especially through working on Hanting.

As I age, my career evolves, my way of thinking, my outlook on life and my values of life are changing. I have become calmer, more tolerant, more considerate and more indifferent to fame and wealth. Perhaps I have become less driven than when I was younger, but I am now more mature and wiser.

This is the most valuable reward I gained from ten years of entrepreneurship. As we grow older, we become kinder and simpler.

28 December, 2017

TO BUILD A STRONG ENTERPRISE

A good enterprise must have sound inner strength.
It must be able to satisfy market demand.
More importantly, it must be adaptable.
Only with these attributes can we ride
market turbulence and grow.

AN ENTERPRISE'S IDEALS AND ORIGINAL INTENT

Making the company bigger and stronger is an objective shared by all entrepreneurs. But how to realize this ideal?

I believe, to make a company big, the entrepreneur should first think big. If you can't think big, you will never make it big.

Some people might ask: I think big so I can make it big? There are some interesting examples. Many people probably have heard of a slogan in the late 1950s: "People can make the land produce as much as they want, so long as they are bold enough." These days, people often think of this slogan as evidence that demonstrates the inflated idealism that disregarded the rules of nature in that period of modern China.

But I actually think the slogan contains some truth. It can be interpreted as: You can fly high and far only when your ideal is high enough. How can you fly high in the sky when flying around indoors is good enough?

Another common line is: Of course, one must have ideals but what if one day you realize those ideals? I think this makes a lot of sense: if we do not have ideals, we will not make it big, and we will surely never succeed.

In the 15th century a famous Chinese Confucian philosopher named Wang Yangming said: "Nothing exists outside of the mind." It means the world is what you can think of and can feel.

Things don't exist if your heart can't feel them. This view corresponds to idealism in the West.

Many people, especially when they are young, think this concept is not scientific and is irrelevant to their reality. However, my experiences in recent years are related to this concept. In the process of managing H World, I have repeatedly experienced my wishes becoming realities.

When our company first started, we put forward a goal: to become a leading brand in the future hotel industry in China and be the first choice for Chinese travellers. At the time, a few established brands were already in the market, like Home Inn, Jin Jiang International and 7 Days Inn. Many of our employees did not believe in our goal, thinking it unlikely to be achieved, and thought making a few dollars was good enough.

When our company reached a certain scale, I pledged to make H World No. 1 in the world and many people did not believe me, either. Being the world's No. 1 means a scale ten times the current size and multiplying our company's current market value dozens of times. Is it possible? At present, the size of our company ranks as the No. 9 hotel group in the world, but market value is ranked No. 4. If there were no substantial structural changes, it is foreseeable for H World to become No. 3 in the world. But is it possible to become No. 1? It's hard to say. I do not have a definite answer yet, but I do have a strong desire and full confidence to lead my team to achieve this goal. Perhaps my determination and the determination of thousands of H World employees is the deciding force to push us to become the world's No. 1.

Here is another example of thinking big. Wuzhong Road in Shanghai is between the H World headquarters and where I live. No other road in Shanghai, probably in the whole of China, is so crammed with H World hotels. Sometimes, as I walked along Wuzhong Road, I would spot a hotel. A thought would come to mind: this hotel looks nice. Perhaps one day we can take it over and make it another H World hotel. Miraculously, these hotels eventually joined our group. I do not know how it happened because I have never pursued them using my connections.

The chance for your dream to come true is a lot higher if you are sincere enough and determined enough. If you can't think big, you will never have a chance to make it big. Only if you can think big, if your ambition is high enough, will you have a chance to make it a reality. Only when you have grand ambitions, grand ideas and a grand vision can you build your grand plan, and only with a grand plan can you make your enterprise great.

If your goal is to open a wonton stall and make 10,000 yuan every night, then there is little chance for your wonton stall to become a business as big as McDonald's or KFC. You will have to adjust your vision if you want to make it bigger. And even if you do adjust your vision, it is not guaranteed that you can make your business as big as theirs. Many large enterprises started small. But in the Chinese market, it is difficult to make a company grow fast enough without having a grand vision.

Before making a company bigger and stronger, we first should consider a more fundamental question: Why do we want to make a company bigger and stronger?

Many people want a company bigger and stronger to make money. Others do it for fame, for face, for beautiful women or power.

After my first entrepreneurial attempt, I acutely realized that the purpose of making a company bigger and stronger is far more important than how to actually make a company bigger and stronger. When people start their entrepreneurial journey, many of them simply want to make money and become famous, and to satisfy their ego. This is normal. It's human nature. But for me today, the purpose of entrepreneurship is to make the world a better place. Otherwise, there is no point. In a hundred years, no one will remember you because you were rich. But you will be remembered if you created something meaningful, for example, if you wrote a novel called *The Story of the Stone*, if you introduced a system of philosophical concepts like Confucianism, or if you unified China, like the first Qin Emperor did 2,000 years ago. You will be remembered only when you create something valuable which benefits others, our country, the world or even the universe. And this is the only reason for us to make a company bigger and stronger.

Some people make their money from irresponsibly mining resources, some operate dyeing factories or laundromats, and discharge untreated contaminated wastewater into rivers. The harm they do to the environment, to the people and to future generations is far greater than the value they create.

I have always said what I want to achieve in the hotel business is to make travellers worry-free. In the past, many hotels made travellers anxious: filthy rooms, unsanitized pillows, unwashed sheets and hidden room charges – a 200-yuan-room that ends up costing 1,000 yuan. What I want to achieve is for travellers to be free from these worries.

H World hotels also provide employment opportunities for many people. We have about 60,000 employees. Their jobs in our company enable them to support their families, to send their children to school, to buy festive presents for their parents-in-law and their own parents. This is my original intent of running the company. It makes me feel that I am creating value for this world, and what I am doing is bigger than myself.

This is my understanding of the purpose of making a company bigger and stronger – to make the world you are in a better place because of you and your company. Otherwise, it is pointless to make a company bigger and stronger. It will only harm the world and a bigger and stronger monster will only harm the world even more. In this sense, a self-centred bigger and stronger is worthless.

5 June, 2018

BIG MARKET, FAST DEVELOPMENT

When an entrepreneur plans to create a large enterprise the first priority is to select a large market.

If you were the biggest pencil manufacturer in China, that would be really something. However, if you make cruise ships or corporate jets, no matter how good you are, the market size is limited and so is the size of your company. If you are in the business of selling items people consume every day, like rice or edible oil or toothpaste or toothbrushes, you have chosen a huge market – this market is sufficiently large to achieve large scale and profit. If you choose a small market, it's very hard to make your company big.

We were especially lucky because China is the largest market in the world; actually, the largest single market. That means that here we use the same laws, language, currency and have the same historical roots. The European Union has about 500 million people, the USA has a population of 300 million. India has 1.3 billion people, but China has slightly more at just over 1.4 billion. Europe is not really a single market because the grouping encompasses multiple languages and multiple countries with their own currencies, and recently it appears to be breaking up. Although the USA is a large single market, its population is a mere 300 million. I estimate that with China's population of over 1.4 billion, many businesses are able to capture markets comprising of half the population; that is, approximately 600 million people. That 600 million strong market is far larger than the USA, which would have a comparable market of about 200 million people. Although India has many people, there are fewer consumers and a limited middle class, on top of which there are problems with transportation, electrical power and religious divisions, so it cannot be considered a single market. In China, any business related to people's livelihood is in a world-scale single market. If a business is to be big, then choose a big market. We Chinese have a distinct advantage in that any field of business can grow to a very large scale very quickly. Look at the hotel industry: the USA has about five million hotel rooms and China has about 17 million, slightly more than three times as many as the USA. But while the USA's hotel chains account for about 65% of the total number of rooms, in China chains only account for 12–15% of the total.

Within this large market the top ten hotel groups in the past were almost all from the USA, and just one from France, while China didn't have a single brand that qualified for the list. And yet in just over a decade, China now has three chains on the top ten list. And this is just the beginning. It is entirely possible that one day two or three of the top five hotel groups will be Chinese. The USA's large single market nurtured many famous international hotel chain brands like Hilton, Marriott and Intercontinental. In the future, China's huge single market will nurture even larger leviathans. It's simple arithmetic, and based on direct observation, that expanding our business is especially beneficial to us. I am often asked where is the best place to start a business, in the USA, in Europe or in China? My answer is unequivocally: in China. China is a huge market so, if you have big ambitions, choose the biggest market to start a business, which will provide the best chance of growing a large business. And if you want to expand a business in a market that is growing rapidly like China's, it means that you want to expand rapidly. There are no opportunities for a slow-growing company in today's society and even less chance for these companies to grow large. A seedling in a forest may have sprouted from the best seed stock but it will be overshadowed and outcompeted by other fast-growing trees. Not being able to receive enough nutrients, it will eventually die.

The law of competition in today's society is no different from the law of the jungle. A small and slow-growing company will have almost no chance to take off and fly high. Of course, if you do not have big ambitions and are happy to remain at the moss or grass levels, you can grow slower. But if you want to make your company big, you must grow fast.

A company can only grow fast in a fast-growing market and China is precisely that kind of market. Why is China the fastest growing market in the world? First, it's because the economy is not sufficiently marketized, which can be regarded as 'institutional dividend.' China's hotels used to be lodging houses and guest houses for government officials. The commercial hotel chains, such as our company, Jin Jiang and Home Inn, started ten to 15 years ago. It is relatively easy to win when the market is not sufficiently developed. As long as we have good products, good capability, a good business model and a good management team, we will grow quickly. This is true in the budget hotel and mid-range hotel market that we have entered and is also true in the high-end hotel market that we will enter in the future.

Second, China is a market that is growing by leaps and bounds. What does that mean? Take China's internet as an example. China's computer technology used to be far behind the United States. But today, when it comes to application technologies in areas such as mobile phones, communication protocol and computers, we are more or less at the same level as the United States. Chinese consumers can purchase almost everything that is available on the

US market and there are few restrictions in the consumer market. And our hotel business is in this market which makes it possible for us to synchronize our development with the global market. Some people said it would take China's hotel industry 40 years to develop, just like in the United States. I said that was impossible. It would take five or six years for a few industry leviathans to emerge. And that is what has happened. This kind of development by leaps and bounds requires our company to grow fast – if you want to grow your company, you must be able to keep up with the pace of the leaping market, instead of following conventional order. This kind of leaps-and-bounds development does not exist in many other countries because they have experienced a long period of marketization, which means more time for preparation and fine-tuning.

China is an interesting place. Geographically speaking, it is lower in the east and higher in the west, drier in the north and wetter in the south. But if we look at it through a business lens, China is a vast open land – like the grassland or the Gobi Desert in Inner Mongolia. Everything can be spread out quickly. And as long as you are fast enough, you can claim your sphere of influence in no time.

As for making your company big, the Chinese market has unique, favourable conditions which relate to Chinese history. The first Qin Emperor unified all of China but there was no one like that to unify Europe. What was the first thing the first Qin Emperor did after he united China? He issued orders to standardize units of weight and measure. From the Shanghai Jinmao Plaza right down to an old couple in a rural production team, the extended period of unified thinking in China has made it easy to amalgamate cultural ideas and consumer sentiment, and this unity of thought is deep-rooted in the psyche of every Chinese person. Whenever a business activity becomes a mode of diffusion, a model or a movement, it's similar to the spread of an idea that will permeate the four corners of the nation. Some, like the supplement Nao Baijin, or Brain Platinum, sprang forth from grassroots beginnings. Others used cities as a base to expand and grow the business, like a hotel chain or an apparel brand.

China's vast open geographical features enable newly-founded or already established Chinese businesses to take cities, seize territory with ease and grow rapidly. When it comes to expanding a business, we currently really do have all the advantages of being in the right place at the right time.

8 June, 2018

SPECIALIZATION IS THE MAGIC WEAPON OF BUSINESS SUCCESS

I have always believed that specialization is the only magic weapon of business success.

More and more success stories of my entrepreneur friends diversifying their businesses are challenging this belief of mine. Am I too stubborn and too conservative to see the truth? Or are these success stories of diversification merely a flash in the pan? If we jump to a wrong conclusion, we will either miss many opportunities, or dither and lose focus.

The concept of specialization comes from the West. Competition brings specialization of labor. In order to survive, every company must be specialized at something and find its niche in the market.

Very few enterprises in developed countries, like General Electric Company, are successful through diversification. But in today's China, diversified and large enterprises like Li Ka-shing's company are not rare. Most entrepreneurs in China enter the real estate market, regardless of their initial specializations in trading of garments or building materials, or the import/export business.

I have a friend who has ventured into fields including real estate, department stores, hotels, e-commerce, mining and private equity investment, and is doing well on all fronts. But close observation reveals that the diversification of his business is not an act of speculation. Each of his business ventures is backed by a set of comprehensive long-term strategies.

In Shanghai I know another legendary entrepreneur. Initially, his business was in real estate. He had assigned an international hotel group to manage his properties, but then decided to man-age the properties himself because he was not satisfied with the international hotel group's performance. He leased the properties to others in the shopping mall industry. Seeing their business booming, he now wants to enter the market too. I heard he is also planning to enter the cinema business because he noticed cinemas in his leased properties are doing well. Readers may sneer at this entrepreneur's constantly changing business appetite, assuming he will fail on every front. But that's wrong, at least for now. The hotel that he manages himself is also doing well.

Since so many Chinese entrepreneurs are successful in their diversified businesses, I think we should avoid holding prejudice and try to find out the reasons behind their success.

First, and most importantly, opportunities are abundant. Many an entrepreneur's decision to enter a market is inspired by business opportunities that spring up right in front of them, not based on business analysis, investigation or strategizing.

Second, at present three types of enterprise – state-owned, foreign-owned and privately-owned – coexist in the Chinese market. The characteristics of privately-owned enterprises, including their flexibility, mean these enterprises are advantaged in certain areas. For example, their decision-making process is faster than foreign-owned enterprises, and their risk-coping capabilities are higher than state-owned enterprises. This is why diversification is more common among privately-owned enterprises.

Third, the competition is not extremely fierce because there are not many competitors that are truly matched in strength. Over the past few decades, across various sectors, few competitive brands and enterprises have emerged.

Fourth, the quality of entrepreneurs, especially the most successful ones, in the privately-owned enterprises is improving. They are no longer the 'farmer-entrepreneurs' who emerged soon after the opening up of China in the early 1980s. They know how to recruit talent and they know how to navigate the capital markets. They know how to utilize management tools and strategies and how to deal with government agencies. These entrepreneurs are extremely energetic and diligent. Like the Shanghai entrepreneur that I mentioned earlier, they are hands-on in their business operation. He always appears to be high-spirited, despite not even taking Saturdays and Sundays off, or having to consume a shot or two of strong Chinese liquor at dinners.

I think these entrepreneurs will diversify continuously. They are currently in the ongoing expansion stage and don't yet know where their limits to expansion are. The next phase is consolidation and development to make every part of the business operations better and stronger. In this stage they may encounter many challenges because very few people can be the most outstanding in every realm when they embark on new ventures. No matter how strong you are, there is always someone stronger, so in the midst of fierce competition most people will voluntarily, or under duress, concentrate their efforts in areas in which they have expertise. This is the inception of specialization. Of course, there are a small number of companies that have grown into diversified conglomerates like General Electric or the Cheung Kong Group.

Another way to diversify is through investment, not simply via an investment put on the balance sheet, but actual investments. For example, there are those Fosun International has made using financial means to control an enterprise, using first-rate talent to manage the enterprise, then using excellent operational results to acquire more funding in the capital markets and, consequently, control even more enterprises.

China today is at a stage where there are opportunities wherever you turn. Gold mines and coal mines are virtually sitting on the surface of the Earth – just dig down a little and you'll strike it rich. For many entrepreneurs, there is nothing wrong with their diversification strategies. Their baskets contain many eggs, which is better than just one egg because not only can they earn more wealth, their ability to withstand risks is strong.

But sustainable business operations can only be achieved with specialization.

Outstanding entrepreneurs are a rare commodity. Over-diversification spreads the outstanding entrepreneurs thin on the ground to the point of mediocrity. Moreover, regardless of how vigorous and industrious we are, the energy of one person has its limits. There is a limit to what the hands-on approach to territorial expansion can achieve. Moreover, focused and rigorous specialization will help build more competitive positions in the market.

In the future, brands, scale, capital and talent will be key factors in productivity, and these factors point to the need for specialization. Ultimately, these trends will apply pressures that will force entrepreneurs to choose greater specialization.

16 June, 2010

AIMING HIGH

An ancient Chinese teaching says that if someone sets a high objective, the final result may only be ordinary, and if an ordinary level objective is sought the result may be low. To lead a business to grow stronger it is vitally important to set objectives high and have strict requirements.

I am famous for setting high objectives for my teams. If I feel someone's performance is not good enough, I will criticize or dismiss that person. I used to have a bad temper and would occasionally scold people. I have scolded almost all of my subordinates, and female subordinates have been driven to tears. Now I don't resort to scolding anymore and my subordinates can't get used to it. Anyone in my company who I have scolded would think, "The boss still values me because he still scolds me." Why do I scold people? When I make a request that I consider to be nothing out of the ordinary and they feel it is too difficult, we reach an impasse. When a business is being set up, the pace is fast and there are countless things to deal with, there's a sense of crisis and, when it surfaces, I start scolding people.

I founded three companies and at the start no one appreciated my rigorous demands – some even said I didn't know what I was doing because I always made unrealistic demands. I'll give an example. We purchased a four-star hotel on Zhongshan West Road in Shanghai that was owned by two French brothers. The younger brother was the manager and he was doing a good job. When we took over, the hotel's gross operating profit (GOP) was about 30%. After our team took over, the GOP rose to about 40% but I set a target of a 70% GOP, which meant every $100 of revenue returned a gross operating profit of $30 and I wanted to push up the GOP to $70. My team thought that was impossible.

At that time a former employee of a state-owned corporation managed by the central government in Beijing, who had just taken up a senior position in our company, said to me, "Mr Ji, you don't understand this industry. There's no way a hotel can generate such a high GOP." I responded, "No. You shouldn't think about whether or not the target is appropriate, you should think about how to achieve it."

Of course, when I set the higher target, I also worked closely together with staff to analyse how to achieve a 70% GOP. For example, the hotel's control room operated 24 hours a day with three shifts. I could see that these idlers just kicked up their heels to drink tea and read newspapers. With three shifts, having at least two people on each shift, it added up to six staff at a time when it was becoming more and more expensive to employ people. That was simple to fix by moving the control room screens to the front desk and record all the channels. Initially, the recordings were kept for a week but now we can keep them for a month, or even three months because, after all, hard disks are cheap. The fire alarm system is now also located at the front desk and it's very loud when it goes off so the front desk staff will immediately hear it and no longer need to constantly watch the monitors. The changes cost a few thousand dollars but reducing six staff meant the annual payroll saving exceeded tens of thousands of dollars.

The front desk originally operated on three shifts with four or five people on each shift and there were plenty of managers, with just a few people doing the actual work – I changed it to self-service registration. Guests can register, select a room and pay for it on their way to the hotel. When they arrive at the hotel, we only need to photocopy their identity document and give them the room card. A well-designed automatic registration system reduces the staffing requirements from dozens to just a few. The hotel has now exceeded my 70% GOP target.

I studied mechanics at the Shanghai Jiao Tong University, so my maths is pretty good, and I know something about modelling and numbers. The 70% GOP figure was based on calculations, not pulled out of thin air. This business model for hotels can actually achieve a 75% or 80% GOP, so in fact I held back. I set high objectives for teams so that they can break through the constraints of the past. If I am told that this is the way things operate and there is only one possible program, I will ask: "Why is this the only way?" If you just follow convention and continue to work in a rut, it will be impossible to make breakthroughs and outperform your predecessors to occupy the position of an outstanding achiever.

Many businesses that retreat or contract in the face of adversity will find it hard to grow. Only by aiming high can businesses grow and flourish.

10 June, 2018

THE DIALECTICS OF BIG AND STRONG

From establishment, to expansion, to stability, an enterprise passes through different stages. At every stage, the entrepreneur faces the same core dilemma: Should I make the company bigger first or stronger first? Different strategies are required depending on the stage of the enterprise's development.

For a newly-established enterprise, rapid expansion is the first priority. In a primitive market like China, a company that is not able to swiftly seize its territory will be crushed by others in no time. This is like playing a video game. Without a controlled territory, a company will have no chance to survive. This is the strategy I follow. When H World was just established, our first strategy was '120% speed and 80% quality,' since we could not achieve '120% speed and 95% quality.' Territory seizure comes first. The second strategy is to target regional centres and seize territory around first- and second-tier cities, including second -tier cities that are nodes to first-tier cities. After territory seizure is achieved, we will change the strategy to '95% speed and 95% quality.'

When an enterprise plateaus, the first priority becomes making the company stronger.

Once you finish territory seizure, you should work hard to improve quality. This is an effective formula in our times. As a company reaches the sustainable growth stage, making it stronger is vital.Take the real estate sector as an example.

At present, the most important task for a real estate company is not territory seizure – the larger the territory they seize, the quicker they fail. The change of business model in China Vanke is a good example. It has morphed from a real estate developer to a real estate operator – it is a more advanced business model. In the past, they built the properties, sold the properties, took profit and left. Now they are doing things differently. They build the property and stay – their businesses encompass property management, retail, hotel and shopping centre management.

Many real estate developers in China now are developing their own hotel brands. This is a new strategy to strengthen the company in response to new industry trends. In the past, people made profits by selling houses. These days, they provide more services and seek deeper knowledge of the market and explore more possibilities.

Most established enterprises in China followed the same path – territorial seizure, then growth. I admire the spirit of Japanese artisans – the spirit of operating one solitary sushi restaurant for three decades. But this business model is not sustainable in the Chinese business environment. When you are not 'big' enough, you will be crushed before becoming stronger. What I mean by 'crushed' is not that your company will be forced to close. For example, if there are 20 entrepreneurial companies, the first three that are able to attract investment can survive and grow. Gradually, the other 17 companies that were not able to attract investment will either shrink or collapse. This also applies to talent recruitment. If your enterprise is not big enough, it is unlikely to attract talent because most talented personnel prefer to join large enterprises.

Another aspect is that if a company is not strong enough, it is not possible to sustain its expansion. Solid beams and pillars are very important to the sound structure of a building. If you want to expand your business, you must also make it stronger. In the hotel sector, it's common that some hotel chains at the initial stage of their business aggressively seize territory but neglect quality control in their products and services as the companies grow, granting franchise contracts without proper due diligence. In the end, the size of these companies is indeed big, but so too are their problems.

H World encountered similar issues, such as receiving consumer complaints as well as complaints from franchise operators about unsatisfactory investment returns.

When a brand faces a crisis, many people may choose to retreat but my choice was different. In my view, if we do not try to save the industry, no one else will, and China might not have our own budget hotel brand. So, we invested a lot of money, a lot of energy and even sacrificed short-term profit to upgrade hotels under our direct management and encourage our franchised operators to upgrade their hotels. As a result of our efforts, the revenue of our individual hotels has been steadily going up, after the initial downturn.

If we are single-minded about growing big, expansion is not hard. At present we open two hotels every day and will probably open three a day next year. And it is achievable if we want to open more. But is this pace sustainable? Can we be sustainable after our expansion is successful? This is an important matter.

How to maintain the tempo of developing both size and strength? All brands follow a curved line progression – from establishment to growth, to maturity, then to decline. How do we ensure the continuation of the curve? My view is that when the curve is pointing downwards, you have to find a new function, a new power, a new direction so the curve takes off until the next time it reaches the peak before the next trough arrives and the rhythm continues. For the curve to continue its 'ups and downs' sustainably, an enterprise must possess robust innovative capability and resilience. Only when an enterprise is both big and strong, can it become a great global power.

For example, the territory seizure for budget hotels in China is largely over. Its future development is likely to follow a horizontal trajectory, instead of an ascent trajectory. As a response, we found an upward new curve – mid-range hotels. Our mid-range hotel portfolio consists of five or six brands. We purchased Orange Hotels, created the Ji Hotel brand, and are working with Accor Hotels. Three to five years ago, mid-range hotels generated a near zero profit for our group that couldn't really be included in our accounts, but now they are contributing one third of our total profit and will soon be contributing 50%.

The number of our mid-range hotels is increasing. Now I am looking for ways to generate profit from hotel management contracts. In the past many people in China's hotel industry made profits from directly operating hotels or franchise agreements. However, most global hotel groups make money through hotel management contracts. I am in the process of planning and nurturing high-end hotel brands, hoping to make profit through management contracts, like Marriott International does. Recently, H World introduced a new brand – Joya Hotels. The first hotel under this brand was opened in the trendy Xujiahui district in Shanghai. By incorporating Oriental elements, Oriental aesthetics and Oriental style, I intend to present a product that is unique to both Eastern and Western customers.

This is the third stage of our enterprise as I see it. To generate management cash flow and profit, we not only create new brands, we also purchase and merge with suitable high-end brands, including luxury brands. My eyes are also set on the fourth and the fifth stage of our company. I have successfully seized a large territory in the Chinese hotel market. Now I am aiming for a bigger territory – the global hotel market. We set up our global headquarters in Singapore. The first step of our global expansion is first to enter Asia, then on to Europe and finally the United States. This will constitute the different waves of our company's future development.

You may not be able to think far ahead like this when you are first establishing your company. But you must plan for the second and third stage of your company's development as soon as your company reaches a certain scale. Only a visionary entrepreneur can make a company grow bigger and stronger.

12 June, 2018

THE LIMIT OF VELOCITY

In ideal circumstances, the formula for matter moving in a straight line is: $V_t = V_0 + at$. Where a is acceleration and t is time. That is, the velocity at a particular time is the result of the initial velocity plus acceleration by time. Theoretically, as time approaches infinity, speed approaches infinity.

In reality, this can never happen. This is due, first of all, to the fact that classical mechanics only applies to slow moving bodies and cannot describe motion that approaches the speed of light. The speed of light is the limit for ordinary matter; to approach the speed of light, matter must change form. In the real world, the velocity of matter is always limited by resistance forces.

Even with a tailwind we can rarely ride a bicycle much faster than 40 kmph. The faster the speed, the greater the air drag resistance, until it balances out your pedal power. Thus, velocity hovers at a limit – such as 40 kmph.

It really means that if we are moving too fast, a greater resistance is produced that will prevent a further increase in speed.

This rule constantly manifests itself in everyday life.

"When a tree stands out in the forest the wind will topple it" is an aphorism that uses this logic. The height of trees has limits: the higher the tree, the easier it is to blow over. Thus, the trees that we can see all have limits on their height.

According to the Peter Principle: "In a hierarchy every employee tends to rise to his level of incompetence."

This expresses the same idea. What limits you from rising up further, is the height you have reached.

The Tower of Babel cannot be constructed. Not because God is thwarting the project; rather, because the higher the tower is built, the heavier the tower becomes which, ultimately, crushes the foundation and supporting structure, causing the tower to topple. Even in an environment with no gravity, structures cannot be built to limitless heights because the higher the structure, the less stable it is, and even the slightest disturbance will lead to system collapse.

What is true for trees is also true for companies. The larger the company, the smaller the ability to innovate; too many layers of management engender a bureaucratic culture that causes the efficiency of the entire organization to decline. The leviathan General Electric cannot do everything, so it must abide by the principle of being best, or at least second best, to be able to maintain its advantage and stay competitive.

Throughout history it has been the same for empires as well. The Roman Empire expanded rapidly and cultivated an excessively lavish material culture that eroded management and weakened controls, which led to a diminution of the military's fighting strength. Ultimately, the incursions of northern barbarians led to collapse. Genghis Khan more or less made the same mistake: rapid expansion and rapid retreat to the starting point – the grassland steppes of Mongolia.

The educator Huang Yanpei describes a similar dynastic cycle that prevailed throughout Chinese history. A dynasty expanded, became extravagant and then collapsed. The rich become richer, officials become more corrupt, the impoverished ordinary people become poorer, and the miserable lives of the people become worse. This led to imbalances in society which could only be changed through violent means to redistribute wealth. This is the result of a dynasty reaching the limit of its lifespan.

Family legacies are also similar. A Chinese saying holds that wealth never lasts more than three generations. A family's loss or diminishing of competitiveness is usually the result of prosperity.

Prosperity can cause later generations to lose their fighting spirit and their motivation to strive and work hard. People born into poverty surge out from the lowest strata; they have ambition and are motivated.

Are individuals any different? Our businesses, our ranking and our wealth all follow a rule similar to the Peter Principle. The speed of which we are so proud of is precisely what is blocking our progress. Here speed is used in its broadest meaning: the rate of development for a company; the level of an official position; the amount of wealth accumulated.

Laws of the natural world are verified in human society as well. A man's got to know his limitations. That's why I always emphasize that people need to be respectful. If we don't respect the humanized God, we still must respect the material God – the laws of nature.

26 December, 2010

BUILD A TEAM OF TALENTED KINDRED SPIRITS – THOUGHTS ON A PLANE IN AMERICA

Some members of staff, such as Cheng Jun, who had been working with me since the early days of H World, left when Zhang Tuo was the CEO. And when I came back to be CEO, Hai Jun and other old comrades left. I loathed to see them leave but each goodbye triggered soul-searching: What went wrong? Is 'not having the same goal' a sufficient explanation? How can I be happy when comrades-in-arms leave before we achieve the final victory?

I reflected upon these questions.

Those friends had joined H World for various reasons when the company was first established and was facing an unknown future. They took risks and blazed paths through all kinds of obstacles. They laid a foundation for today's H World and made remarkable contributions to the development of our company. Along this journey, some of these friends left because they felt they did not receive the promotion they had expected. Some were recruited by our competitors when the growth of our company was slow. Some of them are full of passion and love the thrill of entrepreneurship. They embarked on new adventures or joined other startups when they felt the excitement was fading as H World became bigger and more rules were implemented. Some friends do not have extravagant material needs. They left H World to live a simpler stress-free life after accumulating some wealth from the stock market.

Some friends left because they had been affected by changes in the management team. Some left us for remuneration related reasons. Some left for personal reasons ...

I have to admit that the departure of every veteran H World member brings me immense sadness. Yesterday, I walked along New York streets in drizzling rain. A sense of melancholy descended as I walked past the Waldorf Astoria where Hai Jun and I had stayed, and that Japanese restaurant in which both of us had a little too much to drink. I envy the enduring business of Accor and the life-long friendships among its founders. It is my ideal to achieve both. But I also understand the reality of present-day China – a hubbub of chasing wealth has enveloped the entire society. The lure is real when opportunities are abundant, and many people are anxious to achieve quick success.

Perhaps some of the people who left H World were disappointed in me and H World. Especially when the expectation of striking it rich overnight did not turn into reality, when the value of H World stock was low and the company's remuneration system was undergoing changes. Our company's rapid growth inspired some people and they decided to leave H World to embark on their own adventures. I sincerely wish them well. While in my heart I did not want to see them leave, our teambuilding has to continue because H World has goals to achieve and responsibilities to fulfil.

Among our H World colleagues I am probably as much praised as blamed. In fact, I am not heartless. I take the bond between people to my heart, but people may not realize this, probably because of the work relationship and the distance between us. Some people probably think I am too demanding and too harsh.

I am demanding because of my responsibilities and high expectations. How can the company survive if we are not better than others? In the past few years of entrepreneurship, I have been largely taking a practical approach by settling on a broad-stroke style in our work. But, by nature, I am a perfectionist. I want to be perfect in everything we do and make everyone happy. It is therefore inevitable that I am demanding at work. My motto is 'aim high.' This is the truth whether for startups or for a company's sustained operation. 'Being outstanding' is the only path to being great.

Some people do not like my harsh attitude. But this is my leadership style and has nothing to do with attitudes such as being disrespectful. No one is perfect and I am certainly not a saint. My harsh attitude comes from candidness, trust and high expectations. I rarely treat our ordinary employees with fury or reprimand people for whom I do not have high expectations.

The hotel business is not one that brings exorbitant profit overnight. The work is tiring and tedious. The business model of direct management is very challenging for us. Moreover, rapid growth in multiple regions brings enormous management pressure. I have no choice but to do my utmost.

In fact, I truly love this industry. I love my work and feel I have found the worthiest thing to do in this life. Every day I go to work my heart is filled with hopes and plans. When I finish work, my heart is filled with satisfaction and joy (of course, there is also frustration and exhaustion, occasionally). I am willing, and have the responsibility, to lead our company and our team to advance forwards and achieve greater success. Everyone's life has a limit and so do companies. I do not expect H World to be an exception that lasts for centuries. But I will do my best to ensure the company operations are on a sustainable path.

Some colleagues have developed personal friendships and often have gatherings outside office hours. This is a good thing. People in modern societies are spending more and more time on work, so friendships between co-workers are certainly good for the company. But some people at times cannot separate personal relations from working relations. They let personal feelings affect their judgment and behaviour at work. Some even form 'small groups' and 'small circles' which, to a degree, prevent talented outsiders from joining the team, affecting the company's sustainable development.

Some company veterans claim credit for their contribution and play politics. By doing so they have become negative factors in the company and should be counselled or even removed.

These veterans must be able to keep up with the pace of the fast-growing company. When new opportunities occur or new positions become available, I will first consider candidates among our existing employees. But if no one within the company meets the requirements for the task, we must look for outside talent.

As for new members of our company, we should calmly observe their performance without prejudice or favour. We must not assume new colleagues are definitely better and wiser than veteran members of the company. The most important quality for new members of our company is *de* (德), literally meaning virtue, which is an idea I often emphasize of having the same values and beliefs. We cannot expect a new member of H World to instantly establish a bond with the company, but at least we should share the same values. As our company grows, we must also have a willingness to welcome new members to our team.

Should we run the company like a family business or use professional executives? This is a topic explored and considered by many Chinese entrepreneurs. Like Alibaba, we have tried both approaches but have yet to find a satisfactory answer.

At present, I prefer a style that combines both approaches, following the traditional Chinese belief, as found in the yin-yang hexagrams, that the universe desires the middle ground, the golden mean. Entrepreneurial team members and professional executives are equally important. Because the company is growing fast, certain parts of the business can't wait, so outside help is essential. And also, because the company is growing fast, fundamental values and institutional memory are inevitably fading, and we need veterans of our company to preserve this institutional memory and to then pass it on. Perhaps a good formula for managing fast-growing companies like H World should include uniting old and new team members and combining Western management systems and tools with Oriental virtue.

An entrepreneur who runs a fast-growing enterprise must be open-minded and willing to embrace all team members, both old and new, in an inclusive manner. The only appropriate parameter that should be used to evaluate a team member is whether this person is valuable to the enterprise. Talent should be attracted and retained as long as they are good for the company.

The Chinese people value the quality of *yi* (义), loyalty. This is a traditional virtue that deserves respect and support. However, we should know there are differences between the 'small *yi*' shared among mercenary associates and personal friends, and the 'large *yi*' that benefits most people. The small *yi* shared by a small group of people might not be good for a large enterprise. In everyday work, some people are reluctant to speak up because they do not want to offend others. This will definitely harm the company and result in a lose-lose situation for the people involved and for the company. If one person fails to point out a mistake, then the person at fault loses a chance to improve. The person who fails to point out others' mistakes loses performance points. And this leads to the company's loss.

Some people harbor 'big company pride,' believing a small loss or a small gain is too trivial for a large company like ours to worry about. Since the concept of a 'company' is more abstract than the real people (colleagues, suppliers and partners) we interact with, in order to avoid offending the real people, to evade trouble, to protect themselves from being viewed as taking advantage of others, some of our team members choose to do nothing when improvements can be made, or benefits attained. Just let it go. No one will notice anyway. Better to be a benign peacemaker. Whoever harbors thoughts like these because of their selfish calculations is hurting the company's interests, sacrificing the interests of many people, including their own. This kind of inaction and self-serving convenience are seriously harmful.

Therefore, we must carefully design the balanced scorecard based on the company's general strategy for all key departments to objectively select good performers. To encourage them to make more contribution to H World, we must nurture them, put them in important positions, trust them, promote them, give them more resources and reward them with remuneration. As for those individuals who are selfish and slack at work, we must encourage them to change. Those who fail to improve will eventually be asked to leave our team.

Building talent echelons is a top strategic priority which is vital to the future of our company. To build three talent echelons with like-minded members, we must first intelligently optimize the management structure of our company, based on our strategic objectives, and effectively deploy staff members. Second, audit the management hierarchy and tailor our strategies according to their functions.

Apart from the top management team, management executives can be divided into three categories. First, the highest level is the core management team that includes department directors in our headquarters and regional GMs. Second, important management personnel including C-level executives and department managers in our headquarters, as well as senior hotel managers and department managers. Third, managers and supervisors in our headquarters, and managers who run one or more hotels are the most important basic level management team.

We first choose candidates for these positions from the existing teams. If no suitable candidate is available, we will recruit externally. For newly recruited personnel, a performance evaluation period is required, as well as viable goals and adjustment plans.

Regular communication with all three management levels is needed in order to ensure consensus. While individuality should be persevered, the core values of the company must be maintained. Quarterly meetings, regular talks, irregular informal interactions, luncheons, milestone parties and birthday parties are all channels for us to communicate with our team members.

Management team members are encouraged to be 'super-supervisors,' which means they not only supervise their subordinates but also keep an eye on a level further below. For example, regional general managers directly manage senior hotel managers and, at the same time, watch over individual hotel managers and people who manage several hotels.

Performance is a metric to evaluate a management team member. Develop a balanced scorecard for each task and position in different departments in order to achieve the company's strategic objectives. While aligning with the company's goals, the evaluation of a management team member must be fair.

Apart from encouraging personal development and self-reflection among employees, the company should support them through training. Methods of improvement include external coaching, such as leadership development and utilizing management tools, taking courses at the H World Academy, engaging consultants, encouraging experienced employees to share their knowledge, and developing a reading habit.

We must build competitive profit-making capacity through highly effective management. And the foundation of highly effective management is the management team. Rewarding them with competitive remuneration is an investment, just like training activities, not merely a cost reported in the company's balance sheet. A competitive remuneration package can help most management team members resist external lures, such as being poached by our competitors, bribery and dubious practices, and focus on self-advancing, so that they and their families can live their lives with no qualms.

Team members in these three levels should be included in H World's Shareholder Program (either Stock Options or Restricted Stock) as part of their remuneration package, in the hope one day to bring them substantial wealth so they can enjoy a comfortable retirement. Through this Shareholder Program, key executives can share the fruits of our company's growth.

In addition, we hire management interns from elite universities. As H World continues to grow, our company must have strong cell proliferation ability in terms of talent-pool building. We need talent with frontline experience, as well as talent with analytical skills who can analyse abstract ideas, and process and synthesize information. The project has just started, and its effect remains to be seen.

For most of our frontline employees, we must provide job security, a relatively competitive remuneration package and a pleasant working environment. As labor costs will increase dramatically, we cannot promise our basic wage increases will be in line with inflation or guarantee the wages we provide are the highest in the industry. But through technical initiatives, organizational transformation and outsourcing, we will strive to control the increase of labor costs while ensuring our employees enjoy a relatively competitive remuneration.

From a startup company with only a few members, H World has become a billion-dollar corporation listed offshore today with hotels operating in provinces and cities nationwide. With nearly 100,000 guest rooms, we serve tens of millions of customers every year and generate hundreds of millions of dollars in sales revenue. We make tens of millions of dollars in tax contribution to our country and provide jobs to tens of thousands of individuals so they can look after themselves and their families. H World is no doubt an outstanding performer in terms of talent, capital, financing capacity, hotel network, client base and brand reputation. We are situated in the most favourable time that we have ever had – the gateway to ever more market opportunities is open to us. As our country's economic power increases, a new spring has arrived, not only for budget hotels, but also for the entire hotel industry in China.

I believe I have enough endurance and persistence to lead the team advancing forward. As the leader of our company, I am acutely aware of my responsibilities. I must have sufficient forbearance in the face of negative people and matters. I must treat veteran team members with kindness and welcome new members with an open heart. I must also resolve grievances, and repel harmful rumours and false accusations.

Without the spirit and energy to tackle these matters, I would have no right to speak of greatness.

I do have regrets over matters in the past, but I am confident and hopeful for the future.

12 May, 2012

ANXIETY OVER INTERNET-BASED MARKETING

It's been 12 years since I changed my arena of combat from the internet industry to the hospitality industry. It was exhausting but the results were not bad: although late-starters, we overtook our peers in almost every aspect to slowly become the top hotel brand in China. And having founded several businesses, I am often asked by new entrepreneurs to share my experiences.

Once, in a small restaurant in Guangzhou, Shen Ya of Vipshop asked me for advice on entrepreneurship and financing. I no longer recall what I told him or whether it helped him, but now Vipshop has a market value of US$5.8 billion which is 3.5 times larger than us, and even larger than Ctrip! I busted a gut for ten years in a traditional business yet was so easily overtaken by an internet business run by a younger generation businessman.

Then there was an IDG annual meeting where I solemnly vowed that I would grow H World to be a US$10 billion corporation. There was thunderous applause, which was hugely encouraging and made me feel pretty impressed with myself. The next speaker was Lei Jun who had started Xiaomi Corporation well after I had established H World. The previous round of financing exceeded US$10 billion. The company hadn't even gone public and it was already worth US$10 billion.

The hotel business is by no means easy; it is all hard work, both complicated and trivial, with a multitude of interlinked issues.

And for budget hotels it is even harder, because quality has to be good and prices have to be low; if costs are just a little bit high, profit evaporates. Your eyes have to be wide open 365 days a year, and there's no room for slip ups. You're doing business every single day, so when you fall behind for one day you have to work even harder to catch up.

Look at other businesses. They hype up an internet angle, make a new internet play and then their market value easily overtakes ours by leaps and bounds. Just from stock prices that are several times higher than ours, or even dozens of multiples. It's not a question of who is smart and who isn't. If Heaven rewards the diligent, as the saying goes, is our hard work and effort wasted? What's Heaven up to?

Another source of anxiety is online travel agencies (OTA). The widespread use of mobile phone apps has given OTAs miraculous abilities to be both general service platforms as well as mobile phone portals. Mobile phones have small screens and limited storage capacity, so customers don't usually keep single-use apps like ours on their phones. Watching the proportion of business going to OTAs is making me increasingly anxious. OTAs already make twice as much as we do on each room and with the growth of the internet, they will be able to grab an even larger market share.

Will OTAs have an easy ride? Not necessarily. After James Liang went back to Ctrip he burnt the midnight oil to implement bold changes and made acquisitions and investments. In addition to dealing with the competition from Qunar and eLong that is nibbling at the edges of Ctrip's business, he had to keep his eye on Tencent and Alibaba looting market share under the cover of a crisis. It really does call for blood, sweat and tears.

Will BAT – Baidu, Alibaba and Tencent – have an easy ride, too? Good old Jack Ma was completely burned out dealing with Tencent's WeChat and he was obviously anxious: internally he was pushing his messaging app m.laiwang.com; he was also rushing into promoting mobile phone games; he purchased WeiBo; and it was even rumoured that he was investing in Qihoo 360.

What about Pony Ma? He's not necessarily having an easy time! Just look at what he once said: "In the age of the internet and mobile internet, a company that appears stable is actually facing great risks because it is very dangerous to not have a handle on trends. What was accumulated in the past can easily disappear like a wisp of smoke."

Everyone seems anxious and baffled. We are all looking for answers and solutions. The source of our anxiety is the internet, mainly the mobile internet. It's the same as the surge of the internet 14 years ago, when every revolution in information technology brought with it unlimited scope for the imagination, while at the same time instilling fear of being made obsolete and facing the dangers of a time of transformation.

When a problem cannot be solved, take a moment to reflect and look back at history, and perhaps we will find a new direction and an answer.

Before 1949 there were quite a few business titans in China: Zhang Xiaoquan, the king of scissors; the Wu Fang Zhai dumplings shop; the Rong Clan flour and cotton magnates; the foremost Peking duck restaurant, Quanjude; the matchstick king Liu Hongsheng; and Aw Boon Haw, the Tiger Balm king. They all ran businesses that were intimately related to the daily lives of ordinary people. They thrived in the era of national capitalism and quickly became captains of all kinds of industries. After the establishment of the PRC in 1949, most of their businesses were nationalized and to this day some are still leaders in their fields. We recently invested in Quanjude, which is an excellent century-old establishment. Quanjude actually has 150 years of history, which far exceeds Jack Ma's dream of a 101-year business.

Let's consider the titans of clothing, food, housing and travel in the current era.

Uniqlo is currently worth US$40.8 billion; McDonald's is valued at US$95.1 billion; the recently listed Hilton is US$22 billion; Delta Air Lines US$23.5 billion. It looks like each industry has some winners. These traditional companies have some commonalities: long histories, stable profits and significant scale and market capitalization.

Now consider how quickly internet companies come into existence. In an era of constant technological innovation, the emergence to obsolescence ratio of high-tech companies is very high: Hewlett Packard, once the darling of business schools is now unstable; Google has replaced Yahoo!; and Facebook has stolen Google's limelight. Nokia once had a market value of US$200 billion but was squeezed so hard by Apple that it was sold to Microsoft for US$7 billion. And Microsoft, for that matter, is not doing so well, either, now struggling to stay warm while lingering at death's door. And what will happen in 50 years or 100 years? There will certainly be many more new enterprises that employ new technologies to dislodge today's big shots. Few of today's flash-in-the-pan success stories will survive.

The world-class hotel chains are mostly over 40–50 years old. Hilton Hotels was established a century ago in 1919. What will things be like in 50 or 100 years? I am sure people will still need to sleep and they will still stay in hotels when they go on business trips. Businesses like ours, which cater for basic needs, will definitely continue to exist. As long as we do not make errors and strive to build upon a solid foundation, H World will have a chance to join Hilton Hotels in the ranks of international hotel groups.

Admittedly, online businesses are doing well and their scale can be huge, reaching 100 billion dollars, but the competition is fierce, and the life cycle will be relatively short. Like fresh flowers, they are beautiful, but they only make a single appearance.

Internet businesses are beautiful and marvellous. I am also jealous of the intense interest they generate. I would love to achieve the same perception but unfortunately it has not been my destiny. I am sentimentally attached to the wonderful hospitality industry that I am involved in. Until such time as a way to avoid sleep is invented, hotels will definitely continue to exist. Businesses that are intimately entwined with people's basic needs will last longer, be even more stable and more diverse.

Taking these issues into consideration, I feel more at ease. But we cannot allow ourselves to stagnate or ignore the outside world. We must do our primary tasks well, perfect our basic skills and embrace the internet.

A newly fashionable acronym is O2O – online to offline – and it refers to joining offline business opportunities with the internet to make the internet the front desk of offline transactions.

Traditional service industries are silent in the face of popular O2O businesses such as dianping.com and group buying websites, for example, as if this has nothing to do with them. Actually, the concept of O2O encompasses a great deal, so if a supply chain has online and offline aspects it can be considered O2O.

There is no reason to behave like an ostrich when facing these types of changes in the mobile internet industry. Internet OTAs can earn about twice as much money per room that we actual hotels can earn, and after market value enlargement they will be able to reach seven or eight times higher. If we don't take the initiative, our profits will diminish as mobile internet companies ride the crest of technological transformation and, ultimately, we will end up fighting over crumbs.

Ten years ago, when I had just entered this traditional business, I suggested using the information technology spirit to transform traditional industries. In today's hotel industry in China those that truly have competitive strengths are the ones who adopted this spirit.

Today, I need to make an improvement: use the internet's spirit to transform traditional industries. And not just use internet technology, but more important is to adopt the attitude of the internet.

The internet attitude influences thought processes, as opposed to the thought processes of industrialization.

In the age of industrialization, the characteristic way of thinking was large-scale production, large-scale sales and large-scale dissemination. But in the internet age, this important trinity has been deconstructed.

Industrialization resulted in sufficient productivity to ensure the elimination of shortages and even created large surpluses of products. Products are increasingly in the form of information, making it impossible to create monopolies; fundamentally, the media's monopoly has been broken, as consumers have transformed into both information producers and distributors.

That means influencing consumer behaviour through unidirectional broadcasting to promote hot products no longer works.

The age of consumer rights is being ushered in, and with it comes consumer equality, democracy and freedom. The power of brands, distributors and retailers, that used to play a key role in the supply chain, is being diluted and weakened and, ultimately, will be terminated. In the age of consumer sovereignty, consumer information is increasingly symmetrical, the traditional interest groups in the value chain are finding it harder to consolidate their interest barrier, while traditional dominant brands and retailers are gradually losing their ability to lord it over others. Discourse authority has slipped from the hands of retailers into the hands of consumers, as consumers use self-media to establish and strengthen their rights.

The internet attitude is users above all else.

Of course, businesses used to talk of customers being paramount and products being king, but such slogans were either self-promotion or a reflection of the entrepreneur's personal creed. In the digital age the customer being paramount must be complied with. We have to sincerely win over users, because their praise and positive reviews become valuable assets.

The mobile internet industry is continuing to overturn existing business value systems and points of reference. In the past, brands and retailers habitually blew their own trumpets, but the essence of the 'fan economy' is providing a sense of participation. We must actively invite our users to participate in every step of the value chain from concept to design, right through to production and sales. The mobile internet industry has also overturned the rules of value creation. We have to return to business basics to find out what annoys our customers and what they yearn for, to be able to create value for our customers. As Lei Jun, the founder of Xiaomi, put it, you have to make products the customer will scream for. If you merely provide a product that has value for the consumer, there will be a plethora of similar products and your fans will have no incentive to buy your product.

To differentiate from the currently popular O2O concept to better define the path forward in O2O for traditional businesses like ours, I propose the O2O2O concept.

The first O is for offline and refers to our products and services, which is our foundation. In the internet age we must look to the internet (online) to promote and sell our offline products and services. This is the first O2O (offline to online).

After customers purchase our products and services online, they will have to come to our offline physical entity to enjoy our hotel experience, which is the second O2O. Combining the two gives us O2O2O. This can be represented by the following diagram.

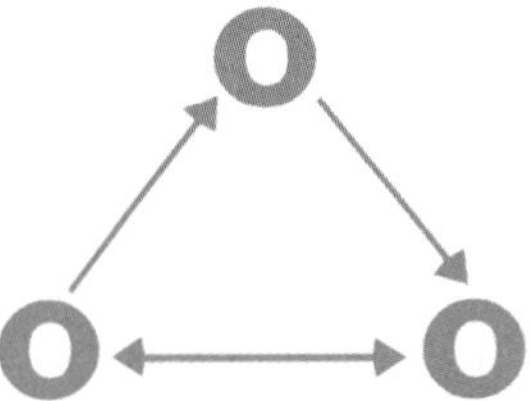

The lower segment is our offline foundation, upon which our very existence depends, and is the basis of competition. The apex is where we must make good use of the internet toolset to raise our brand recognition, boost operational efficiency and improve every stage of the customer experience.

Many new internet based O2O businesses are engaged in creating something from nothing. Taking advantage of the surplus of goods and services, getting great discounts from suppliers to attract more customers, providing low wholesale prices and low selling prices is euphemistically called *tuan guo*, that is, team or group buying. Collecting customer reviews, grading suppliers, finding ways to collect money from suppliers or users is a 'review network.' As soon as they can aggregate a huge customer base, they monopolize communication channels between the businesses and customers in the same way as distribution channels did in the past, and thus have a strong say in transactions and derive high profits, both from customers and from businesses, mostly by extracting large commissions from the businesses. In the past era of industrialization, GOME Electrical Appliances and the Suning Commerce Group are examples of companies monopolizing the channels of commerce.

These new O2O methods can help small-scale enterprises and widely dispersed suppliers; at least the pros outweigh the cons when the profits do not dip below a critical level. But when large brand groups come to depend on these new channels, it will spell disaster. These new intermediaries can easily acquire and retain customers.

Impelled forward by social media interactions and mobile applications there will also be 'debranding.'

The traditional Chinese service industries are actually experiencing the two opposite extremes of branding and debranding at the same time. The long-term contempt for, and suppression of, service industries in China has given rise to an obvious branding trend; however, the internet, and especially since the rise of the mobile internet industry and social media platforms, has led to a dilution of brands, which has resulted in a trend of debranding. Within this trend of opposites, we can respond by turning these opposite forces into an upward spiral of growth.

For traditional service industry companies to find their own positioning and core value under these new circumstances, they will have to adopt the characteristics of the internet. My positing of the O2O2O model (which is actually the O2O model stated more explicitly) is likely to be suitable for the majority of businesses in the traditional service industry.

In future, will there still be a need for this kind of mutant intermediary and a middle-man channel? Will the brand groups of the future still employ this model? This is a topic worthy of consideration and exploration. Hotel groups, for example, have evolved from a heavy reliance on real estate assets to today's reduced emphasis on real estate, relying instead primarily on branding and management. Will future hotel groups further evolve into a 'brand + management + channel' model?

Thinking along these lines, we will further experiment and explore. The ideal for H World is to become 'the King of Offline!'

I firmly believe no technological development can replace an offline experience. Hotels, for example, offering good products and services, or restaurants serving delicious food, will always be the most important core value of offline industries. Online platforms will never replace this kind of experiential service. The mobile internet industry will provide us with an effective means to communicate with customers and have transactions with them without any need, or perhaps just a small role, for a third party in between. Via the mobile internet, we can present our core value directly to the end customer, making our services convenient, efficient and affordable. This concept will enable H World to stand out in the international hotel industry and become a company worth dozens of billions of US dollars.

Anxieties engender reflection; reflection generates breakthroughs; breakthroughs are the path to a bright future.

To be the King of Offline is the best cure for our anxiety about the internet.

1 March, 2014

BIG WIND AND STRAIGHT TREES

Every year at this time, a typhoon-like seasonal wind passes over Provence. The wind is so ferocious that only if one is in the middle of it can one fully comprehend its force – it turns my outdoor furniture upside down, and can almost blow a slight person away. In China, crops are flattened, and trees and bamboo groves bend to the direction of strong winds. In Provence, however, the equally strong wind has no effect on trees – they are as straight as ever after the strong wind, proud and confident.

This was intriguing to me so I investigated and found three reasons. First, the soil in this area is quite hard. Tree roots are tightly holding the soil. Second, these are mostly old trees with well-established roots. Third, these trees are flexible. When the strong wind blows, they dance with the wind. When the wind passes, they remain unharmed.

This conjures up the waves of the internet, Chinese enterprises, and the succession of adjustments and fluctuations of the Chinese market.

An enterprise is like a tree. The market and customers are like its soil. In order to withstand the wind, the enterprise must firmly hold on to the market and its customers. An enterprise's inner-strength and values are like tree roots. They must be deeply rooted to keep the tree standing. And the wind is like the succession of adjustments and fluctuations of the market. When the wind arrives, we must have the flexibility to dance with it. Only with these qualities can our company proudly stand, tall and straight, when the wind has passed.

A company must have sound inner strength; it must not only be able to meet market needs, but also be flexible and adaptable. Only then, can we confidently dance with market wind and grow despite the wind.

11 July, 2014

SOME POINTS TO CONSIDER BEFORE YOU START

1. BUSINESS MODEL

The business model is vital to entrepreneurship.

A successful business model has to be used at the right time – not too early and not too late. Every business opportunity has a window. A good business model that is used too early becomes a business martyr. Too late, and it will be hard to dominate the market, and even miss business opportunities.

Most business models are introduced to meet market needs and do not necessarily create new consumer behaviour – they simply apply new technologies to alter the rules of the game of existing business models. For example, you can sell clothing online, but you cannot ask people to wear scarves instead of clothes.

A good business model is one that reaches a 'harmonious point' for various interests: good and cheap products for customers, a small investment with a big return for businesses, high commissions for intermediary agents who want rewards for little effort. Finding the harmonious point for all parties in the ecological chain in the industry is very important. For example, what is an adequate investment? What is the best price for customers? What kind of services should be provided and what should be cut? How much to charge franchise partners? How to make the business attractive to franchise partners while generating substantial profit?

A good business model should be able to stand the test of time and implementation. Like a new piano that requires fine-tuning, it is normal for a business model to bounce between ideal and reality a few times. It requires constant fine-tuning and continuous upgrading.

A good business model must be unique and innovative. An entrepreneurship that relies on low cost and high efficiency only works in certain environments – China, for example – relying on flexible market-oriented mechanisms to compete with rigid non-market-oriented mechanisms. Success comes in different ways, but copycats only ever end up with a second-rate business at best.

2. CLIENT RELATIONS

In a segmented market, the total number of customers is actually fixed.

How to maximize customer attraction and increase loyal clients and followers is the most important question for entrepreneurs. Perhaps attract them with good products, like Apple products; or with a good story, such as renaming the town Zhongdian in Yunnan Province, Shangri-la; or with products that appeal to client values and ethics, such as the Japanese brand Muji; or a product with a high cost-performance ratio, such as budget hotels. I summarize our approach in three words: focused, refined and scream. This means that in the age of product oversupply and information explosion, we have to be focused to make refined products, because only refined products can captivate clients, and only refined products that can make customers scream can truly captivate them.

In the hotel industry, customers include both hotel clients and franchise clients, whose needs should be considered. Franchising is a reputation-based business. A damaged product brings a damaged reputation, which is terrible because it is almost impossible to rebuild trust.

In addition, there are plenty of competitors lurking in the background, waiting for you to make mistakes so they can attack and tear you apart.

As for Customer Needs Analysis, I do not rely on the opinions of marketing companies or consulting firms. Instead, I opt for role play, imagining myself as our target clients, then designing scenarios to identify demand, not only what they want, but also what they need, including what appeals to their values.

After the product is made, it is also vital to obtain onsite experience of customer feedback. No reviews and market surveys are as good as onsite experience. We should not only observe the product and communicate with users, but also should experience the product ourselves. For example, we used to have TVs in our hotel rooms. The power button on the TV had a glaring blue light that you would not necessarily notice during a routine room inspection. Only when you spend the night in the room and are deprived of sleep by the bright blue glow, are you aware of the problem.

3. PROVIDE REFINED PRODUCTS

The manufacturing industry makes visible products, an item of clothing or a pair of scissors, for example. Internet companies sell software products, such as WeChat and Keynote. The service industry sells services, which sometimes is a combination of software and hardware. For example, the products of the hotel industry include its own form of 'hardware' such as hotel rooms, and 'software' such as hotel services.

A hotel industry product is a combination of many aspects. Even the outfits of front desk staff, the service attitude of the hotel staff, the quality of a hotel breakfast and the speed of hotel Wi-Fi are all part of the product.

Just as the great poet Su Dongpo wrote, "The ducks are first to know the warming Spring river water," hotel clients are the most observant reviewers of a hotel. Every detail is important, just as every requirement of different types of clients is important, and they must not be overlooked. For example, the ideal height and size of a toilet seat is different, depending on the height of guests. If the toilet seat is too high, the guest will have to tip-toe. Leisure travellers prefer big wardrobes with enough space to store clothing for different occasions, but for business travellers, it is more important to not leave things behind so a wardrobe without doors is more practical.

Good hotel products do not have to make customers 'scream.' Instead, they can attract customers with subtle and thoughtful details. To achieve this, first adopt common sense and avoid pretentiousness. For example, when we took over the Manxin Lijiang Holiday Hotel, all the power switches in the guest rooms were on digital control panels. They were so complicated that even a university graduate with a science major like me had difficulty turning the lights on or off when I wanted to. A hotel feature like this does nothing other than annoy guests.

Second, we must understand human nature, especially human weakness. For example, people are lazy and like to indulge in convenience. Adding an escalator can effectively direct human flow to the second floor – which is different from what a lift can do. People also like to know they will get more than they pay for. We can offer some complimentary items. For example, our Hanting Hotels are praised for offering free bottled water and free Wi-Fi access. Another example is reward programs, which are attractive even for well-to-do people like me. I like the idea of being able to buy plane tickets with reward points.

Third, we should make products at a reasonable cost. The balance between cost-control and function is vital, especially for budget to mid-range hotel markets, and it is even a decisive factor in the life or death of a business model. For instance, the operator of another hotel brand manages budget hotels at the same cost we pay for running our mid-range Ji Hotels. Its RevPAR is even lower than our budget hotel brand Hanting. Readers can just imagine how miserable the return is for owners and investors.

The balance of function and cost is equally important. For example, should we put a private bath in each guest room? This was a subject of much debate when we were designing our luxury brand Joya Hotels. Eventually, we decided to exclude this item because according to our business model, very few people use baths and putting a bath in each room increases the cost. Of course, having a private bath in the room certainly has its advantages, but we had to forego this item in the design for our luxury brand in order to be consistent with our business model.

Fourth, our products and services must satisfy the aesthetics and values of our mainstream clients. In the years when having a noble bearing was the norm, guests expected to be served and to be treated attentively. Therefore, making doormen, bellboys and concierges remember the guest's name was widely promoted. A symbol of that era is Ritz-Carlton's motto, "We are Ladies and Gentlemen serving Ladies and Gentlemen." Guests today expect more privacy, convenience, self-service and environmental friendliness. Overly attentive services only cause annoyance. A team of staff hovering over one or two guests is often viewed as wasteful. The over-elaborate formalities of the past are now considered outdated. And our Ji Hotel brand is tailored to meet this trend among modern day travellers.

Thanks to the internet, client reviews are more important than ever before. A good product does not even need advertising or promotion. Through WeChat, Weibo, Facebook and other social media platforms, reviews, good and bad, spread widely in no time. The hotel industry is in the business of experience. The water temperature, the fineness of bed linen and the firmness of the bed are all part of a guest's experience. Guests may not praise us for giving them a good experience, but one slight flaw in their experience is enough to give rise to grievance.

The importance of our product quality cannot be overemphasized. The product, in effect, is the realization of the business model on our customers. In this regard, all entrepreneurs must be experts of their products. To use today's fashionable term: Product Managers.

Take a people-oriented approach, make refined products, gain customer approval to develop a good reputation that can be widely shared. This will lead to brand recognition. A recognizable brand is the prerequisite for brand promotion. This logic and route are never outdated. All sophistry, trickery and pseudo innovation will eventually be exposed.

We must not take shortcuts. We must strive to create a brand that lasts; the foundation and key to our success is the good quality of our products.

4. FLAGSHIP STORES

Flagship stores are important when establishing a chain business! Everyone is familiar with the New York City Fifth Avenue Apple store. And many Chinese people also know of: the Grand Hyatt Shanghai which is in the 88-storey Jin Mao Tower; the Carrefour Gubei hypermarket; the IKEA Xuhui Store on Caoxi Road in Shanghai; the Wangfujing McDonald's, Beijing's first, and once the world's largest; and Shanghai's first KFC on the Bund that was opened in 1989 in the then Dongfeng Hotel, formerly the Shanghai Club building.

Flagship stores, sometimes called demo stores, in addition to being used as a venture for product presentation, are also a showcase of the company's business model. Aspects such as style of interior design, product display, costs, line of operations, customer feedback, rent and profitability are fine-tuned and tested in flagship stores before being applied widely elsewhere. How can we expect others to invest in the business if we do not know enough about it ourselves?

Flagship stores are best set up in cities to influence rural areas. Stores located in Shanghai and Beijing have a greater impact than in regional cities such as Nantong and Kunshan. As for location and the visual aspect of flagship stores, the more centrally located the better and the more visible the better.

The standards of site selection and investment for flagship stores can be higher. As a flagship store is to be used as a template for other sites, it should be more refined, taking the diminishing effect into account in the process of duplication. However, the overall model should not be changed. Otherwise, the purpose of a flagship store will be lost. For example, in our Ji Hotel on Zhaojiabang Road in Shanghai, the room décor accessories and homeware are of a high standard. And because of its good location, its RevPAR is higher. While being used as a demo Ji Hotel, this hotel adheres to our overall business model for the brand.

The first hotel bearing our brand in a province or a regional city is very important. Regardless of whether it is a directly operated hotel, it is in effect the flagship store of our brand in this region. This hotel must be centrally located and highly visible.

The standard and quality of the product must adhere to our business model.

The impact of a flagship store, such as profit, image and customer experience, can be very effective marketing components that will help form a good reputation for the brand, which is the most effective tool to attract franchise partners.

It is very important to pay attention to the launch of a flagship store at the initial stage of the entrepreneurial adventure. Entrepreneurs should spend a lot of time in flagship stores to reflect, improve and upgrade their products. I spent a lot of time at the Jianguo Hotel in Xizhimen in Beijing and the Hanting Hotel in Xin Hong Qiao. Many of my new ideas and improvements emerged during my time spent onsite at flagship stores.

5. THE BRAND STORY

Every brand is unique, and every brand tells a story of its own. As entrepreneurs we must learn to tell stories. Use engaging language to describe your passion, your ideal, your ideas, your design and your products.

Since your audience includes investors, team members, clients, the media and the public, your story may have different versions, but the main storyline should be the same. The language of your story should be succinct, animated and straightforward. We can use metaphors, jokes and charts to help us tell the story.

I remember when Zhou Quan of IDG first came to our business model presentation. He said, "Clearly state what you want in three sentences." I was taken aback – make a decision on such a large investment based on just three sentences? Simplicity is the ultimate sophistication. Investors listen to people talking about business models all the time and have seen all kinds of trickery. It often takes only three sentences to reveal whether or not an idea is worth pursuing.

I am very good at telling stories to my employees. When Hanting was first launched, I told everyone that we want to make it a leading company in China's hotel industry. After our company was listed on Nasdaq, I said to everyone we want to make H World the world's No. 1. Listeners have doubts but I always back my claim with evidence and a road map. Step by step, when we eventually made what seemed like a fairytale into reality, our team members gained more confidence, which will strengthen their resolve to follow us to reach the next goal.

The story for the media should deliver a shock effect. After Ctrip was launched, I once said, "Ctrip is the gravedigger of travel agencies." The line is still shocking to this day. We must stay attuned to hot topics in the media and cater to the interest points of both the media and the public. After all, few companies can generate hot topics like Apple.

The most important stories are for our customers. For example, the motto for our Hanting brand is, 'Surf well, sleep well and shower well,' for Ji Hotels it is, 'Life of simplicity,' and for the budget hotel brand Hi Inns it is, 'Say Hi to friends around the globe.' Our Manxin Hotels are for 'romantic hearts and free spirits,' and Joya offers 'luxury lite.' We must find a unique aspiration point for each brand. This can be what customers need, or the brand's characteristics, or a simple sentence that connects with customers.

Of course, most importantly, your stories must match what you offer. The worst thing we can do is to promise too much but deliver little, or to tell wonderful stories but deliver a dreadful product. No one will believe stories like that and no brand like that will last. This is the most vulnerable weakness of companies that launch their brand before launching their hotels.

Pacing and restraint are important for storytelling. We can share stories about what we did and what we are doing, but not always about what we will do. We must not lie, but there are stories we may choose not to tell, or stories that do not tell all. Exposing our strategic goals prematurely risks inviting our competitors to launch their attack.

6. TEAM

Team building is particularly important at the initial stage of entrepreneurship.

At this stage, it is not possible to attract talent with a high salary package. Very often talent recruited at the cost of a high salary package cannot cope with the challenges that occur at the beginning of entrepreneurship.

The key to attract talent is inspiration. We use ideals, passion and our charisma to attract talent to join start-ups. That's why team members who join a company at its very early stage tend to be very impassioned, but professionally are not always the best in the industry. Some even have obvious flaws. To work with these team members, we should put their ability to good use while setting their weaknesses aside because every bit of resources count.

To improve collaboration with team members who have plenty of passion but not enough experience for the work at hand, we ensure good communication, adequate training opportunities and reflection. We can invest in our goodwill and spare time to interact with our team members by engaging in activities such as attending dinner parties, joining excursions and group reading sessions. We can also develop shared interests such as running, playing soccer and badminton.

Entrepreneurship is a terrific learning experience. Many individuals make accelerated progress in what they do through entrepreneurship. Most successful businesspeople in China today are not from large companies. Instead, they made their way up from small enterprises. Good examples are members of Jack Ma's startup team, who are known as the Eighteen Arhats, as well as most of H World's senior executives.

For key members of our team, while it is not possible to offer them a high remuneration package, we should share the fruits of success with them instead of swindling them. Stock options are a good tool. In asset-heavy businesses, options can be slightly less and under 5% is quite reasonable; businesses relying more on human resources need to offer 10-20% options.

Passion is very important at the initial stage of entrepreneurship. It is part of a leader's job to inspire people. And sustaining team members' passion is equally important. Activities such as reading groups, beer parties and outdoor training are all effective ways to sustain entrepreneurial passion.

In the offices of startups, lights are always on and working overtime on weekends and public holidays is common. The word 'overtime' does not exist in a startup's vocabulary and is not even in their dictionary.

7. COMPETITORS

"Who are our enemies? Who are our friends? This is a question of the first importance for the revolution," wrote Chairman Mao. Who are our allies? Who are our competitors? This is a question of the first importance for entrepreneurship.

Your competitors not only constantly remind you to work hard, they also define your territory and expansion strategies.

In some areas, the difficulty of success for a startup increases if one of your competitors is already dominating the market, such as BAT, Ctrip and H World. However, with the development of technologies and the evolution of business models, it is still possible to overtake these big players by adopting new technologies and new business models. The leading Chinese language travel search engine, qunar.com, the food delivery service Meituan Dianping, and the e-commerce giant JD.com are all good examples.

For a startup to survive in a traditional industry, hyped remarks and gimmicks are not enough. It must have real knowledge and offer genuinely good products. Basic matters such as cost-control, efficiency and a good ability to execute projects, are important.

A startup business in a traditional industry can borrow ideas from a trend and ride with the trend. This will be useful in terms of financing, marketing and recruiting. For example, Ctrip in its early days was, in effect, a call centre which worked as an agent for traditional hotels, but its financing value was calculated, based on the evaluation of an internet company. In addition, our market strategy took advantage of the internet craze in all aspects, including our talent recruitment and incentive mechanism.

Pace of growth and development strategy should be planned with your competitors in mind. Ideally, we want to win on both fronts – quality and speed. But if our competitors are moving fast, we should at least ensure our development speed is at the same level. We must not be preoccupied with quality at the expense of development speed because it will lead to a strategic defeat while tactically winning. IBIS is an example on this issue.

Avoid head-on confrontation with competitors. We must learn to sidestep and be different. Self-harming tactics are not good strategies. For example, Hanting consolidates its presence in first- and second-tier cities, while Home Inns take on markets in second- and third-tier cities. Our strategy of taking control of highly visible buildings has been very successful. Transportation services in southern cities are convenient. In regions where we did not have a strong presence, such as Guangxi and Hubei, we carefully developed products that are tailored to third- or fourth-tier cities to seize these territories. This has proven to be a successful strategy.

20 September, 2014

ENTREPRENEURS AND PROFESSIONAL MANAGERS

It is very difficult for people who do not have sound management skills and knowledge, and solely depend on entrepreneurial spirit, to grow startup companies to large enterprises. It's risky, too. At the same time, the advantage that professional managers possess does not always apply to the initial stage of entrepreneurship. Sometimes it can even become an obstacle. Planned or not, the three enterprises I have been involved with are very good at managing both.

Entrepreneurs usually have backgrounds in areas such as marketing, technology or particular industries. They are passionate about their products and markets but are not interested in the company's day-to-day operations. They tend to think they are smarter than others. They like to take risks. They are vigorous in work. They have big personalities – their strong points and weaknesses are equally noticeable – and they like to do things their own way.

They give open promises to their companies. This means their companies will not only take up most of the time in their lives, but also become their lives. Many of them consider running a company a challenging game and the source of deep happiness.

Professional managers are well-educated people – many have graduated from elite universities in the United States – and have years of experience working in multinational companies. They have received structured professional training and attach importance to numbers and logic.

They are different from entrepreneurs when it comes to passion, risk-taking, decision-making, innovation and vision.

Some founders (mostly owners) of entrepreneurial enterprises in China tend to firmly hold on to power and also rely on nepotism. They do not trust professional managers recruited externally and are reluctant to relinquish control of company operations. When professional managers clash with family members of the company founders or company veterans, these entrepreneurs have a tendency to side with family members and the veterans. This means professional managers recruited externally cannot possibly carry out the work they are hired to do. Animosities will inevitably occur if one side tries to push their own policies through. Eventually, it is always professional managers who leave the company in disappointment. Some professional managers, especially the ones hired by entrepreneurial enterprises controlled by venture capital investors, attempt to erase all contributions made by entrepreneurs, overstate the company's problems, and put all the blame on their predecessors and the entrepreneurs. Some even attempt to hijack the company to glorify their own careers for their own short-term interests.

In China, both entrepreneurs and professional managers are rare commodities. They should treat each other equally and with respect. Neither the attitude of the rich looking down on educated people, or the attitude of 'sea turtles' looking down on 'local turtles' (overseas trained people looking down on those who are locally trained) is constructive because neither of them can replace the other. Whoever does not respect this rule will pay severely.

In China's primitive and fast-growing business environment, only learning from each other and growing together can bring success to everyone. In the current environment, ideal entrepreneurs should possess global knowledge. They are not only familiar with the local business thinking and environment, but also have an in-depth understanding of traditional

Eastern culture and history. They should not only understand Western business protocols and language, but also know how to utilize modern management tools and strategies.

A deciding factor is a company's shareholding structure. Companies in which venture capitalists or private equity take up 70% of the shares face different fundamental questions from companies whose founders own 70%. The board of a company is a product of its shareholders and the management team carries out decisions made by executive board members. A company's strategies, objectives, values and culture reflect the wishes of its shareholders.

Therefore, I believe an ideal enterprise should have a large shareholder who is able to work with professional management talent to ensure the company's resilience, stability and sustainability. A soulless enterprise lacking ideals is merely a cold money-making machine and a tool of wealth accumulation.

25 April, 2018

A LEGENDARY FOUNDER OF A COMPANY AND HIS TIMES

These days, a founder of a company is often bestowed the epithet 'legend.' In fact, legend simply means you are a product of the times you live in.

Take me as an example. As a child I grew up in rural China. Perhaps I was a smart kid, but I was not particularly handsome, nor did I possess irresistible charisma. In my view, many company founders and 'legendary' entrepreneurs look the same if they all take their clothes off and jump into a public bath. The so-called 'legend' is part of the publicity generated by the companies we founded and the media. It is also a result of the influence on society of our viewpoints. There is another reason. In times of change, leaders are important.

People like me would probably be useless in a calmer environment, for example, in a large company based in a Western country that has an annual growth of 5–7%. The outside environment is stable and safe, and internally no changes are on the agenda. In a country like this, my CEO is probably more suitable to be the boss than I am. But China is an ever-changing environment and it needs people like me. What are the distinguishing features of us entrepreneurs? We possess a sense of crisis and we are acutely responsive to risks and opportunities. The Chinese word for 'crisis' is literally 'risks and opportunities.' Artists are sensitive to feelings and we are sensitive to the business environment. This kind of sensitivity is a hard-earned intuition that is a result of long-term thinking, constantly battling with life-and-death situations for our companies, confronting challenges and bearing the pain of hardships.

Take me as an example. I do not spend all day monitoring details such as reservation figures and stock prices. Instead, I constantly observe changes in consumer trends. If I become numb and less alert, or if I become subjective and narrow-minded, the company's direction will be negatively affected.

Entrepreneurs sometimes make seemingly 'irrational' judgments. Many of my ideas did not come from Harvard MBA classes. Rather, these ideas came from reading Buddhist texts, or from everyday life experiences, or my conversations with artists or from my fitness trainers. For example, my Pilates trainer recently told me I should try to use the smallest amount of effort to execute the best movements. This suggestion suddenly struck me – that's right. A good movement has to be completed using the smallest effort. And a movement that has to be completed with the greatest effort certainly will not be perfect; at least, it cannot be sustained because it may be compensated by something you are not aware of. Hence the saying, the Tao models itself on nature. A perfect movement has to be an effortless movement, for in nature everything is harmonious and perfect.

In recent years, I have started to embrace some seemingly irrational ideas. Sometimes when my discussions with our CEO reach a deadlock, she will say: "I do not really understand what you are saying, and I do not agree with your views, but since your being-correct ratio is higher, let's follow your idea." Perhaps this kind of ability is part of the 'legend.' However, we must not forget, as founders of entrepreneurial enterprises, that we are created by the times we live in and we did not create our times. Individuals are always insignificant in a society, even though they are regarded as heroes.

One hero alone cannot create history. Heroes and the people create history together.

18 April, 2018

COMPANY FOUNDERS MUST BE DEEPLY IMMERSED IN THEIR OWN PRODUCTS

It is vital for company founders to be deeply immersed in their own products. I personally inspected all of our directly operated hotels. A lot of my experience and ideas come from repeat observation and continual analysis. Take the approach of a guest room floor layout. It is common practice to put two rooms between two load-bearing walls. For example, two rooms each 3.5 meters wide can be placed between walls that are 7 meters apart. But is it possible not to be constrained by the walls? What if the walls are 8 meters apart? Then the rooms will be too big if each room is 4 meters wide. What should we do if some rooms might be excessively wide? What if one room in the layout happens to be very dark?

These are in fact geometry questions. It's all about how to draw lines and produce the best results.

Immersion also applies to room designs. When I started to work on Hanting, I realized that low cost is not the only factor to consider. Our products should also be visually appealing and follow aesthetic trends. For example, at the time painting loud and bold colors on hotel walls had been out of fashion and subtle color tones were preferred.

In the early days of Hanting, we planned to open a hotel on Wuzhong Road in Shanghai. I personally inspected the site. There is an atrium with a skylight in the middle of the building and the floor plan was challenging for room layout. I came up with the idea of a corner room layout to maximize space and turned a very long room into a suite. The result was good – the suite is the most popular room. We put in a two-metre-wide bed instead of the standard 1.8-metre bed, which looked too small for that space. It is visually more balanced and our guests like the result.

I am also involved in bathroom designs for our hotels. We had used glass panels to divide the toilet and the bath. But glass panels are difficult to clean and make people feel cold in winter. We later abandoned the design.

I am also sceptical about consulting firms and market survey results. I believe it is the ability to feel and to perceive that makes a great entrepreneur. The conclusion of a market survey can be exactly the opposite if the parameters are altered. How many people should we survey? Can we choose the right people to survey? If the people surveyed are not my target clients, then we are asking the wrong people. For a survey for Hanting, you should ask people who graduated from universities, or young professionals who work in Jin Jiang or Huaiyin. The focus group will be different if the survey is for Ji Hotels.

Just like me, people who work closely with me also have indepth knowledge of our products. I often say to Zhang Min: "It is hard to become a good CEO of a hotel without in-depth knowledge of the hotel."

As a company founder you can find the right direction for your company by being deeply immersed in your own products.

21 April, 2018

MY EXPERIENCE ANTICIPATING THE FUTURE

When I founded Hanting I had set three-year and five-year plans that stipulated when to open how many hotels and when to list the company, and these milestones were planned in great detail. Miraculously, these milestones were all validated in practice.

I think the accuracy of my planning is not because I am more rational than others; rather, it stems from my holistic thought processes.

Before Hanting, I had already founded Home Inn, so I already knew how to avoid detours and setbacks. When thinking about Hanting, I had a clear picture in mind about the changes in the business environment and, as a consequence, what changes needed to be made. After deciding on the products, it was easy to work out when to open how many hotels, how much money to invest, how many staff would be needed, how much working capital would be needed and how much capital we would have to bring to the party. After that, the funding, the scale of the listing and the schedule for listing clearly came into view.

When it was time to put it all into practice there were times when reality lagged behind the vision I had in mind, requiring me to step harder on the gas pedal. Sometimes I felt the pace of development was too fast and would negatively impact product quality, necessitating a reduction of speed. For example, there was a point when our expansion in first-tier cities was too fast so we immediately reduced investments in first-tier cities. This speeding up and slowing down approach allowed the whole company to advance at an appropriate pace.

Plans being precisely realized can be merely a coincidence. But behind this coincidence is the integration of long-time reflection and experience.

This strikes me as having a lot in common with a good doctor dispensing medical treatment. When a good doctor takes on a patient, he will have a plan and the ultimate treatment result is usually quite close to the plan, or perhaps even exceeds it. This is because the doctor has experience and knows exactly what the effect on his patients the treatment and medicines prescribed will have. The doctor sees different individuals and cannot always be successful, but if he can achieve a 90% success rate he can be considered a good doctor.

I named our hotels. Home Inn, Hanting, Joya, H World are all my idea. Literally, they mean Like Home, A Small Courtyard in the Cosmos, Joyous Pearl, China Lodging. My literary talent is meagre, but I feel that my name-picking ability is not too bad, because I allocate sufficient time to think it through, just like no geometry question was too hard for me to solve when I was a child. Why? I think when eating, I think when performing ablutions, I even think when sleeping, and I will not stop thinking about the question until the answer comes to me. If I keep applying my mind to it, a solution will surface; it's an invariable model that closely resembles running a business.

Planning will succeed because I put my heart and soul into the task. When you are single-minded, and you can be single-minded for a sufficiently long time, miracles will happen.

5 May, 2018

CHAIN BUSINESS MANAGEMENT

I have been managing chains for over a decade, and although it's the hotel business, when reflecting upon the overall experience, I feel other chains ought to be able to gain something from our experience. I believe the management of large chains must begin with four areas: beliefs, economics, knowhow, community. These four aspects correspond exactly with the essence of the four organizational principles of a society: belief corresponds with religion; economics corresponds with business; knowhow corresponds with the military; community corresponds with family.

1. BELIEFS

Beliefs are very important, the soul of an organization. Religions are held together by shared beliefs, beliefs that touch upon fundamentals like life and death, meaning and soul. This identification with metaphysical values transcends all material matters, which is more enduring and more reliable. Some of the great religions have lasted for thousands of years.

Although chains are business organizations, beliefs are equally important for them.

A company's system of values determines all the possibilities of that company. For example, what is a company's purpose? Is it to be listed on the stock market and maximize investments to create greatness? Or how does a company treat its customers, employees, shareholders and society? Does it treat employees well or exploit them? Does it cheat customers or give them something they value? Does it engage in selfish profiteering or the sublime creation of something beautiful?

Chains are distributed over vastly different geographical locations with employees who come from diverse backgrounds, have different family circumstances, have reached different educational levels, adhere to different religions and have unique characters, so it is quite a challenge to promote shared values.

Actually, everyone yearns for something lofty and grand, something that they can devote their entire life to. When an ordinary life is merged with greatness there will be no loneliness and meaning to life can be found.

Large chains face many levels of the public, so company values must be clear and simple, colloquial and catchy. In addition to memorizing the statement of values, post them on walls and print them on name cards.

Take H World's corporate values as an example.

The founder's original aspiration: a group of like-minded friends happily working together to create something great.

Values: truth, compassion and beauty.

Vision: become a great international enterprise.

Mission: create a beautiful life.

2. ECONOMICS

Planning the allocation of benefits is, of course, very important for a commercial enterprise. On the macro level it is all about balancing the interests of the customers, employees and shareholders. Make too much off the customers and competitiveness is lost; too little and the company will have no profits. Employee benefits and remuneration should also be appropriate and reasonable. For example, if H World's 60,000 people were given a 10 yuan – about US$1.50 – increase in their daily meal allowance, that would cost 220 million yuan (over US$32 million) over the course of a year.

However, if the working conditions are harsh, employees will be unable to provide satisfactory service to customers, and even qualified staff will be hard to recruit. Labor costs have grown dramatically in recent years and may continue to do so in the future. Our salary levels cannot far exceed that of our peers, though we can achieve a remuneration level that is above average for the industry. Shareholder profits can only be realized when a balance between the interests of customers and employees is achieved.

Every retail outlet of a large-scale chain is an organic economic entity that involves the allocation of benefits between the property owners, the staff and customers. If there is not a transparent and well-designed system for allocating benefits, it will be impossible to replicate the units that link the chain, leading to many retail units losing money and a deterioration of the chain. Without profits there will be no customers, leading to the inability of the chain to continue in business.

When acquiring business sites, you are often in competition with a whole range of businesses. Businesses with higher sales revenue per square metre squeeze out businesses with lower sales revenue per square metre. Strong brands squeeze out weaker brands. This is especially obvious in the food courts of commercial centres. The owners of shopping malls have minimum requirements for brands that want to rent space from them and will not accept bad brands. And even if a bad brand does manage to open an outlet, the average amount a customer spends and the flow through of customers will be too low to sustain the business and, ultimately, it will face closure. Therefore, a chain's economic calculations must be sound to be able to withstand being put to the test. Performance evaluations are essential to allocating employee benefits. Work more, get more; work less, get less. The greater the contribution, the greater the reward. For example, our house cleaning staff are paid by the room, our front desk sales staff get commissions by selling membership cards, our hotel managers are on a balanced scorecard. Different positions are evaluated differently to reward diligence and punish laxity, to ensure a basic fairness in the system of benefit allocation.

In the H World system, the primary consideration is to guarantee the interests of our clients – hotel guests and franchising partners.

We strive to provide our clients with a product at a reasonable price. For example, we try to avoid using intermediaries and sell at the net price by achieving high efficiency, low cost and reducing unnecessary added costs for our customers in our distribution channels. Do we allow unprofitable hotels to participate? The answer is obvious. If the property owner doesn't make a profit, how can the basic employee interests be guaranteed? How can the business be sustained? And how can it bring profits to our brand and management? As we operate, we assess the property owner's cost and return on investment. We do not accept unprofitable hotels because that would be a violation of the most fundamental business principles.

Apart from paying staff wages slightly above the industry average, we rely on improving skills and promotions to continuously raise the remuneration of key staff. This kind of strategy is particularly useful in the rapid development phase. In the new normal speed of development this should be changed; we would share with employees the benefits gained through fine-tuning that increase efficiency.

Currently, shareholders are rewarded with rising stock prices and an annual set rate of dividend distribution. While the company needs as much capital as possible for expansion and investment at its development phase, it must guarantee shareholders a set ratio of dividends, because that is the goal of the shareholders investing in the first place.

China has very few excellent suppliers, and as demands for quality increase, costs will soar. Thus, attracting and retaining partners in compliance with our requirements in the supply chain is more often achieved by providing benefits. Of course, large purchases increase scope for negotiation; but if we assist companies in the supply chain with low efficiency to raise their game, we can reduce our own costs while ensuring that the supplier's interests are not harmed.

For an enterprise with healthy profits, there is no need to say much about their contribution to the nation and the community. In a market economy where core units of society are business entities, a company's profitability can never be overemphasized. Apart from tax contributions, our contributions also include employment opportunities, maintenance of social stability, improving the quality of life (service industry) and enhancing capabilities (manufacturing industry).

3. KNOWHOW

Large modern chains must have appropriate technological tools and strategies to function properly.

Here, knowhow actually refers to two different kinds of management tools. One is the multilevel structures of the organizational framework modern enterprises commonly employ, that is, headquarters, branches, regional offices and retail outlets, and so forth, that have rules and a mechanism that regulates workflow, audits, approvals and appraisals.

Modern enterprises include regionally dispersed chains that depend on an organizational format that differs from family clans or nomad societies. From top to bottom, from headquarters down to retail outlets, centralized management is the usual organizational system. The pros are that through a chain's network abstract thinking and wisdom performed and generated by the critical few can be transmitted. Collaborative governance can be shared and emulated efficiently, at a low cost. The con is that it is easy to become rigid and dogmatic.

Therefore, it is a marvellous thing to be able to mobilize the brainpower and ingenuity of frontline staff to bring into play the wisdom and strength of all the staff of a chain, in order to achieve a shared goal. Will the spread of mobile technologies make it possible for traditional enterprise structures to become flatter and more direct, by reducing middle management layers to give end users even more ability to make their own decisions?

We will explore and experiment with these ideas for future management practices.

On another level, knowhow refers to the latest IT technology, including IT, communications, sensors, control equipment and robotics.

In a massive chain system that consists of many physical points and an ocean of data, we cannot examine every single detail. However, we must effectively gather and make use of this information in order to guarantee service quality and be able to control all the outlets in the chain. The most effective way is through IT. Let me put it this way: modern chains were established with the support of IT knowhow. Chains like Walmart or banks or, of course, H World, all have extremely strong back office IT, without which there could be no links in the chain.

The use of cloud computing is a key aspect of IT knowhow that is especially suited to chains dispersed over a large territory. Centralized data enables data mining and analysis. Application software is easy to maintain and update, convenient to deploy and implement and, moreover, it can differentiate configuration and boundary conditions, and enable different units of the chain to customize to their requirements. It increases safety and stability to avoid the danger of data loss or damage at the individual store level and greatly reduces the store level hardware costs, with a negligible maintenance cost. As far as large chains are concerned, the investment and operational cost can effectively be reduced.

Knowhow, such as IT, makes an undeniable contribution to reducing the complexity of management. Many mature workflow practices can be consolidated through software which reduces the workload for staff training and lessens the requirements for staff.

It is no exaggeration to say that a first-class chain enterprise must possess an outstanding IT team. IT projects must be supervised by the most senior level of the company, or the owner, and must be mainly developed inhouse. It is irresponsible and ineffective to pile IT work on the IT manager (or whatever title that person has) or get a subcontractor to do the work.

4. COMMUNITY

China is a country in which worldly wisdom is extremely important. On their journey from their ancestral halls to modern urban offices, in the hearts of many people there still remains the warmth of the old hometown.

Large chain enterprises are the same as any other business, in that social groupings such as coming from the same hometown, being alumni of the same school, masters and apprentices, colleagues or simple friendships, all have a considerable impact. We notice again and again that when the employees of a retail unit are united, the results of the retail unit and the quality of service provided are invariably very good.

Haidilao Hotpot is a business that has made exceptionally good use of small communities. From the very start they only hired staff from the Sichuan Province and this cohesive unity of people from the same place meant they spoke with one voice and presented a homogenous picture to the outside world. The company even remitted bonuses to the mothers of staff to effectively rope in family members to give their support.

In all gatherings of people, such social communities are unavoidable. They may weaken the consistency of a chain, but blindly attempting to suppress or attack social communities is not a solution. Skilfully guiding these communities and putting their community spirit to good use will save effort and lead to better results. For example, recruiting service staff from the same hometown means that they will be able to help each other and pass on experience through their informal hometown networks; similarly, the master-apprentice relationship supports managers and staff training. Training staff gives the master a sense of accomplishment and makes the apprentices grateful, which serves to make relationships in a chain even more harmonious; for people who graduate together are likely to have a good mutual understanding beyond friendly competition and can more easily help each other when they have problems or encounter difficulties.

As long as the work gets done properly there is nothing wrong with these groupings. In remote chain outlets, these lively grassroots communities are a manifestation of human warmth that we should respect and guide to transform into the glue that stabilizes the chain. Retail stores are the point of contact with the ground for chain management. Through them, there is an opportunity to reduce the scope of authority of the head office as much as possible, reduce the number of departments to a minimum, reduce costs as much as possible and enhance socialization whenever possible. There is also an opportunity to allow functional departments with exceptional competitive advantages to provide services to other enterprises, thereby turning cost centres into profit centres that may even be able to list in their own right.

These four aspects are an organic whole. Not one can be omitted, though companies can at different phases, in different regions, in different lines of business, place emphasis differently. The art of management is to mix these ingredients appropriately. The ability to create the greatest value is the best formulation.

Using shared values to point the way and fully utilizing existing knowhow and tools, we can mobilize communities to act in unison with an enterprise's goals, arouse the enthusiasm and energy of frontline staff to achieve value creation for companies, and share the value created with all those who have contributed. These are not only best practice for large chain management, they are also best management practice for all companies.

1 February, 2018

THE BUSINESS CORE LIES IN CREATING VALUE

When I had just stepped into the hotel industry as an IT professional, I thought I was descending from a higher plane, about to bring a fresh new take to the boring, safe hotel sector. "Using IT to revolutionize the traditional hotel industry" was the best summary of this idea. With the passing of more than a decade, the internet, IT technology, and numerous entrepreneurs have indeed changed the face of the hotel industry. The rise of domestic hotel brands and chain groups is the result of the last wave of innovation, and China now has three companies ranked among the world's top ten in terms of scale.

Talent and capital are forever the main driving forces behind changes in industry structure. Heavily backed by SoftBank, the Indian company OYO barged into China's hotel industry like an Indian elephant in a china shop, creating waves across the sector. The praise it received mostly came from PR articles, while industry insiders were sceptical and doubtful about its success. Despite the debates, that did not hamper its rapid expansion, and its financing looked to be going smoothly as well – its latest valuation is reportedly already at ten billion dollars.

We actually had contact with them very early on and found these young Indians to be really impressive! Their approach was highly effective in the Indian market, and since we also had plans for gradual globalization, we invested in them. We hoped to gain insights into and enter the

Indian and broader Asian markets through this investment. Naturally, we shared our experiences and insights with them without reservation.

Little did we expect that these young Indians would turn around and aggressively enter the Chinese market. Though they initially targeted segments we all dismissed – the cheapest hotels with a RevPAR below 100 RMB and fewer than 50 rooms – their growth was rapid, and their rhetoric even grander. They claimed to be China's fastest-growing hotel company, already surpassing Home Inn and H World and clinching the No. 2 spot in China. They even suggested that becoming the world's No. 1 hotel company was just around the corner. At times, they even leveraged the name of H World's investment in their promotions, which caused us much embarrassment.

Would OYO truly disrupt the Chinese hotel industry like we did, over a decade ago? Is the ultra-budget hotel market truly worth pursuing? How crucial exactly is scale for a hotel group? Where exactly is the future of the hotel industry headed?

With these questions in mind, we began our journey of reflection and exploration.

1. REVIEWING THE OLD FOR NEW KNOWLEDGE

When we ruminate about the future, we must first start from the past – reviewing the old in pursuit of new knowledge.

China's hotel industry began with state-run guesthouses, primarily serving government officials and public receptions – much like the old courier stations of the past. There were also small motels and lodgings for the general public, though their facilities were relatively rudimentary. One of my most vivid memories from that era was the housekeeper carrying a massive key ring to unlock doors for you. You did not have your own room keys. Rooms were frequently shared among multiple guests, and unmarried couples needed to present a marriage certificate to stay together.

State-run guesthouses and basic lodgings represented an early, somewhat primitive phase. It was the entry of foreign-invested hotels that kickstarted the industry's first major revolution. With professional managers, standardized operating procedures (SOPs) and globally recognized brands, China's hotel sector evolved from guesthouses into an era of organized hotel companies. This period was marked by the entry of high-end international chains, including brands from Singapore and Hong Kong (PRC). Local governments and developers sought to leverage these brands to boost awareness and property values. Every major development zone would look for an international hotel brand as a platform and endorsement. These hotels were typically upscale or luxury full-service brands.

The third wave coincided with my own entry into the industry – the era of large hotel chains. Brands like Jin Jiang Inn, Home Inn and H World spearheaded the rise of budget and mid-scale hotels. Today, the scale of these companies numbers in thousands of properties and ranks among the world's top ten. Jin Jiang Inn is now the second-largest hotel group globally, and H World has made its way into the world's top five in market value.

Now, let us take a look at the numbers.

Currently, China has about 1 million accommodation units with 18 million rooms, averaging 18 rooms per unit, including farm stays, family hostels and guesthouses. On average, the scale is extremely small – so small that it has lost its basic profitability model! The average occupancy rate is 55%, hovering on the brink of the break-even point. The slightest misstep could lead to losses, and even when business is doing well, profit is meager. It seems that the Chinese hotel industry is a sector with very low margins.

The chain hotel rate is very low, at only 26%, while in the USA it is 71%. Even in Europe, it is at 38%. In terms of consumer markets, China is the largest single market globally and, logically speaking, it should produce the largest hotel chain group in the world. However, the chain rate is very low – even the three largest groups combined only account for just 7.5%, with low concentration. Such chain hotel rates and concentration indicate that China's hotel industry is still in its nascent stages, with immense potential.

The insufficient chain hotel rate and low concentration have made online travel agencies (OTAs) driven by internet technology a crucial force in China's hotel industry.

Currently, about 30% of hotel rooms are sold through OTAs. When a booking channel accounts for 30% of hotel sales, it becomes a crucial player. And this proportion is steadily increasing; in the next three to five years, OTAs will most likely account for 40% to 50% of hotel bookings. At present, China's largest OTA, Ctrip, is valued at over 20 billion USD, which is much higher than the combined market value of the top three hotel groups.

With the immense opportunities and potential in the hotel industry, 'countless heroes are bowing to it.' The wind tunnel in physics experiments can lift very heavy objects into the air if the wind speed is high enough – even a human or a pig. The phrase '风口上的猪' (fēng kǒu shàng de zhū), or 'a pig on the wind,' likely alludes to this concept. Over the past few years, many 'entrepreneurial pigs' have tried to catch the wind, including foreign imports like Airbnb, hipster inns, as well as so-called influencer hotels, IP hotels, white label hotels, light chains and soft brands, making the industry bustle with hustle. Even BAT's A (Alibaba Group) has entered the game, launching an OTA called 'Fliggy' and a no-staff hotel called 'FlyZoo Hotel.' This shows that the hotel industry has huge potential but is also on the cusp of an impending storm.

Where is China's hotel industry heading? What does the future hold?

2. THE ORIGIN OF BUSINESS

Humanity has no ability to see the future. All predictions of the future are speculations, and all accurate predictions of the future are coincidences. But, if we execute the most recent prediction, we may just receive the greatest reward from thc heavens.

So, when we attempt a prediction, going back to the source of origin is the most reliable choice. And the origin of business is obviously the customer; their needs are the starting point and foundation of business.

Let us take a look at what hotel customers really need. I have ranked them based on my own understanding:

The first one is safety: Are there fire safety measures? Identity verification for guests? Is there any renovation pollution?

Second, cleanliness: A hotel filled with unpleasant odors, unclean sheets, or even cockroaches and rats sharing your bed would be unbearable for most people.

Third, location: For example, if you are working in Haidian, Beijing, the chances of you living near Guomao are low. The daily commute alone would take around two hours due to congestion.

Fourth, price: Of course, facilities are very important, but I believe this is related to price. Higher prices usually mean better facilities, and vice versa. There are many inconveniences when travelling, and everyone wants a more comfortable, convenient stay, but you are limited by your reimbursement standards and cash in your wallet.

Fifth, brand: The meaning of a brand is to communicate clearly what kind of product, values and aesthetics it offers. Over the years, Hanting has crept deep into people's minds as a well-recognized national hotel brand, and Ji Hotel has become the preferred choice for business travel among the middle class. Guests in mid-range or higher hotels are more willing to go out of their way or pay extra to stay at their preferred brand. Many people prefer staying at Hanting in third- or fourth-tier cities, instead of unbranded star-rated hotels, because the quality is guaranteed.

An excellent brand can surpass the first four considerations and become the guest's first choice. This is the charm of a brand!

Of course, the hospitality of hotel staff, the exterior and interior design, the aesthetics of the hotel, and the quality of food and beverage offerings all play a significant role in guest choices. But the four factors I have listed are the most basic and important. Ultimately, hotel guests pursue high cost-effectiveness – good things that are not too expensive.

The hotel industry has two types of clients: those who pay to stay as guests; the other is the hotel investor. Investors earn money through investments, and evaluate their choices through return on investment. H World has more than 4,000 hotels and over 7,000 investors. What are these clients' needs? Simple – making money. No one is willing to invest without profit. Return on investment is the primary consideration for the second type of client.

So how can we ensure good investment returns? High income, low cost. Here is a formula: High income = High RevPAR = High average room rate × High occupancy rate = Quality product × Loyal customers. Without a good product, you can't sell at a high price, and you lose the premium allure. Customers will not be loyal, and you will have lower returning customers, and thus you will be unable to achieve high occupancy rates. Therefore, high returns revolve around focusing on product quality and customer loyalty.

Low cost, first and foremost, refers to low construction, renovation and rent costs (if leasing), then low labor costs. Operational costs are also important but relatively easier to understand and control.

Whether it is the high cost-effectiveness required by guests, or the high return on investment needed by investors, in essence, it is all about high efficiency. Whoever can achieve high efficiency and performance to customers and investors in this industry will succeed. In all businesses, efficiency is fundamental. A highly efficient company will always outperform a low-efficiency one. Only high efficiency can generate low input and high output.

In the hotel industry, whether an existing company or a new business, the odds of survival and success depend on whether it meets the fundamental needs of customers – improving the hotel's cost-effectiveness and increasing investors' returns. These principles are easy to understand but putting them into practice is not so simple.

3. H WORLD EMPOWERS SUPPLY-SIDE STRUCTURAL REFORM

H World has always spent its efforts focusing on high efficiency. While we dare not claim to be No. 1 in the world in many aspects, we are definitely at the globally leading level.

Our IT systems, membership systems, direct sales, procurement, product development and massive store management all rank among the world's best. Among our peers in the Chinese hotel groups, we have the highest RevPAR, the highest GOP margin and, naturally, the best return on investment.

I have not seen a large hotel group anywhere in the world where all their systems are developed in-house. Our entire enterprise has already been digitized, and our IT scope goes far beyond traditional enterprise resource planning (ERP) systems. H World's membership system is unique to us, with over 80% of our guests being members, and the majority are paying members – this may be unmatched globally. Our direct sales ratio is also over 80%, mainly through H World's official channels like our app for bookings. Our procurement volume is enormous, purchasing over 100 million bottles of mineral water annually – we could probably open our own little water factory at this point. As a result, our procurement costs are very low. You could even say that no one can match our procurement efficiency. In product development, it is not even up for debate. Driven by the large Chinese market and its rapid development, our brand innovation and development are probably world-class. It is impossible anywhere else in the world for other companies to create more than a dozen brands in just over a decade, from the budget-friendly Hanting, mid-range Ji Hotel, to the upscale Crystal Orange Hotel, and even the five-star Joya, with many of these brands already undergoing umpteenth iterations. And since we adopt a management franchise model, we are effectively managing four to five thousand hotel fronts – there are not many like us in the world.

H World's development is primarily focused on incremental markets, leasehold renovation and branded operation management. Our products are consistent and the boundaries between our brands are clear.

However, in response to the enormous existing market, how do we address this? Being complacent, self-indulgent and self-content is not H World's style. We are willing to be proactive, push for progress together, and be socially responsible for the broader world.

China's hotel industry has a trillion-yuan market size, but profit levels often hover near the break-even point. There are 18 million hotel rooms, with an average of just 18 rooms per hotel, and an occupancy rate of only 55%. This means that the government's 'supply-side structural reform' is also applicable to the hotel industry. Supply-side structural reform means advancing structural adjustments using revolutionary methods to improve the quality of supply. It is about using incremental reforms to promote adjustments in the existing stock, which means improving the quality and efficiency of the existing stock, while eliminating outdated capacity.

So, H World is more than willing to leverage its existing efficiency advantages, contributing its own strengths to the journey of the domestic hotel industry's progress.

Hanting, Ji Hotels, Crystal Orange Hotel, Joya and our other core brands continue to focus on the incremental market, using quality growth to enhance the existing market. Our soft brands, such as Madison, Starway and Elan, span from one-star to five-star, mainly targeting the existing market. H World uses its brand to endorse these, thereby maintaining higher-quality standards.

If China's hotel industry is like an ocean, H World's brands only cover a bath-ladle of its water. Even if we reach 10,000 hotels in the future, we will still only have captured 1% of the market. That is why, when we encountered Xia Qingning and his amazing team, we did not hesitate to invest in them. We hope that H Hotel can assist even more existing individual hotels, allowing them to share in the efficiency advantages H World has already achieved. Like cloud services, we aim to empower many small and medium-sized hotels to improve quality, increase returns and raise their efficiency.

H Hotel is a highly compatible soft brand, which can also be described as a hotel alliance. It is a partner and enabler for individual hotels, not another OTA. Competition in the OTA market is already saturated and adding more OTAs will not bring fundamental change to the industry. In fact, unhealthy competition, such as subsidies and price cuts, will harm hotel profits, eventually making hotels pay the price.

H Hotel does not intend to engage in hyper growth by shovelling in capital and offering subsidies, insisting on 'value creation' as a central vision – creating value for guests and owners. We add value to the existing stock and share in the value created. I once told H World's development team: The key to leasing properties is to look at their acquisition cost. If the rent is only 10 RMB per square meter, the line of owners wanting to lease to us will stretch beyond our office's entrance.

If a franchise chain company wants to grow exponentially in record time, it can do so by waiving franchise fees and offering subsidies, easily signing up four to five thousand hotels in a year. But what real value does franchising bring to these hotels? Aside from putting up a sign, has it improved the product? Has it brought in more customers? Has it reduced costs?

We cannot allow such deceptive practices, nor can we tolerate 'burning money to harvest from the crop' strategies. Otherwise, it will end in chaos, with so-called 'entrepreneurs' and 'investors' walking away from the table and going elsewhere to 'harvest other crops,' leaving its owners and consumers to hold the bag.

This is why H World is willing to share our insights and systems to the public – it does not cost us much. Whether we procure 100 million or 200 million bottles of water, the workload is the same; the cost may even decrease. Our cloud-based hotel management system (PMS) can serve 5,000 hotels or 20,000 hotels without much difference, apart from needing more server bandwidth. We aim to improve the quality of the entire hotel industry, actively respond to supply-side structural reforms, to create value for both owners and guests, instead of exploiting them as tools for financing or cash grabs. We do not want to be the 'pig on the wind' but are committed to being the steady 'workhorse.'

4. CONCLUSION

If a company, startup or existing, fails to create value, I do not think it has a chance or future! No matter who invests in it, no matter how much money has been shovelled into it, it has no chance.

So, to build a fireplace, burning firewood is a far better idea than burning money. To build a wall, using cement is better than using paste. Not all bubbles are beer; a lie repeated a thousand times is still a lie – it does not make it true.

I firmly believe that the core of a business lies in value creation! And it should make people's lives better through the value you create. Going one step further, it may even influence the course of human civilization. This should be the ideal and aspiration that an entrepreneur, a business, should possess.

23 August 2019

TREATING CHINA AS THE GLOBAL MARKET

1. THE INTERNATIONALIZATION CONUNDRUM

At first glance, this topic may seem like it is about blind faith stemming from unfounded confidence, but it is actually not.

As H World's scale gradually expands, as its market value steadily increases, the question of internationalization naturally arises.

First, the large global hotel groups, along with the globalization of customers and brands, started their global expansion process early on, particularly driven by European and American companies. Due to the spearheaded dominance of the American economy and culture, the largest hotel companies are based in the USA, and these companies have been the most successful in global development. For H World to join the ranks of global giants, considering internationalization is the next logical step.

Second, there is the need for brand development. H World started with Hanting; the mid-range Ji Hotel brand is also a successful case study of its incubation. But nurturing high-end and luxury brands takes time. Acquiring a mature foreign brand, for example, could yield better results in less time. Therefore, we can extend beyond our domestic borders in the process of internationalization, as well as import successful brands into China through acquisitions and mergers.

With such a background and thought process, we began exploring internationalization. We opened Ji Hotels in Singapore, and sought to bring Joya to Japan. But the intensifying trade disputes between China and the United States forced us to rethink our internationalization strategy. Should we really internationalize? How do we do that? What are the risks involved? Can we replicate our success in China internationally? What advantages do we have for successful internationalization? How much financial and human resources are we willing to invest?

Confronted by a confusion of constantly changing circumstances, I found myself full of thoughts, perplexed and uncertain ...

2. ZHOU CHUNYA'S WAKE-UP CALL

One day, I met a few friends for tea. We were curious why China's famed artist, Zhou Chunya, simply could not find an international art gallery to court the international market?

His answer left everyone at the table astonished: "I treat China like the entire world. In early 1989, when I returned from Germany, China was so behind the times. But I had a belief: Through everyone's efforts, little by little, we could change the circumstances in our respective industries. I would sacrifice my generation to give our next generation a better life (including spiritual)."

The entire art collection and dissemination system was established by Westerners. Many international galleries had already set up in China, bringing good Chinese artists to foreign countries. As a result, artists looked up to Western galleries and curators, like a fine horse anxiously waiting for the right person to recognize its worth.

The creations of Chinese artists mostly stem from our own culture, be it contemporary, modern or ancient. Our historical and cultural roots nourish these local artists, and local collectors more easily resonate with these cultural works.

China's history is storied enough; China's culture is deep enough; China's social changes and cultural diversity provide ample creative wellsprings for artists; China's population is large enough, ensuring enough of a pool to produce outstanding artists; China's collectors and wealth are substantial enough, presenting a large enough market ...

For an artist to be the best in China, they are already world-class. It is not Chinese artists who need to go to the West to hold exhibitions, but Western galleries that should come to China to do so. Western collectors should come to China to seek out great artists and excellent works.

In fact, artists like Zhou Chunya already command the highest prices among contemporary Chinese artists. Even so, his works are still highly sought after, difficult to obtain.

One answer that wakes people from their dreams! Why should I yearn for what is afar when I already have it near? What a pointless endeavor! In the current international situation, we should stay rooted in China and treat China as the whole world.

3. THE CHINESE ADVANTAGE

First of all, China is the world's largest growth market.

China is the largest single consumer market globally, even bigger than the 300 million people in the USA, and the 500 million in the European Union. Due to its large population, every niche market is large enough to support world-leading companies. For example, the potential customer base for budget hotels is 1.3 billion, for mid-range hotels it is 400 million, and for luxury hotels, there are tens of millions of potential customers. Therefore, it is inevitable that Chinese hotel brands will become world-first in scale in the future.

Since China's marketization started late, all businesses can operate on two levels at the same time: one is the basic version, and the other is the upgraded version.

For example, most hotels in China are independent hotels with basic facilities, management standards and sanitation. The 20 million hotel rooms are the sum of 810,000 hotels, with only 25 rooms in an average hotel. With such accommodation, one can imagine the vast potential for improvement on the supply side. The hotel industry's chain rate is only 17%, four times lower than the 71% in the USA. Supply side improvement, including the shift from independent hotels to branded chains, is the relatively elementary basic version.

The almost 400 million-strong middle-income consumer base possesses considerable spending power, with strong brand awareness and high-quality demands. However, they have few products and brands tailored to them, which is a market gap. For example, the market share of mid-range hotel chains in China is 2%, and after excluding low-quality supply, it is only 4%. Meanwhile, in the USA, the ratio is 28%; that is seven times more. Our Ji Hotels were an immediate success after their launch, instantly becoming the first choice for many franchisees, and rapidly penetrated into third- and fourth-tier cities, even exceeding our expectations. This is a market-driven consumer upgrade – the upgraded version of the business.

A large market size, with all businesses having twice the opportunities – just as Vice Premier Liu He of the State Council said: China is already the world's largest growth market.

If we do not soar in this market, where else could we go to fuss over?

Secondly, these companies of ours have greater advantages in China.

Whether it is consumer insights, employee communication, policy and regulations, or regional culture, it is the local entrepreneurs who would surely be more familiar with them. Many foreign companies have struggled to adapt the moment they step on local soil, and more so for foreign internet companies that have gone completely under.

In the economy and mid-range hotel sectors, Chinese companies dominate the market. No foreign brand has the opportunity to participate in the main battlefield. International brands such as Marriott, Hilton and Accor barely maintain a certain market share due to their partnership with local companies.

In the high-end and luxury segments, international brands are still predominant, which has to do with the cross-cultural background of local consumers, as well as many owners blindly worshipping foreign brands to elevate their status. But this business model is changing. Mature consumers will eventually choose their lifestyle based on local aesthetics. High-end hotels are proportional to economic development; after China adopts reform and opening-up policies, when China's economy rapidly grows to more stable heights, China's homegrown high-end hotel brands will emerge. With the development of China's economy and wealth standards, the high-end and luxury sectors will eventually be dominated by local brands.

Furthermore, China's competitive environment has forged high-level companies.

Whether in terms of education or the use of tools, China is always in sync with the world, not lagging behind. Its large scale has sparked the aspiration of many ambitious individuals to try to make their mark; the intensity of fierce competition has fostered a group of world-class entrepreneurs and companies. On the other hand, many European and American companies are mired in a low-growth period. A lack of pressure and crisis awareness has led to innovation fatigue.

H World excels in many areas, such as its membership system, IT applications, direct sales and product innovation, surpassing many foreign competitors.

Enterprises and entrepreneurs are driven by the market. The vigour and complexity of the demand side will inevitably force the emergence of the most outstanding outcomes.

Finally, one must stand at the world's peak to do business in China.

Ren Zhengfei strongly opposes the so-called 'autonomous innovation", which is to ignore outside information and create something ourselves, i.e. blind faith stemming from unfounded confidence. Be it innovation or inheritance, all the best things in the world should be learned and absorbed. Knowledge, information and wisdom have no distinction between good and bad, nor national borders. As long as we can use them to nourish and benefit us, they should be absorbed without hesitation.

During H World's early development, I spent a lot of time travelling to Europe and the USA to visit hotels, meet with peers, and study their products. In a way, H World's starting point was already built on the shoulders of giants. We listed on Nasdaq and attracted the world's top investors as shareholders. H World's senior executives include people from Singapore, France, Malaysia and Taiwan (PRC), many of whom were educated in the USA and Europe. On the branding front, we partnered with Accor in China, to great results. If there is an opportunity to acquire excellent international brands in the future, we will also gladly partake in that venture, and bring them to China to take root, grow and flourish.

4. TREATING CHINA AS THE GLOBAL MARKET

Today, the world's largest hotel group – Marriott – is primarily rooted in the US market. It practices internationalization, albeit to a limited extent. Similarly, Europe's largest hotel group – Accor – is entrenched in the European market. Hotel groups, in reality, are a representation of a region or a country's overall strength, including factors such as population, economy and cultural influence. Smaller or weaker nations would be hard-pressed to produce world-class hotel groups.

Whether or not Chinese hotel groups will become world-first in the future – that will ultimately depend on China's national strength in the years to come.

However, I firmly believe: China is big – big enough to be treated as a global market. Chinese people are exceptional – exceptional enough to become world champions. At the same time, we are not narrow-minded. With a global perspective from the world's peak, we will absorb the world's brands, talent, capital, knowledge, information, wisdom and, harnessing the concept of 'treating China as the global market,' channel all our focus into building it to a world-class standard.

2 July, 2019

SUPPLY-SIDE STRUCTURAL REFORM IN THE HOTEL INDUSTRY

1. DEFINITION

If we used a formula to describe what people commonly refer to as 'supply-side structural reform,' it would be 'Supply-side + Structural + Reform.' Its meaning is: Using reform-driven approaches to advance structural adjustments, reducing ineffective and low-end supply while expanding effective and mid-end to high-end supply. The goal is to enhance the adaptability and flexibility of the supply structure in response to changes in demand, improve total factor productivity, and make the supply system better suited to shifts in structural changes.

When this concept was first introduced, I thought its application was targeted at steel, coal and iron ore industries – sectors that produced predominantly low-to-mid-end products, experienced overcapacity, high pollution and high energy consumption. At the time, I had not yet associated it with the hotel industry.

While I was preparing for a speech a few days ago, I took a look at data on China's hotel industry. It was then that I realized that the hotel sector, too, is in need of supply-side structural reform.

2. SCALE

The USA has a leading hotel industry association, the American Hotel & Lodging Association (AHLA). Its provided statistical data on the US hotel industry is as follows: 54,200 hotels, 5 million guest rooms, 8 million employees, 1.1 billion rooms are booked annually, 61% are small-scale businesses.

From this data, we can estimate that: The average hotel has 92 rooms, employee-to-room ratio is 1.6, occupancy rate is 60%, number of rooms per capita is 0.015 (based on a population of 330 million).

As for China's hotel industry data, we have aggregated data from various sources and performed some analysis, so the data should be relatively accurate and objective. China has 810,000 hotels, with a total of 20 million guest rooms; the average hotel has 25 rooms, and the number of rooms per capita is 0.014 (based on a population of 1.39 billion); the average room rate is 174 RMB, occupancy rate is 55%, RevPAR is 96 RMB, and market size is 700 billion RMB (excluding F&B services).

Ctrip's market coverage is 390,000 hotels, 13.71 million guest rooms, with an average of 36 rooms per hotel. Ctrip does not cover 420,000 hotels, 6.29 million guest rooms, with an average of 15 rooms per hotel.

For star-rated hotels, the China Tourist Hotel Association's data shows that: As of the end of 2018, there were more than 11,000 hotels that were star-rated nationwide. The hotel groups that were included in the statistical scope include more than 30,000 hotels and more than 3 million rooms.

For brand chains: 60,000 hotels with 3.35 million guest rooms, occupying a total market share (chain rate) of 17% (US hotel industry chain rate is 71%).

Comparison of Tenant Numbers Between China and the USA in 2019

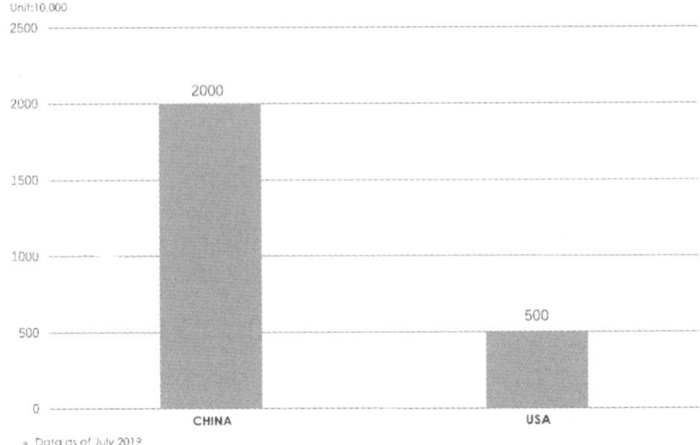

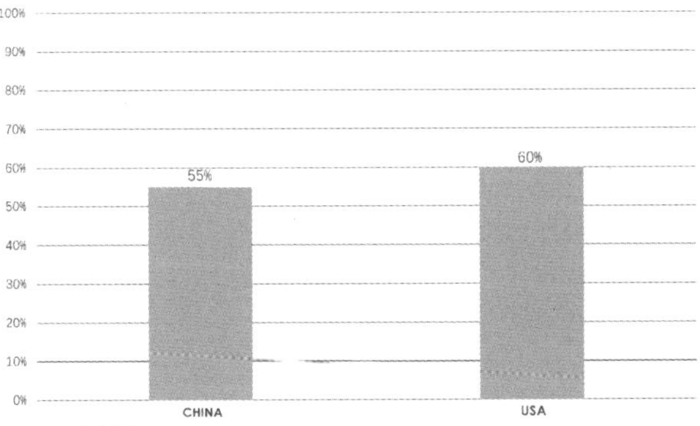

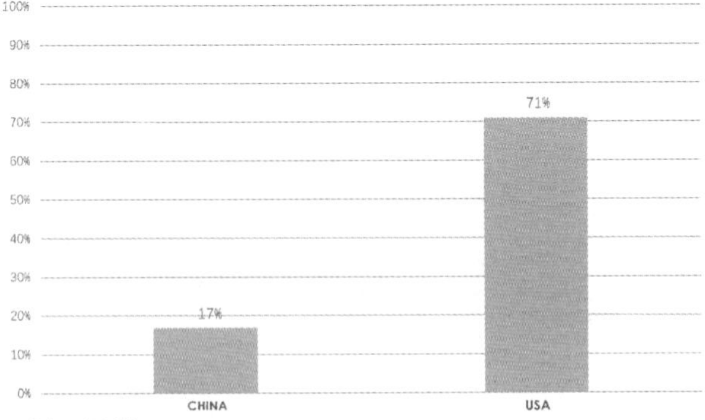

3. SUPPLY SIDE

We have always assumed that the number of hotel rooms per capita in China was lower than in the United States, but that is not the case.

In terms of total volume, the per capita hotel room ratio in China is about the same as in the USA, around 1.5%. This means that China's hotel industry is comparable in scale to the fully marketized and developed US hotel industry and does not suffer from shortage or oversupply.

If we look at size, the average number of rooms per hotel in the USA is 92; in China, it is 25. Among all 54,200 hotels in the USA, 61% are small and medium-sized enterprises, which means that the vast majority of hotels in China are even smaller, essentially micro-enterprises.

Many of these are farm stay, family-run inns, small-scale operations in rural areas and individually owned properties. They solve a portion of employment opportunities and alleviate peak holiday demand but, from an industry scale, this 'supply side' segment should not be tallied; they are more like scattered, independent operators, and do not constitute an organized, systemic capacity capable of large-scale development.

Now let us compare occupancy rates. The difference of 5% (55% and 60%) between China and the USA seems small, but this apparently insignificant difference is critical. The hotel industry has high fixed costs (depreciation, amortization, labor, energy). At an occupancy rate of 55%, many hotels are barely breaking even, but at 60%, they can turn a profit. Which is why this average occupancy rate of 55% in China's hotel industry is often literally teetering between profit and loss. It is also the case in reality – the entire hotel industry is indeed constantly ping-ponging between profit and loss.

Accordingly, the hotel industry ranks second to last in income levels, just above agriculture, forestry and animal husbandry. In 2017, the average income in the hotel industry was ¥43,382 per year, only 64% of the national average.

The supply side has quantity, but lacks in quality, with low profitability and subpar wages. This is a very classic supply-side issue that calls for reform.

4. STRUCTURAL REFORM

Here, we quote General Secretary Xi Jinping's speech at the 12th Meeting of the Central Leading Group for Financial and Economic Affairs in 2016. The General Secretary emphasized that the fundamental goal of supply-side structural reform is to enhance social productivity levels and implement a people-centred development philosophy. While appropriately expanding overall demand, efforts must be made to reduce overcapacity, inventory and costs, and to deleverage, as well as to address, weaknesses. High-quality supply should be strengthened in the production sector, ineffective supply should be reduced, effective supply should be expanded, and the adaptability and flexibility of the supply structure should be improved. Total factor productivity must be enhanced so that the supply system can better adapt to changing demand structures. This statement precisely outlines the solution to China's economic issues, and it also applies to the hotel industry, word for word.

Firstly, incremental reform should be used to drive stock adjustments.

As a representative of chain hotel groups, H World primarily operates through franchise management. Most franchisees lease properties, then renovate them before joining one of H World's brands. The majority of H World's brands, such as Hanting, Ji Hotels and Crystal Orange Hotel, have distinctive product characteristics and strict hardware standards – it is very hard to meet brand franchise requirements without renovation.

These branded chain hotels are undoubtedly the best products in China's hotel market, with most of them new additions.

It is because of these quality new additions that consumers can be provided with the best choices, pushing out certain segments of subpar inventory, and offering directional guidance for the entire industry. A few years ago, many budget hotels were renovated in the style of Hanting. In recent years, many mid-range hotels have been designed following Ji Hotel's aesthetic style. These are all examples of how incremental reform drives stock adjustments.

H World adds 1,000 new hotels annually, and the combined total of all major chains is estimated to be between 5,000 and 10,000, accounting for 5% to 10% of the 100,000 hotels (chain hotels) nationwide. This level of growth can be considered reasonable.

Secondly, industry structure should be optimized, improving industry quality, optimizing product structure and enhancing product quality.

This is the strategy for addressing stock adjustments.

The majority of existing hotels are in a state of low product quality, inefficient management and weak profitability. Without renovation, they cannot be branded, and renovation lacks investment motivation. At this point, apart from the 'soft brands' launched by H World, such as Starway and Madison, H Hotel is the indisputable alternative. By leveraging H World's accumulated industry experience, management capabilities, platformization, IT technology and vast membership and other efficiency factors, these can help well-established and enterprising existing hotels improve their quality, thereby fulfilling industry and product structure optimization.

Thirdly, the flow structure should be optimized, reducing transaction costs and increasing effective economic output.

OTAs account for about 30% of the hotel industry. This number will reach 40%–50% in the future. As the concentration of OTAs and customer proportions increase, the bargaining power of independent hotels weakens, and the probability of commission rate increases will only amplify.

This requires that the Chinese hotel industry transitions from independent hotels to chains, from solo efforts to partnerships leading to mutual benefit. Building their own membership systems and direct sales systems, reducing dependence on intermediary channels, and further lowering transaction costs by directly connecting with end customers, allowing them to offer products best suited to the demand side – only then can the entire industry's efficiency be improved.

Fourthly, the consumption structure should be optimized, achieving continuous elevation of consumer goods, and meeting the demand side's need to improve the quality of life.

After more than a decade of chain development, branded budget hotels now account for 25% of the budget hotel sector, making it the most highly chain-affiliated segment.

However, mid-range hotels only account for 20% of all hotels, and branded mid-range hotels only account for 10% of mid-range hotels. This ratio is relatively low, signalling significant potential for growth.

Regarding high-end and luxury hotels, due to the rapid rise of the real estate landmark model in previous years, they undoubtedly face an oversupply and misalignment in product structure. Although the market has cooled slightly recently, it will still take time to digest these large investments and inventory.

China's consumption structure is still dominated by budget and mid-range hotels. Quality branded budget hotels continue to penetrate further, increasing the chain affiliation rate. There is an insufficient supply of mid-range hotels and mid-range branded hotel chains, both in terms of incremental and existing stock; there should be an expansion of high-quality supply in this segment. As for high-end and luxury hotels, there is not much point to incremental growth anymore. Reforming and adjusting the product structure itself is more crucial, especially improvements in utilizing space, staff efficiency and sales channels.

National-level supply-side structural reform is equally applicable to the Chinese hotel industry. In the future, H World will continue to uphold its core brands, while actively developing soft brands and sharing its existing capabilities to participate in the structural reform of numerous independent hotels, aiming to enhance quality and efficiency.

The above analysis will not only guide H World's future development, but also hopefully provide some reference for our peers in the hotel industry. We hope to contribute our modest efforts to improving the level of China's hotel industry, and work together to help China's hotel industry stand tall in the world!

8 July, 2019

THREE STAGES OF THE HOTEL INDUSTRY

1. REINFORCED CONCRETE

The modern hotel industry is deeply intertwined with real estate. Whether it is César Ritz, the king of hoteliers, or many of the hotel brands we are familiar with today, like Hyatt, Shangri-La and Four Seasons, they are all associated with luxury properties in prime locations. The hotel industry is simply an extension and adornment of the real estate industry.

China's hotel industry has also just passed through this stage. Developers and some government departments used luxury hotel brands to sell houses and raise land prices.

I call this phase the 'Reinforced Concrete' stage of the hotel industry. The assets were heavy, development was slow, and it only catered to high-ranking officials, wealthy families and the rich. Arrogance, opulence and hierarchy marked this era.

2. STEEL STRUCTURE

Today, most world-class hotel groups adopt a light-asset model, with franchising and management as the main development methods.

The assets belong to the owners, as do the investments. The hotel group provides branding and management, charging franchise fees (typically around 5%) and/or management fees (typically around 10%). It may seem like the fees are not high, but through scale, they can quickly form economies of scale. In economic cycles and unexpected events, management companies face less risk and more easily weather any sudden storms.

Currently, the top ten hotel groups in the world basically utilize this model. Operating at a scale of thousands of hotels, with networks spanning nationally and globally, and profits amounting to billions, their market value can reach the hundreds of billions-dollar level. The three major hotel groups in China have also developed in this way.

I call this the 'Steel Structure' stage of the hotel industry. The weight is much lighter than reinforced concrete. Due to steel structure's higher unit load capacity and lighter weight, it can be used to build higher buildings (allowing for larger scale) at a quicker pace (faster development), with better earthquake resistance (risk resilience).

These hotel groups mainly rely on business travellers, and their core service audience is the newly emerging white-collar class. Standardization, simplicity and friendliness define this stage.

3. COMPOSITE MATERIAL

We know that composite materials are lighter and have a larger unit load capacity than steel structures. Composite materials are widely used in aircraft and spacecraft. The wings of an airplane, for example, are made of composite materials: light, flexible, strong.

H World's key innovation is to create a future-oriented hotel group. This type of hotel group has never existed in human history; it is built using composite materials.

These three materials – brand, traffic and technology – respectively correspond to our three key strategies:

offline dominance, membership-driven and fully digitalized processes. They also represent the three key capabilities we emphasize: product capability, return capability and innovation capability. This 'alloy army' built from these three materials will have unprecedented potential and scale! An organization made from this alloy will also possess unparalleled organisational power!

H World's 'Thousand Cities, Ten Thousand Hotels' is the foundation and base, and the central channel and primarily membership-based sales model are the key enhancers, while technology is the high-tech additive and catalyst. The quality of the alloy depends on the purity of each material, so each strategy must be pursued to the extreme. For example, the brand must rival the top international hotel groups (such as Hilton and Marriott), traffic must align with OTAs like Booking.com, and technology must meet the standards of Oracle Hospitality.

The future hotel group will not only serve business travellers, but also millions of families and billions of consumers. Many investment banks classify the hotel industry under real estate, but this is still traditional inertial thinking stuck in the first stage. The hotel industry should be classified as a consumer business because it already serves hundreds of millions of customers.

Besides traditional business travellers, leisure vacationers, exhibition and conference participants, blue-collar workers, migrant workers, students, visitors visiting relatives and friends, dating couples, square dance grandmas, delivery drivers and patients' visitors, will all be our consumers.

So, H World's potential customers in China are not four to six hundred million people but the entire population of 1.4 billion people. Hotels are no longer luxury goods reserved for the few, nor are they a consumer good for some, but they are a necessity for the broader public to enjoy a better life.

Our hotel development is not about repeating the paths of our predecessors – it is to achieve ten thousand, even tens of thousands of hotels in a short period of time.

Steel structures can build skyscrapers, reaching hundreds of stories. But, aircraft and spacecraft made of composite materials can reach the skies and stars.

No matter how far our dreams may go, our alloy army will reach there! This is what I mean by the future hotel group – the alloy army built with composite materials.

This will be another upgrade of the hotel industry, the third stage of development.

28 August, 2020

THREE ESSENTIAL ELEMENTS OF A BUSINESS

1. BUSINESS MODEL

In the hotel industry, Hyatt, which focuses on luxury hotels, represents one business model, while H World, which is based on budget, national and mid-range hotels, represents another.

Neither model is inherently better than the other, but the outcomes of the two are vastly different. If the world or target market has a high demand for luxury clientele, the victor will certainly be the luxury hotel model; if the market demand is for budget-conscious and mid-range clientele, then the winner will undoubtedly be H World.

Accor started with the budget-friendly ibis and Novotel but is presently focused on luxury and high-end brands. This reflects an evolution of their business model. Whether this shift in decision is right or wrong, only time will tell.

Startups essentially try to innovate and experiment with business models. This is the most important crucial factor in this process.

No matter the business model chosen, it determines the scale and potential size of a company from its inception. If the business model is wrong, failure is inevitable.

2. EXECUTION

Then, with the correct business model, can a company's success be guaranteed? Not necessarily. It still depends on its execution.

Several domestic hotel chains basically follow similar business models, but their operational results vary greatly. This is the difference in execution.

Execution is essentially the organizational capability of a company, in terms of how to effectively organize resources, including manpower, finances and time, to complete a task. Every company has the same amount of time within a certain period, making it a level playing field in that sense. When investments are equal, the most important factor is talent. How do people organize among themselves? Collaborate? Interact and communicate? Get along? Rectify mistakes and offer criticism? How are rewards and punishments handled? How are promotions and appointments managed? How are successes and failures addressed? Will strategies permeate down the hierarchy? What is the professional competence at the ground level?

Even with the same business model, the difference in execution becomes the key factor that drives competitive advantage.

3. ADAPTABILITY

With the right business model and strong execution, can one rest one's laurels in this current day and age? Not at all!

The world today is full of change. The development of technology has shattered traditional boundaries. Amazon, once just a bookseller, now sells everything. Alibaba does not just serve small businesses and retailers – it also sells fresh produce and offers booking services.

Kodak failed to adapt to the digital revolution, and Nokia was utterly crushed by Apple. These are typical cases of lacking adaptability. The traditional hotel industry, once flourishing, has lost its former glory and competitive edge in the new era – another example of insufficient adaptability.

In a world full of blurred boundaries and uncertainty, adaptability is crucial. The adaptability of a company is essentially its ability to innovate.

Innovation is not just about breakthroughs in technology or inventions. For a company, especially one of a certain scale and age, it is more about how well it can adapt to a changing environment.

Being sensitive to environmental changes, valuing key shifts and technology, one must maintain a sense of crisis at all times – complacency is poison. After fully understanding the changes, one should adjust the business model timely to adapt to the new environment, accumulating talent, preparing crucial resources for new business models, and developing new products and technologies to meet changing customer demands.

The business model corresponds to a company's strategic ability. If the strategic compass is wrong, a company will never succeed.

Execution corresponds to organizational ability. Without it, the best strategies are useless. One may have the will to fight but lack the ability to do so.

Adaptability corresponds to the capability to innovate. Without keen perception and adaptability in a constantly changing world, a company is easily overtaken by competitors in other dimensions, often without realizing what happened. This is particularly true for seasoned industry leaders who are most vulnerable to making such mistakes.

The business model, execution and adaptability are the three key elements of a company.

18 January, 2020

BUSINESS COMPETITOR STRATEGY

Over the years of running a business, I have been constantly reflecting on this profound question of corporate competition. In December 2022, while conducting an investigation of lower-tier markets in Hunan Province, I had the following thoughts and conclusions. I have compiled them here for everyone's reference.

Apart from monopolistic enterprises, in a normal, free-market competitive environment, corporate competition can ultimately be boiled down to three key aspects: firstly, low cost; secondly, high selling price; thirdly, innovation (breaking free from price/cost competition).

1. COST LEADERSHIP

Cost leadership is just low cost. Every business hopes to minimize cost for their products, but when quality standards are consistent, simply slashing cost is neither feasible nor advisable. Cost leadership must be supported by a systematic framework, or quality must be sacrificed for lower costs. Only high-efficiency systems can create a cost leadership advantage. Raw materials and processing, from procurement to delivery to maintenance, from logistics to warehousing, from business model design to chain expansion and replication, even from organization to culture – all must be efficient to form a systematic capability that achieves true cost leadership.

China is a major manufacturing nation with a complete and well-established supply chain (especially in traditional industries like hospitality that have low technical entry barriers) and cost advantages in natural resources, equipment and labor. We must cherish and make good use of these inherent advantages, and perhaps even consider the model of German brands using Chinese-sourced supply chains: made in China, assembled in Germany.

But I must remind everyone: The Chinese population dividend is slowly disappearing with the advent of an aging society. Labor costs of construction and factory workers are in danger of a gradual rise. We need to embrace more assembly production and automation methods to reduce our reliance on manual labor.

China's second major advantage is its large market and scale, which can lead to a high degree of centralization. We open over a thousand hotels every year, and each brand typically has hundreds of locations, allowing for centralized design and production. For example, we can hire the best designers to create prototype designs, produce large quantities of components by moulding, and purchase items in bulk at the best prices. The supply chain system at H World is built on this logic, and it has undoubtedly become a strategic department for cost leadership.

In day-to-day hotel operations, besides the elimination of the rigid organizational structure of traditional hotels, we also rely on many automated and unmanned measures in IT technology, among other aspects, to further reduce the labor-to-room ratio and lower job requirements. We use flexible staffing methods like hourly workers and temporary workers to reduce labor costs. As the supply of frontline labor diminishes, this advantage will become increasingly evident.

In addition to manufacturing and service costs, there are also sales costs and customer retention costs to be considered. Our membership system and direct sales system are great ways to address these. Over 80% of our guests come from within our system – an impressive achievement globally. We must continue to stay the course with this initiative without faltering. OTA is an effective channel, so it should be reasonably regulated rather than eliminated. Keeping it between 10% to 15% is a relatively healthy state.

Management costs and platform costs must also be borne by each hotel and strictly controlled. A few years ago, the number of people at HQ grew too quickly, resulting in overstaffing and redundancies. The organizational structure was not entirely reasonable, and there were too many management layers at the storefront level. Across the organization we made appropriate changes, and have seen improvements, but we must always remain vigilant and not become complacent.

Every penny we spend must create greater value to maintain the cost advantage of the chain enterprise. Otherwise, we risk becoming a bloated organization that consumes the hard-earned money from storefronts, ultimately harming the interests of franchisees and, in this way, the company will lose its competitive edge.

In cost leadership, H World has done exceptionally well, something we should be proud of. We must continue to uphold this fine tradition.

2. THE POWER OF 'PREMIUM'

Ordinary product pricing has cost-based pricing (based on cost plus a certain percentage as operating profit), competition-based pricing (based on competitors' prices) and demand-based pricing (pricing according to market demand). The ideal approach, though, is to be able to surpass cost, competition and demand to set prices. This requires premium pricing capability, and the most competitive form of premium pricing is brand premium.

Hermès is the quintessential example of brand premium. Functionally, a Hermès bag serves the same purpose as any other; its quality and production costs do not seem to be significantly higher, nor is its craftsmanship particularly more complex. Yet, to afford a Birkin bag, one might have to sell several head of cattle!

BMW and Mercedes-Benz in the automotive industry have clearly achieved brand premium pricing in the Chinese market. Compared to similar automobile tiers, these two brands cost 50% or more. If you are looking for an entry-level functional car and want to avoid paying excessive brand premiums, other brands would offer better value.

When comparing traditional star-rated hotels, all branded hotels win the competition by a landslide! They surpass an entire tier – this is the result of years of dedicated effort by China's hotel brand companies.

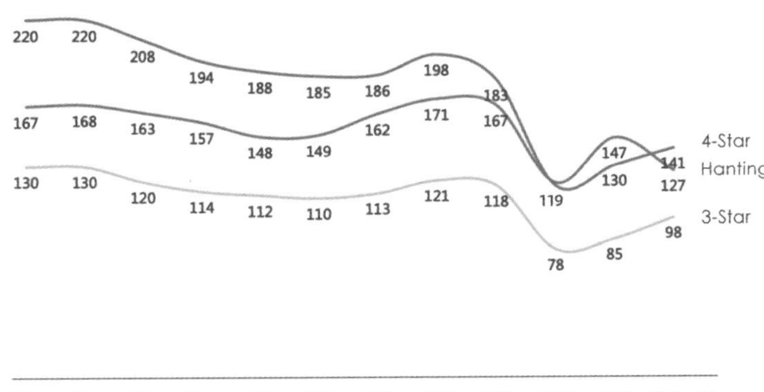

Hanting VS 3-Star/4-Star

(Attribution: Ministry of Culture and Tourism, H World Group)

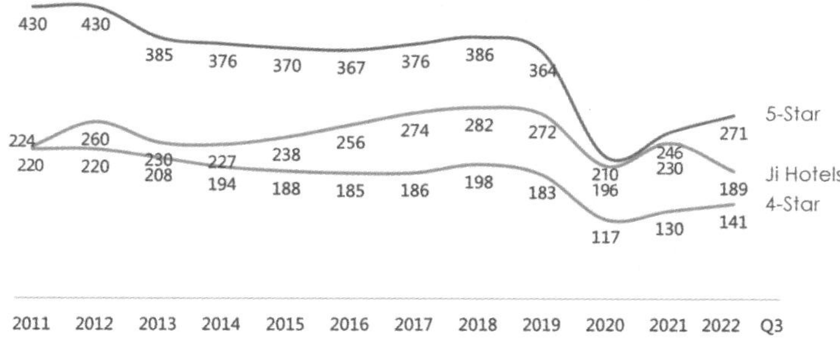

Ji Hotels VS 4-Star/5-Star

(Attribution: Ministry of Culture and Tourism, H World Group)

Compared to other brands in the same tier, our core brands do have a brand premium. However, in recent years, hotel brands across China have been expanding aggressively, building new properties non-stop, resulting in the rapid increase in homogeneous supply within a short time. This has limited our ability to fully monetize our brand's premium value, since we have yet to establish a fundamental distinction from our competitors. This is also why we must further strengthen our brand development efforts, including flagship storefront construction, new product development, product consistency, maintenance and upgrades of existing products, and market investments.

For a brand to dominate its category, it requires time, a stable and consistent brand proposition, and relentless reinforcement of its brand story. Hotel products are highly experiential, making it absolutely necessary to continuously invest in the product, maintain brand freshness, uphold the brand's core identity and preserve its distinctiveness.

The generational evolution of Chinese consumers is strikingly evident, meaning brands must constantly innovate and intently align with the core demands of each generation. There are vast regional differences across China and, at the same time, it requires brands to maintain a certain universal appeal in both trend and region. There are many similar brands and products in the market, requiring that brands stand out amid homogenization, showcasing a distinct identity in product design – the brand characteristics must be a cut above the rest (Ji Hotel for example, has gradually developed a unique product identity that is difficult, if not impossible, for others to replicate).

Compared to independent and star-rated hotels, H World's brands hold a clear advantage in brand premium. But against our competitors, even our flagship brands have yet to create a decisive gap. There is still work to be done! We must continue investing in our brand, make time our ally, and allow talent, resources and the accumulation of experience to forge a gold-standard brand in which we can take pride.

3. INNOVATION CAPACITY

Innovation is the defining factor that separates great companies from good ones. Achieving cost leadership and pricing premium alone does not guarantee that your company will become great – all it means is that you are a strong contender within its industry, like being at the peak of a parabola, an unstable equilibrium point where sustainability cannot be maintained.

When everyone competes fiercely on cost and pricing, an industry inevitably turns into a low-margin battlefield – the so-called 'Red Ocean Market.' Survival is possible, but it is a brutal struggle, beset on all sides by danger. Companies grind their efforts to the bone to earn meager profits.

So how does one escape the Red Ocean? The answer is innovation – to break free from existing constraints, carving out new frontiers at a higher dimension, and redefining the rules of the game. It is a dimensional leap, just like the old saying: "Break free from the Three Realms, beyond the Five Elements."

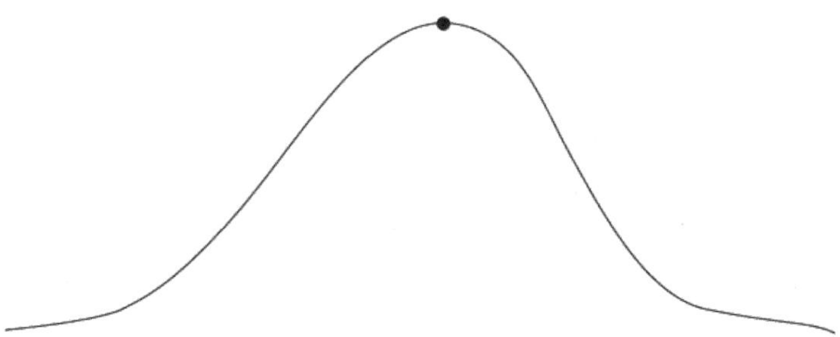

Although innovation can be divided into many levels – technological, tactical, strategic and even at the business model level – the most important, fundamental innovation comes from a 'leap' of perspective. Behind the proverbial wheel of all innovation is essentially a change in perspective and cognitive ability. Only by changing the way we think, can we bring about structural and revolutionary innovation.

You can only reach this perspective 'leap' by evaluating yourself, the company, the world and all things from a higher plane. You must break free from mediocrity, be unconventional yet grounded, balancing pragmatism with visionary ambition, and exist in the space between worldly engagement and detachment. Many see Elon Musk as someone who thinks and speaks quite differently from the average person; this is precisely because he is a revolutionary character.

One could say that, without innovation, H World would not be where it is today. We changed the expansion model of traditional hotel brands, from leasing to franchise management. We transformed the structural framework of conventional hotels, from spatial design to organizational structure. We redefined the growth trajectory of hotel companies by utilizing venture capital and private equity to accelerate development, capturing business opportunities quickly and establishing a vast hotel group network in a short span of time. Our innovations in products, services, organizations and culture are too numerous to count – but above all, we redefined the concept of a hotel company.

This is what I often describe as 'one body, two wings.' While traditional hotel companies are building cars and trains, we are constructing airplanes and spacecraft.

H World = Marriott + Oracle Opera + Booking.com. H World is a hybrid entity, a new species. It is a fusion of a hotel management company, a hospitality brand company and a software as a service (SaaS) provider.

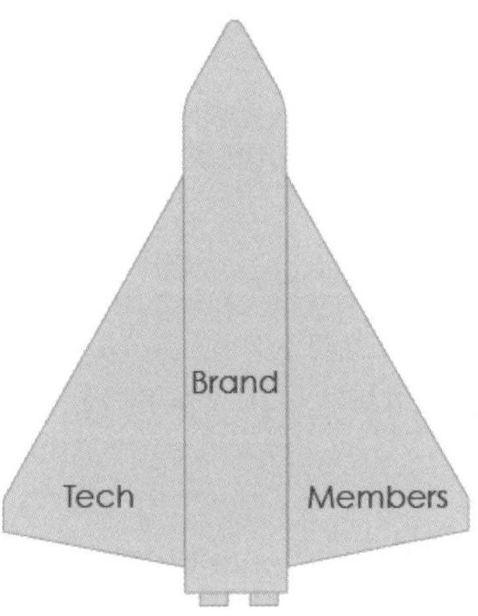

Beyond our brand, H World's powerful membership system and IT technology platform are our two wings that propel us into the sky. We do not just sell hotel rooms or issue franchise licenses – we provide fundamental solutions for hotel owners. Our solutions can truly empower owners to achieve the greatest returns on investment.

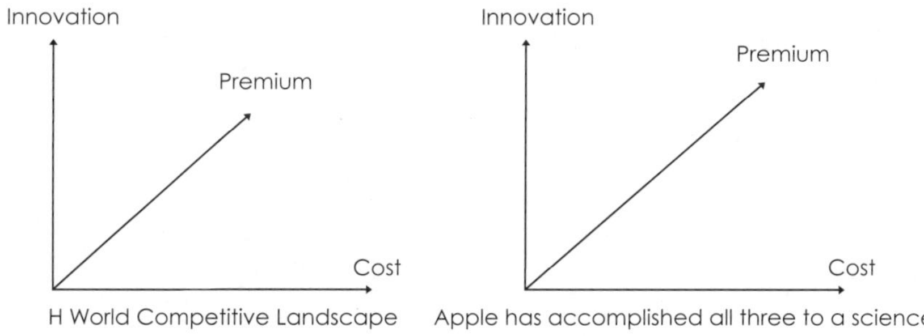

H World Competitive Landscape Apple has accomplished all three to a science

Competitiveness	Definition	Key	Case Studies
Cost Leadership	Low Cost	Systematic High Efficiency	H World, Apple
Premium Capacity	High Selling Price	Brand Premium	Hermès, Apple
Innovation Ability	Rulemaker	Higher Dimensional Understanding	Musk, Apple

I believe that once H World fully masters its 'perspective leap strategy,' the global hotel industry will enter a new era. A groundbreaking phenomenon will arise from China!

30 January, 2023

H WORLD PHILOSOPHY

The H World Spirit is an amalgamation of the spirit of the wolf, the dragon and the horse. We must not lose the initiative and fierce spirit of the wolf, but we should also maintain the perseverance of the horse and the superior quality of the dragon.

H WORLD'S ENTERPRISE PHILOSOPHY

1. ENTERPRISE PHILOSOPHY

Metaphysics is the framework, its tangible details the specifics. When the framework is set, the details naturally fall into place. The ideas that bring great change to this world are the metaphysical forces – ideologies, religions, philosophies.

> The pragmatic, evolutionary method expounded by Hu Shih and later partially accepted by the Nationalist Party; and the Marxist revolutionary approach adopted by the Chinese Communist Party. The contemporary history of China from 1921 onward is primarily a story of the struggle between these two parties and their different approaches.
>
> — Immanuel Chung-Yueh Hsu,
> *The Rise of Modern China*

> Those questions are not questions to be discussed in my place. They should be discussed with the Premier. I discuss the philosophical questions.
>
> — Mao Zedong meets Richard Nixon,
> 21 February, 1972

> It doesn't matter whether a cat is black or white, as long as it catches mice it is a good cat.
>
> — Deng Xiaoping

Mao's chief concern was philosophy. In truth, the foundation of his success during the Anti-Japanese War and the Liberation War was his philosophical outlook.

Though Deng Xiaoping authored fewer works than Mao, his reforms were no less guided by philosophy.

This holds true in business as well. Steve Jobs, the creator of Apple's miracle, traveled to India in his youth, and was later deeply influenced by Japanese Zen. The simplicity, smoothness and elegance of Apple's designs are unmistakable applications of Zen principles.

For a kingdom, an enterprise, a politician, an entrepreneur or an artist, their success and historical status are decided by their philosophies, not by guns and power, nor by money and charisma.

For an enterprise to endure, grow and reach great heights, it must embody some humanistic essence beyond mere commerce. Businesses driven solely by profit are fragile. People come and go for gain alone. Without belief and ideals, a company cannot thrive.

Therefore, a company's reach and strength are determined by its philosophy. The height and depth of that philosophy dictate the enterprise's power and potential.

Nowadays, a popular term used to describe a company's mission is 'culture.' But 'corporate culture' is too broad, overused and imprecise. Culture is the visible expression of philosophy, not its driving force.

A company is a commercial entity, not a religious one. Yet it too requires guiding principles – metaphysical ideas to steer its practical actions. Here, we prefer the term 'enterprise philosophy' over 'corporate culture.'

2. MY PHILOSOPHY OF LIFE

An enterprise's philosophy is inseparable from the founder's reflections on life. Their outlook on life, the world and the universe ultimately shapes the philosophy of a startup.

> Seek truth, ultimate goodness, beautiful perfection.
>
> — The sum of my life's philosophy

As humans we must strive to seek truth. Not knowing what truth is, means we cannot distinguish good from evil, thus cannot create happiness in our limited lives.

What is the meaning of life? Does life have meaning?

In a universe where life flows without end, the mere existence of life already carries meaning. But for the individual, the subject cannot define its own meaning. Life has no inherent meaning; meaning is defined by the object. Different objects, therefore, have different meanings.

To the subject, life is a process, not the meaning. Our entire lifetime is a journey, an act of cultivation. How do we experience this journey? How do we complete this practice of individual cultivation? Many people have never truly reflected on this. They simply hope to live a little longer, eat a little better, live a little more comfortably, earn a little more money, climb a little higher, and in the end, drift through life in a fog.

But I believe this: Since life is a process, it should be lived more brilliantly, boldly, freely and to the fullest. Why have I started so many ventures, and kept moving, never settling? It is rooted in this reflection on life. Since we only walk this Earth once, why not explore all the possibilities? Why not let the flower of life bloom without restraint?

Yet our happiness and joy must not be built upon the misery of others. We must not harm others to satisfy personal desire. More than that, we should strive to bring good into this world. Good design, good products, good brands, good companies; to continue the family line, to write and publish our thoughts to make true friends, to be good people, to do good things, so the world is better for our having been here.

Whether or not there is an afterlife, whether or not there is a Heaven, we should live with clarity. If there is no afterlife, no Heaven, then we have lived fully and left without regret. And if there is, then we shall have earned a better next life. If Heaven exists, and we are good enough, then it should hold a place for us.

It is from this reflection that I have distilled my philosophy of life: to seek truth, to pursue ultimate goodness and to fulfil perfect beauty. These higher reflections on the meaning of life began in the second year of my undergraduate days, under the sycamore trees of the campus of Shanghai Jiao Tong University, along Huashan Road, and have stayed with me throughout my life. Though years of tempering have brought refinement and elevation, the essence remains unchanged. My life's actions have always unfolded from this metaphysical essence into practical, tangible form.

3. H WORLD'S ENTERPRISE PHILOSOPHY

H World's Enterprise Philosophy: Seek truth, ultimate goodness, beautiful perfection.

It is the application of my personal philosophy of life to the enterprise.

It is a crystallized and distilled high-vantage perspective of H World's ideas and ideals.

To elaborate on its expression: the search for truth, the practice of goodness and the realization of a beautiful life.

4. THE DEFINITION OF AN ENTERPRISE

'Seeking truth' is, at its core, a reflection on meaning. Just as a person contemplates the meaning of their own lives – what is the point of working and striving so hard to build a greater, stronger enterprise? Where is the value in that? These are all questions of meaning.

Most people believe the purpose of building a company is to make money. But that is merely the superficial goal. What comes after making money? More money? Many become slaves to wealth. In reality, wealth is nothing more than a numerical tag society assigns you. It is a function of its reward-and-punishment system. Profit is the result of running a business, a reward given to shareholders and entrepreneurs. It is not its purpose.

Those who came before us have had many similar thoughts. Let us look at their conclusions.

Steve Jobs once said: "We try to use the talents we do have to express our deep feelings, to show our appreciation of all the contributions that came before us, and to add something to that flow. That's what's driven me."

Albert Einstein wrote: "A hundred times every day I remind myself that my inner and outer life are based on the labors of other men, living and dead, and that I must exert myself in order to give in the same measure as I have received and am still receiving."

Peter Drucker put it more succinctly: "The large industrial enterprise is... the representative institution of an industrial society. It determines the individual's view of his society."

I fully agree with these interpretations of an enterprise's meaning, expressed by people I deeply admire.

Beyond that, I also believe that a business ultimately serves the broader good, through its incentives for entrepreneurship and innovation. We build companies for the progress of society, to make it fairer, to improve the lives of even more people, to allow each person, through labor and creativity, to live a meaningful and dignified life.

This is the meaning of enterprise as I have come to understand it.

Once meaning is found, what follows will naturally lead us to our guiding principles: our aspiration, our vision, our values and our mission. These elements form the integral parts of H World's philosophy.

5. H WORLD'S ASPIRATION

The story at the start of the venture – H World is my third major entrepreneurial attempt. It is no longer about chasing the dream of wealth, nor about proving myself again, but about hoping to do something different, something challenging, passionate and meaningful. At this moment, one phrase naturally came to my mind: "A group of like-minded friends happily working together to achieve something great!"

That simple idea became my original motivation for founding H World. A line straight from the heart, guiding me through the fog, crossing dangerous shallows, climbing mountains, and will also become the beacon for me and H World in the future. Because of this heartfelt belief, many kindred spirits joined us along the way. Together, we've worked hard, grown side by side, and built H World into the great venture it is today.

6. H WORLD'S VISION

H World's vision is a clearer expression of the last line in our original purpose: To become a world-class enterprise!

If a company, like life itself, has no inherent meaning beyond being a journey, then besides making that journey joyful and fulfilling, we should, whenever possible, aim for its deserved heights – pursuing the pinnacle of perfection and beauty, or 'beautiful perfection,' if you will. If we are going to do something, let it be something earth-shattering! "Turning the world upside down with passion," "Challenging anyone to stand against us."

Today, H World can be called an outstanding 'national team,' but we're still some way from being truly 'world-class.' H World aims to lead the global hotel industry, to become a company worth hundreds of billions. In scale, profit and market value, we aim to be No. 1 in the world.

But being 'great' is about more than just size. It's about how we do things—actions directly tied to our core values.

7. H WORLD'S VALUES

H World's values are built on six core principles:

(1) Creating lasting value.
(2) Equal partners, shared success.
(3) Foundational hard work.
(4) Aim higher.
(5) Results matter.
(6) Building a better life.

Creating lasting value: We focus on generating value for our customers, never sacrificing long-term benefits for short-term gains. We act with integrity, avoiding shortcuts or opportunism. We don't aim to be a fleeting rose in full bloom, but the bountiful rice and wheat fields that endure across seasons.

Equal partners, shared success: We deal with everyone sincerely and equally, without flattery nor falsehood. We treat our guests, employees, franchise partners, suppliers and ecosystem collaborators as true partners in mutual growth.

Foundational hard work: We take responsibility and show courage; we persevere with diligence and resilience.

We do not evade challenges, make excuses or pass the buck. We engage directly with frontline situations and do our own research, committing to ongoing innovation and change, always adapting to consumer needs.

Aim higher: We set ambitious standards that push us beyond easy reach, holding ourselves to world-class benchmarks. We continuously improve and iterate, never giving up, never content. There is no 'best,' only 'better.'

Results matter: We reward merit and loyalty, not on personal ties or hierarchy. Failures from well-intentioned innovation or honest mistakes by those striving are understood and accepted.

Building a better life: No wrongdoing, deceit or cheating. We promote positive energy, celebrate good deeds and grow through virtuous actions.

In summary, H World's values centre on creating customer value, fostering equality and mutual growth, working hard, striving for excellence, focusing on results and building a better life together.

8. H WORLD'S MISSION

H World's mission aligns seamlessly with its philosophy and founding purpose: to achieve a better life! It can be broken down into six connected, yet sequential commitments.

H World creates a better life for our guests!

When people travel, H World hotels become their home away from home – to rest, work, meet, socialize, eat, shower and sleep.

Guests entrust us with their most private and precious moments on their journeys. We take this responsibility seriously, caring for them with dedication and warmth, treating them as close friends and family. Every year, hundreds of millions stay under the roofs of H World hotels, enjoying peaceful sleep, comfortable showers, reliable Wi-Fi to stay connected and delicious breakfasts of good quality.

We operate in the vital 'daily essentials' sector, closely tied to quality of life. It is because of H World that travellers' experiences have been greatly enhanced.

Guest satisfaction is our constant, unwavering goal.

For our employees, H World creates a better life!

H World has over 100,000 staff, where colleagues see each other as family in a respectful and friendly environment. Through their efforts and creativity, they achieve success. They use their pay to support their parents, raise their children and improve their lives. They grow, develop and maximize their talents at H World, taking part in a great endeavour that gives life meaning and value.

Our commitment is to better our staff's lives.

For franchisees and property owners, H World creates a better life!

H World has over tens of thousands of partners, and we view them as steadfast business relationships. Many franchisees gain steady, reliable returns and prosper through our brand. We hope that they will find wealth through a franchise partnership with H World. Property owners entrust H World with management, boosting profitability. H World's brand and management also enhance properties' values and brand prestige.

For our partners, H World creates a better life!

In today's specialized economy, success depends on excellent suppliers and partners. They are the ones who have assisted us in opening numerous locations. It is through them that we can provide quality goods, brands and services at affordable prices.

H World builds trust between suppliers and partners on the foundation of shared values and fair business, fostering mutual benefit and long-term cooperation.

For shareholders, H World creates a better life!

When our guests love us, our employees thrive, and our franchisees prosper, H World's performance naturally follows, enjoying steady growth in scale and profits. Beyond retaining capital for growth, we distribute dividends to shareholders annually, focusing on long-term value rather than short-term stock fluctuations, building competitive advantage through product quality, brand strength, management and chain-wide systems. We are firmly committed to creating lasting value for our shareholders.

For communities and nations, H World creates a better life!

H World's operations rely on stable, prosperous communities and economies. We provide hundreds of thousands of jobs, pay billions in taxes and stimulate significant social investment annually. We prioritize eco-friendly materials, environmental protection and green, healthy practices. We respect laws, customs and traditions, striving to do good and spread positive energy, creating a better world.

H World's operations rely on the steady prosperity of our communities and nation, and are closely tied to both macroeconomic and regional development. We have provided hundreds of thousands of jobs, contributed to tens of billions in tax revenue, driven over hundreds of billions in annual social investment – all making a meaningful contribution to local and national economies. We comply with the law, respect local customs and cultural traditions. With a heart set on doing good and promoting positive energy, we strive to bring a little more beauty into the world, through our own hard work.

H World is dedicated to building a virtuous, self-sustaining ecosystem, where every part of the circle is joyful, healthy, fulfilled, beautiful and brimming with positive energy. Our efforts not only improve ourselves, they can also enhance the lives of those within our ecosystem, turning the world into a better place. Perhaps even spurring the progress of human civilization! This, to us, is the true meaning of achieving grand feats and a beautiful life!

Our aspiration, vision, values and mission organically form H World's enterprise philosophy, summarized by the facets of 'seeking truth, ultimate goodness and beautiful perfection.'

We stay true to our aspiration, remain steadfast in our mission, keep our vision close to heart, and live by our values.

To strive for greater heights!

To strive for a better future for H World!

To strive for a better future for humanity!

Completed 16 August, 2014
Revised 28 January, 2020

H WORLD'S AESTHETICS

I was a believer of 'Only the paranoid can survive.' I used to be a good student at school. After enrolling in Shanghai Jiao Tong University, I read many books on philosophy, including works by Nietzsche, Schopenhauer and Spinoza. Not all of what I read belonged to the mainstream. For example, Friedrich Nietzsche believed he was the Sun. Some people say he was mad, but I disagree. I think people just could not understand him, and people tend to label individuals they cannot understand as mad. When I read *Thus Spoke Zarathustra*, I thought he suffered from depression because he was a genius. A work like that cannot be written – it is a stream of brilliance that comes directly from the mind of a genius. The scene he describes is beautiful. For a while ideas in these works, including ideas of pessimism and nihilism, had a profound impact on me. I later encountered the teachings of the Chinese philosopher Wang Yangming and felt his moderate wisdom of the East was enlightening. Everything, in fact, is about the art of balance. If we choose to let spiritual ideas dominate our lives, we will become puritans. If we allow ourselves to indulge in carnal desires, we will become people who linger in karaoke night clubs all day in search of pleasure. I pursue balance, in life, and in business. Balance allows structural steadiness which ensures endurance.

I once wrote an article titled "Ten Sins of Hotels," to list what in my view are excessive hotel amenities and services. I criticized the inclusion of bathtubs, for they are a typical nuisance: the edge of the bathtub is slippery which is a safety hazard for guests. The costs are high to maintain hygienic standards when guests use bathtubs, and costs of cleaning are high. Few people – under 10% of business travellers and perhaps 20-30% of leisure travellers – use them. They are expensive – a Kohler brand bathtub costs several thousand dollars.

I also criticized hotel lobbies and public areas that take up too much space. In fact, many hotel lobbies in New York, London, and in most hotels in France, are small and elegant. The function of a hotel lobby is to welcome guests and process check-in and check-out formalities. They later became a symbol of extravagance. This trend started with Grand Hyatt hotels. They make the ceiling of their hotel lobbies very high, so magnificent that their hotel lobbies are like churches. This is a waste: a waste of space, a waste of building materials and a waste of labor.

When I later worked on Ji Hotels, we positioned our aesthetics for middle-class guests. For mid-range hotels, all redundant features should be excluded, while all important features should be as perfect as possible. To use a friend's remarks on Ji Hotels: "Not one bit more, or less. It includes everything I need and excludes everything I don't need. And the price is reasonable." I think it is very well said. But behind what to include and what to exclude is a long thought process. Behind the simplicity and modesty is a complex process of weighing pros and cons.

Ji Hotels and Hanting Hotels used to have wooden floors in our guest rooms. We did not use carpets because they are too expensive and not easy to clean. We could not afford to use hardwood floor, so we used laminates. Laminates transmit sound and warp when wet. We later used Bolon carpet. An important factor for us in choosing materials is appropriateness rather than extravagance. (Ordinary carpets are vulnerable to cigarette burns). The warmth from floor heating can easily radiate through the carpet. It is sound-proof and odour-free. (The glue used for wooden flooring emits odour and is not environmentally friendly). The cost of this type of carpet is reasonable.

We have many unique ways to achieve this kind of effect. In the past, guest rooms were appraised on the basis of size. The bigger the room, the more expensive. But this kind of pricing is not viable for us in cities like Beijing or Shanghai. Our solution is to improve room facilities to the best we can achieve in a smaller space. For example, we installed heated toilet seats with bidets, we added vanity mirrors in bathrooms, and we provide TVs with a bigger screen. By adding features that enhance a guest's happiness, the smaller room becomes cosy and comfortable. These measures, such as making decisions on room sizes and choosing interior materials, are part of the art of balancing.

As for pricing, a room that is priced at about US$20 means a loss for us, but no guest will come if we were to price it at about US$150. We will probably price the room at US$50, which is profitable for us and reasonable for our guests. This also is our pursuit of balance.

Investment is the same. When we were working on Ji Hotels, the budget for each room renovation was 120,000 yuan (now approximately US$17,000); we would not spend 140,000 yuan on renovation. Only this kind of careful evaluation and budget control can guarantee the attractiveness of Ji Hotels to investors. Otherwise, no one will be willing to invest.

The same logic also applies to aesthetics. There are beautiful plants in my garden, but they are not easy to grow, which means they are not suitable for a hotel environment. Instead, I will probably choose a pine bonsai, which is a hardy variety. I want to achieve what the pine bonsai does; it is not affected by the environment, it's hardy and it meets the aesthetic taste of China's middle class. This taste will change with time and we will follow the changes.

16 August, 2014

THE POSITIONING STRATEGIES OF H WORLD'S BRANDS

H World offers two types of products. One is about the avant-garde, lush, passionate, colorful or a little luscious – like our Manxin and Orange brands. The other type is about moderation, appropriateness and intrinsic quality. It offers what all guests need, but nothing more – that is our Ji Hotel brand. Both types of products have markets among middle-class guests.

Our high-end brand, Joya, uses Oriental aesthetic elements and values to interpret the modern lifestyle. In the past, high-end hotels in China uniformly adopted Western aesthetics. Our Puli brand is an experiment which incorporates Oriental elements. It is popular among both domestic and international travellers. The Joya brand follows the same approach. So, what is the Oriental aesthetic? I think it is about balance, grace and tranquillity, while ensuring convenience and comfort. We incorporate Oriental elements in our hotel design. For example, instead of putting sculptures in the room, which is common in Western-style hotels, we place a bonsai in the guest room.

I also fantasize about one day building China's ultimate ultra-luxury hotel south of the Yangtze River. It will be surrounded by forests and lakes and linked by zigzag bridges. At the fringe of the forest, there will be a few elegant Oriental-style structures. The scent of flower fragrance will waft in from afar, a faint trace of music in the air. Perhaps Mozart, or perhaps the Chinese guqin zither.

The hotel floor will be tiled with imperial kiln golden bricks made in Suzhou, using traditional techniques. Underneath the floor, heating will regulate indoor moisture in winter, and even during the plum rain season, to eliminate the dampness in the air. It is, however, unnecessary to maintain constant temperature indoors, in order to allow guests to appreciate seasonal changes. The lake will be outside the hotel. Guests can take outings by boat. The calming sound of a flute, or perhaps a French horn, will accompany them. Leisurely, they float, under the boundless sky. This ultra-luxury hotel will be the most dazzling diamond on the H World crown.

16 August, 2014

H WORLD'S BUSINESS APPROACH

1. CHINA STYLE SERVICE

Working in the hotel industry in China often makes me feel I was born at the right time. Nowhere else in the world offers as many opportunities as today's China.

As China's urbanization continues, we still have plenty of opportunities to open new hotels in cosmopolitan cities like Shanghai and Beijing, not to mention opening a large number of hotels in other cities.

Until now, there are still very few established strong brands and companies. This means we can strike and establish new business models and new companies, unlike in developed countries in the West where new enterprises have to battle with an army of industry giants. It is hard for new companies in a traditional industry to grow without the help of new technologies and innovations.

Apart from opportunities brought about by urbanization, there are also opportunities generated by China's system dividend and the large market produced by the population dividend. In China the population that has sufficient purchasing power is about six hundred million strong. This scale cannot be matched by the USA, the EU, or even India. Nowhere else but China.

The development of the hotel industry in developed countries has slowed down and the market has been divided. China is the fastest growing country among newly emerged nations and possesses the greatest market potential. The main battlefield of the international hotel industry has moved to China, but international brands have achieved little impact on China's budget hotel market.

Everyone is getting ready to fight in the mid-range market and some international brands, such as InterContinental Hotel Group's Holiday Inn Express, Hilton's Hilton Garden Inn and Marriott's Courtyard, are doing well. After they gradually exhaust their mother companies' reputational goodwill, I believe China's mid-range hotel market still belongs to local brands.

In the high-end hotel market, international brands have established their dominant status. However, as the investment spending to boost economic growth decreases, and the crackdown on extravagance continues, there will be fewer operators who are willing to invest recklessly without expecting return. Our approach that champions luxury lite, Oriental culture and philosophy, and moderate investment will give us a chance to gradually gain market share.

China is a developing country with a huge population. The major part of the hotel market is in the budget and mid-priced markets. As long as we can dominate these markets, we can dominate the majority of China's hotel market. Therefore, the focus of our work is budget and mid-priced markets. The key to H World's future success is managing our brands well in budget, mid-priced, mid-to-high-end hotels.

The main current and future consumption trends in China are staying at budget and mid-priced hotels. Our strategic resources, including human resources, materials, management and capital, should be tilted toward these two areas. This conclusion will not change in the next ten years.

As for our presence in the high-end hotel market, we can proceed gradually through different channels, such as building our own premises, entering into joint-venture arrangements, or through acquisitions. That is a matter for another ten-year plan. As soon as we are ready to act, we will definitely bring revolutionary change to the industry. We won't just drift along, nor will we be opportunistic, either.

2. A GLOBAL VISION

We talk about globalization, not only because we aspire to build a great, world-class enterprise, but more importantly, it is because businesses, clients, talent and capital have all gone global. We must gaze at the Earth from outer space.

First, we must employ global wisdom. Of course, we should carry on China's traditional wisdom of 5,000 years. But we are not populists, and we believe Western wisdom is an invaluable asset of the world which should be learned from and utilized without prejudice.

Second, we must have a global vision. Instead of getting bogged down in particular issues, our strategic thinking must be broad and deep. The marketization in China today has been witnessed in developed countries in the West before. Their achievements and structure today will probably be our future, too. We should learn from their merits, but more importantly, from their demerits.

Third, there is a globalized market. As China continues to develop, more and more people will travel overseas. Visas for many countries, including EU countries, are becoming easier to obtain. More Chinese companies are going abroad and cultivating markets in the Middle East, Europe, South America and Africa. The number of international business and leisure travellers coming to China is also increasing every year. Today, international hotel brands have come to China. Tomorrow, we will inevitably go abroad.

Finally, there is globalized talent. We should attract them to come to China, but we should also send our talent abroad. Some of our staff members studied in developed countries in the West, some of them used to work for multinational companies, some of them have foreign citizenship.

Many members of our supplier teams are globalized talent. We must embrace the idea of attracting more globalized talent, and be ready for it. At the same time, our core management executives must not confine themselves to one city, or one province. We have the ambition to go global – one day we may open new hotels or manage hotels in other countries.

Our globalization road map looks like this: We accumulate cash flow, scale, financing capability and customers through our budget and mid-priced hotel business. We will achieve our globalization goal using our high growth, high PE and large positive cashflow to acquire (through share purchases).

Therefore, we are in no hurry to open new hotels in the United States, in Europe or even in Southeast Asia. Instead, we must first win the battle in China. We must work hard on this fertile land to ensure a great harvest. We will have a chance to be a global leader, only by being the greatest in the Chinese market.

3. STRIVE TO BE NO. 1

The trilogy of single, self-operated hotels: eat enough, eat well, eat healthily.

To establish our presence in a region: complete budgeting, increase RevPAR and increase our market shares.

There are three stages for us to either operate a hotel or cultivate our presence in a region. Each stage is higher than the previous one. The first stage is to complete the budgeting. We will have no right to begin talking without a complete budget. The second stage is to defeat our competitors over RevPAR. The third stage is to also beat our competitors over control of market share. If our competitors control more market share than we do, it means we have not done a good enough job. If we adequately complete the three stages, then we will not be afraid of any competition.

Home Inn is a competitive partner that accompanies the development of H World. I founded Home Inn. I later left and launched Hanting (now H World). Both groups are representative of China's hotel industry. Sometimes I joke that the relationship between Home Inn and H World is like the hand combat invented by the fictional Kungfu master Zhou Botong in a Louis Cha novel.

At present, two state-owned enterprises, Beijing Tourism Group and Jin Jiang International Hotels, have acquired Home Inn and 7 Days Inn, respectively. These are the three large hotel groups on the market – Jin Jiang International, Beijing Tourism Group and H World. Future competition on the Chinese market will likely to be among these three large groups.

Because of the diversity of different brands, we will have different competitors in the diverse markets of budget hotels, mid-range and mid-high range hotels. H World is far ahead in many aspects, but newly emerged entrepreneurial companies with mid-range hotels, as well as foreign brands, are still very competitive in the mid to high-priced hotel market. We must learn from them and cannot afford to be complacent.

Our most likely competitors in five or ten years' time, are likely to be international groups such as InterContinental, Marriott, Accor, Hilton and Hyatt. We will encounter them on the high-end and luxury market as well as in the process of our globalization.

The sharing economy, represented by Airbnb, has taken off and the OTA market share of hotel distribution continues to grow. These business models will continue to be the hotel industry's long-term strategic competitors.

A company's competitive strategies are decided by two factors: the market and the competitors. When the competition is not too fierce, the company can establish itself at a leisurely pace. It took Accor 40 years to open over 4,000 hotels in Europe where the market is less competitive, but we took only eight years to open 2,000 hotels in the very competitive Chinese market.

On the fiercely competitive and fast-growing Chinese market, our first tactic is blitzkrieg. Take Ji Hotels as an example. Our hotels must seize the highest point of the market at lightning speed before our competitors have time to respond. Many foreign brands are unable to use this tactic.

Our second tactic is flanking manoeuvres and encirclement. Both Home Inn and Hanting started from fringe area properties and properties surrounded by narrow streets. These were properties in which others would have no interest. This is what I mean by flanking manoeuvres and encirclement. We never confront our competitors head on when we do not have the strength. We take the same approach in the mid-range market. Once we have a demo hotel up and running, we quickly finish our strategic plan in node cities. Instead of confining ourselves in one area, or one city, to reach commanding heights, we first establish a national network and brand recognition online and offline.

The third tactic is 'Ten times Growth.' According to Moore's Law, the number of transistors on a microchip doubles every 18 months. This computing term also applies to China's hotel industry. In today's China, we can no longer simply evaluate the development of many industries based on conventional wisdom. Rapid burst development and revenge-and-compensation style growth are making the development pace of many traditional industries similar to the fast-growing IT industry. Of course, we hope our development is good both in terms of quality and quantity. However, resources are not always sufficient. If we wish to maintain the development speed at 100, then we cannot expect the quality to also be at 100. To be able to maintain 80 is already very good. This is the 80/100 formula, based on my experience. If we focus on trivial errors and get bogged down in partial perfection, we will lose the opportunity to gain an overall victory.

Both speed and quality are important. However, at a company's development stage, speed is more important.

Having said that, we must make up for the quality shortcomings as soon as we are in control of the overall situation, in order to complete the process of moving from explosive growth to lean management.

H World's development, as well as the hotel market in China, are at the stage that require lean management which is from the 'good enough' phase at the initial start-up to achieving 'enough good;' from 100 at speed and 80 at quality, to 100 at speed and 100 at quality. If the quality cannot match up with the speed, then we would rather reduce the speed to 95 or 90.

What will be the key factors for our success?

First, location. We must seize the best locations in first- and second-tier cities. It is even more important for our operations in third- and fourth-tier cities to seize key locations. This is because in these cities the client base is lean, the replacement cost is low and the dilution effect can be more in evidence.

Second, brand. When location is not a competing factor, then the role of branding becomes noticeable. A brand has two components: product (quality) and brand awareness (volume). A hotel product includes two components: hardware refers to facilities and software refers to services.

In short, to build a successful hotel business, we must choose a good location, present a good product and operate on a large scale.

4. THE YIN AND YANG OF BUSINESS

What are the rules we follow when doing business?

First, we form a united front. If a conflict occurs, we must not aggravate it. Instead, we must do our best to find a win-win solution. Only harmony brings wealth. We must make sure all of our cooperation arrangements move toward mutual benefits. We must strive to unite all forces in order to build our company and maximize benefits for our clients.

Second, push the boat along with the current. It is admirable to sail against the current, but it achieves little. We should follow the trend and make use of the prevailing circumstances to achieve our goals. Never cling obstinately to our course and act on impulse. When we do business, we must follow the trend, follow the market, follow the government and follow popular sentiment.

Third, go with the flow. When we surf, we ride with the waves. What kind of flows and tides do we encounter now? The post-80s and 90s generations are our main source of clients. The mobile internet is the technical wave and labor reduction is the trend in cost control.

Fourth, engage in destructive innovation. The business models of H World, Home Inn and 7 Day Inn are destructive innovations in the traditional hotel industry. By changing the product structure, cost structure, development mode and salary model, the entire hotel industry has been changed. The same practice applies to operating mid-priced hotels. We constantly tear down the old structure from within and build new structures, including new ways to consume, new growth models, new markets, new communication methods and new product presentations. Whenever we enter a new territory, from Hi Inn, Elan Hotel, to Ji Hotel, to Starway, Manxi and Joya, we carry out our destructive innovation wherever we go. Without innovation, we will not stand a chance to survive in this industry.

Fifth, obey the Law of the Jungle. Many people only understand the first level of this law, which is 'natural selection' and 'survival of the fittest.' In fact, the Law of the Jungle has three layers of meaning.

The second layer is competition of same species, and coexistance of different species. It is hard for a small tree to grow next to a much bigger tree, but it is not so for grass or moss. This is because different species require different resources. For example, in order to sustain our growth, we must guarantee enough profits for H World's construction teams and suppliers to enable them to hire the best workers so they can provide the best service for us. We must ensure other species can coexist with us so we can have nutrients to grow. Without the ecosystem, we will not be able to grow and advance, and the cost of survival will be very high. Harmonious coexistence is an important principle of the Law of the Jungle, just as important as 'survival of the fittest.'

The third layer of the meaning is a tall tree catches the wind. Destruction pursues the great. Once on an excursion, I saw a big, 2,500-year-old tree fall to the ground due to strong wind and die, while small trees and trees of medium height growing next to it were unaffected. Companies are the same. As an enterprise grows larger and larger, it risks the fate of a large tree. Apart from aging and decaying, the chance of becoming a target of jealousy and attack become higher. The principle tells us: One, the greatest must know how to be humble. Two, the strength that can support a small tree cannot support a big tree. Lofty ideals must be supported by equally great strength.

H World's business philosophy seems to be a set of opposites. One is about harmony and conformity, the other about destruction and competition. The unification of the two opposites is our yin and yang in business.

16 August, 2014

H WORLD'S TAO OF MANAGEMENT

Human organizations possess four strengths which enterprise management can draw on and utilize.

The first is religious belief. The cohesive force that holds religions together is belief. This force is aimed at the heart, encouraging people to do many things of their own accord without the need for coercion. No commercial enterprise, however, can hope to achieve anything approaching the power of that kind of belief.

The second is military commands. The mission of the military is to execute orders, to fight where they are ordered to fight without question, and never to go against orders. Disobeying an order on the battlefield will lead to your execution. This strength is compelled, and despite the cost of violation being huge, implementation capabilities are strong.

The third strength is enterprise profit. The most basic aspect of business is profit, it is the foundation of business. I would venture to say that commerce is the most important force of modern society. The distribution of wealth, the reward of innovation, the encouragement of diligence and the punishment of sloth, these are all allocated through the profits of companies.

The fourth strength is love of family. This is the cohesive force of the smallest level of human organization, a natural and biological force.

Businesses are commercial organizations, but these four strengths can also apply to enterprises.

Only discussing business profit is not sufficiently balanced. I hope that H World can, at different times and in different circumstances, make use of the four strengths – belief, discipline, benefit and love – to become a commercial organization with beliefs similar to a religion, determination to execute plans like an army, and brimming with love like a family.

1. THE CHARACTERISTICS OF THE H WORLD ORGANIZATION

Currently, we have over one thousand establishments located in several hundred cities in China, staffed by several tens of thousands of people who handle almost one hundred million guests annually. The management of a business like this is already highly complex. In addition, we have directly operated hotels. From initiating a project, to construction, to opening for business, the chain of events is very long. The day to day work of hotels is specific and mired in minor details, whereas the educational level of our employees is not high, as many are just middle school or high school graduates. Moreover, our rate of growth is extremely fast – Ten Times Growth – our pace is unprecedented in the whole world. These factors destined H World to be a business with highly complex management requirements that must be supported by a comprehensive management system.

2. THE YIN AND YANG OF ORGANIZATIONS

Number one is unity of ideals and full authorization to act.

Workflow charts and lists of standards are simply insufficient for a business spread across such disparate cities with so many frontline workers – there must be unified values and ideals. H World's philosophy is the systematic elaboration of these values and ideals. At the retail level we must produce a simple, everyday, easy to understand version. Something that will be well-received by everyone and have a real impact on people by arousing goodness and virtue in the innermost recesses of people's hearts, enabling them to be at one with the H World philosophy.

On the foundation of unified belief, we must grant full authority to act, to avoid inflexibility and encourage resilience.

As a business expands, it is easy to become needlessly complex. Excessive checking and approvals, an inordinate number of meetings, too much checks and balances – this can lead to too many layers of management, resulting in bureaucracy. The ideal is 'simplicity is the ultimate sophistication,' so we advocate concise and clear communications with a simple and direct style. Management design should be as flat as possible; give full authorization, and ensure decision-making power is as close to the frontline as possible. The head office principally handles complex, abstract or platform issues; the front-line decides on the majority of day-to-day matters like service levels, revenue and cost controls.

Number two is precise implementation and adapting to change.

When beliefs and values are unified and the management and organization have achieved ultimate simplification, it is not anarchic or undisciplined. On the contrary, military style discipline and the support of strong implementation are needed. An enterprise with tens of thousands of people also needs to be like an army on drill practice: orderly, moving in formation, obeying orders, strictly enforcing standards, focused on company strategy, dedicated to company ideals, as if the whole chain was one person, a harmonious unified whole that does battle wherever ordered. There can't be fiefdoms all over the place that act differently and have a different interpretation of the company's requirements.

On a foundation of precise implementation, we can adapt to change.

In a changeable environment we must deal with change, accept it and change ourselves. We must open our minds, learn new things and accept new ideas. In this era of change, what never changes is constant change. H World is like a heavy-duty truck that has to be driven fast and frequently overtake bends in the road. Our road ahead is not always clear at a glance. Sometimes, the road meanders, and the weather is constantly changing, so we have to be prepared to deal with changes.

Number three is Eastern wisdom and Western techniques.

When using management tools, I advocate Eastern wisdom and Western techniques to assist us. Eastern wisdom begins with the four great schools of ancient Chinese thought: Legalism, Confucianism, Buddhism and Taoism. Western techniques refers to modern management theory and tools like the Balanced Scorecard, ERP and IT.

Number four is the combination of these three factors.

I earnestly hope that this combination of the three factors I propose will create a model modern management company with an entrepreneurial spirit.

The first combination is that of managers and leaders. Leaders inspire the people's conscience, have prescient strategic thinking, are charismatic, passionate and full of ideas. Managers on the other hand, are meticulous, methodical, rational and efficient. Which is why I say combine the inspirational charismatic leader with the highly effective manager.

The second combination is that of rules and innovation. It's 95% rules and 5% innovation. Innovation is expensive, and if innovation is not given a chance to settle in and to produce fruitful results, it will be difficult for a company to continue. The Xerox Research Center and Bell Labs were innovation departments of large enterprises. Although they have given us many wonderful inventions, as far as the companies are concerned, these innovation departments have not resulted in fundamental change, and consequently are falling into decline. But that 5% innovation is crucially important, like the detonator on an atom bomb or the fuse on fireworks. Without constant innovation it's impossible to keep up with the times, and that leaves a company in danger of being toppled by other innovators and never achieving greatness. This 5% innovation determines a company's future and whether it will reach for the stars.

The third combination is that of realism and idealism. Idealism is cerebral, while realism is about action. Heights cannot be attained without idealism, but without realism nothing will come to life. Especially in today's complicated and everchanging business environment in China, ideals are needed to avoid falling into the all too common traps of mediocrity or unscrupulousness in this cruel reality; but without realism to put into practice, an enterprise will merely be a hothouse flower or an antique in an ivory tower.

16 August, 2014

ON MANAGING THE 'CRUCIAL FEW'

For hotel industry practitioners, experience is more important than brilliance. When hiring someone who is smart and capable that person may not necessarily do a good job. This industry is very concrete, requiring two years and perhaps five to accumulate enough experience to get a handle on the job.

I've been inspecting hotel sites for many years, gradually accumulating experience. I've inspected many properties in many cities, gradually forming something like a conclusion, something that could never be formed by deliberation, only by practice.

In addition to experience, steadfastness and diligence are more important than brilliance. The difference between conscientious work and a casual approach is enormous. It doesn't matter how brilliant someone is, a lack of conscientiousness is unacceptable. This industry of ours uniquely encourages long term and continuous commitment. We give options as an incentive and this is a huge stimulant.

To be compatible with these characteristics of people working in the hotel industry, I adopt a management style of focusing on the 'crucial few' when working with senior executives of H World. To manage an enterprise with thousands of employees and so many hotels, two fundamentals must be handled well.

One fundamental is in our hotel outlets. A branch office is built on a team. Our hotel managers must be proactive to be competent and must act like the master of their domain. To achieve this, we have conducted extensive evaluations and provided ample training, although core values still need to be enhanced. Frontline managers have to command and deploy the troops, which is a very important role.

The other fundamental is the management of the 'crucial few,' which refers to our senior executives. In chain hotel management, a small error may lead to a catastrophe. Take buying a hundred million bottles of mineral water as an example – a five cent discrepancy per bottle times one hundred million, means a huge amount of money wasted. A lack of diligence and professionalism among senior staff members in the company headquarters can result in serious consequences. Therefore, these people are the crucial few.

We offer the 'crucial few' very attractive remuneration packages. Our senior executives can't be driven away once they start with my company. They receive a lot of attention from me. It is not possible for me to give the same amount of attention to all of our 60,000 employees. I can only give my full attention to 20 of them. I fully trust them. Each one of them is responsible for one area and are given great decision-making power. In return, they receive very attractive incentives.

However, this does not mean they are under no pressure. Every one or two years, the worst performer among them will be eliminated. This can be cruel for someone in their position, but it will also inspire them to work harder. The pressure they feel will radiate and reach down to lower levels. This is crucial for the company to remain aspirational.

16 August, 2014

THE SPIRIT OF THE WOLF, THE DRAGON AND THE HORSE

In the early days of our company, we often talked about the spirit of the Wolf. As our company grows, I now propose the spirit of the Dragon and the Horse.

We are all descendants of the Dragon. The Dragon is the totem of ethnic Chinese, the spiritual symbol of our people. The Dragon also represents the Sovereign aspiring to rule the world. We must be as ambitious as the Dragon and set our eyes to the global arena and strive to become No. 1.

In the early days of Hanting, I strategized our approach with one Chinese phrase, *qian long wu yong*, which literally means 'the dragon hides in deep water' – that is, it's not time for action. At the time, multiple players were competing on the market. We decided to stay low key to enhance our inner strength. Now I wish to use another phrase, *qun long wu shou*, 'there is no leader among a host of dragons,' to describe ways of nurturing new leaders.

At present, we all need the characteristics of a Horse. First, we need its speed. Ten thousand horses galloping ahead – what a magnificent sight! Second, we need industriousness. The spirit of industriousness in a horse can be seen when we watch mounted troops in action – orderly, devoted, courageously advancing and disregarding their own gain or loss. These qualities are important for a company.

When our company reaches a certain stage, we should adopt the spirit of the Dragon and the Horse. Then we should make one of H World's core characteristics to balance the spirit of the Wolf. For new brands and starups, the spirit of the Wolf is crucial. In some respects, today's H World continues its entrepreneurial practice.

Therefore, the H World Spirit is an amalgamation of the spirit of the Wolf, the Dragon and the Horse. We must not lose the initiative and fierce spirit of the wolf, but we should also maintain the perseverance of the horse and the superior quality of the dragon.

We must integrate seemingly opposites to form a harmonious whole, not only in business but also in management. The Tao of H World is the Tao of yin and yang, which is also the Tao of nature.

16 August, 2014

HOW WE LOOK UPON CUSTOMERS

As far as lodgers are concerned, the most important thing is for products (including service) to meet their needs. Our products (the entire experience including advance booking) must be convenient for customers, reasonably priced, and we must also cater to the emotional requirements of a new generation of customers.

How do we produce good products and good services? I believe there are four points to consider: innovation, training, master of the house and location.

We innovated to be the first in the industry to implement zero-time checkout as well as self-service registration; we innovated constantly for Ji Hotels to adjust and upgrade improvements. Hanting Hotels will soon introduce second generation products including factory assembled whole bathrooms. In the future, making use of new technologies, we will introduce NFC door keys and other features to make things even more convenient for customers.

Training is equally important. In addition to the H World Academy, we also have onsite training to pass on experience to frontline staff in each different kind of post. As we enter mid-range and high-range hotels, soft service needs to be proportionately raised and training is obviously important.

Without a spirit of 'master of the house' and simply relying on systems and workflow, a large chain will not be able to provide service from the heart. We must consider providing a good situation and good prospects for every post and allow staff in every post to feel free and be spontaneous.

Good products and services also include good location. We not only need locations in the centre of first- and second-tier cities, but also in the city centre of third- and fourth-tier cities. We should penetrate deeply into the county level, so that wherever our customers go they can be confident that there will be a H World hotel for them to stay in.

Product design must pay special attention to providing convenience to customers. We all despise the time it takes to register in traditional hotels and the long checkout lines, and then we have to pay for Wi-Fi, we have to provide all sorts of information when booking, and so on. Many of our innovations target these petty annoyances. We must avoid third rate designers who are so fond of showing off, engage in reckless spending and just plagiarize.

Even very wealthy guests care about reasonable pricing. No successful entrepreneur can survive by 'decapitating' customers. Our strategy, developed for operating budget hotels, is honest-to-goodness pricing, which we also apply to the mid and even high-range hotels. We provide customers with accurate information at the outset and do not equivocate. Especially in an age of a high level of information symmetry, this approach is essential.

Giving customers competitive prices means we must be efficient and do not expect others to pay for inefficient internal operations and overstaffing. Everything is done for our guests, be it via an online platform or regional management office. All wasteful or superfluous practices must be avoided. For example, when staff are on business trips, they can catch trains rather than planes; we can accept three layers of management but definitely not four; print on both sides of the page and offices can use what's left over after space is allocated for guest rooms. In addition, we are insisting on direct sales and not depending on agents, including OTA, and even less on traditional tour groups. Direct selling not only guarantees net room price but also a lower cost of customer retention and communication.

Consumers from the 1960s and 1970s generations traditionally paid attention to a high quality to price ratio, but new generation consumers from the 1980s and 1990s have added a demand – emotional appeals. They value quality of life and the experience, and will stay in a hotel just because they like it, or because it exudes a cultured experience. While most people have budgetary constraints, they will sacrifice money for their feelings, or at least slightly increase their budget.

Franchised owners are another category of customer we have lacked awareness about, or perhaps not paid much attention to, or have not dealt with at the same level as hotel guests. Future budget hotels will mostly be under licenced management. At the high end it will basically be trust management, while mid-range hotels will be somewhat mixed, but principally trust managed. The bulk of our profit is derived from franchised customers and management income; we depend on expanding franchise customers to open up new territories and expand our coverage to fourth- and fifth-tier cities. It goes without saying that they are very important.

Franchised customers expect two things: profits and respect. Profit is easy for us to understand, as franchise customers join our program for a stable return on their investment. Thus, for our brand to be able to attract customers, the professionalism and dedication of our management team is extremely important.

Equality and respect are easy to overlook. The franchise market fad and a bureaucratic sentiment resulted in neglect of franchisees and prejudice against them. And some people even use their positions for personal gain, taking (or demanding) kickbacks. This had a hugely negative impact on H World's reputation and destroyed the fairness of the franchise market. We have undertaken numerous remedies and improvements on organization and mechanisms, but it is insufficient. We will continue to explain internally that alliance members are partners and customers who must be treated equally, that every H World customer must be treasured and respected.

I employ three analogies to explain how to treat customers, regardless of whether they are hotel guests or franchise customers: they are as close to our bodies as a quilt; they are as sensitive as the hot and cold water in a shower; they are as convenient as Wi-Fi. In this way we are building Chinese service with H World characteristics.

16 August, 2014

HOW WE TREAT EMPLOYEES

What traits do hoteliers have? Summing up over a decade of observations, I think the most important trait is dedication to the job.

The majority of our senior staff, especially the key members in the regional offices, all joined the company in the early days and have grown together with the company. They worked their way up from entry level, earnestly, conscientiously, steadfast and assiduously; they are good learners, good at thinking through problems and sum up successful experience as well as absorb the lessons of failures; they are tenacious when confronting setbacks and challenges. The atmosphere in our company is fast-paced and intense, and the pressure is enormous. Some people can't keep up and are eliminated; some people can't cope and give up; but the people who persevere all succeed! Not only do they progress through the company, more importantly, they surpass themselves and are rewarded with a sense of accomplishment.

Ordinary people who try hard, learn continually, and are tempered by fierce struggles can become a store manager, or a city manager, or a branch manager, or even a regional CEO.

We should recruit dedicated people and hunt out those who are good at learning. Basic level staff have three fundamental expectations:

1. Competitive salaries. They wish to be paid a little more for the same amount of work.

2. Stable work. Most people count on their salary at H World to support their family, and do not expect to get rich suddenly. Work is the most fundamental method to make a living, so they hope for stable work.
3. A relaxed and happy work environment.

We have tens of thousands of employees, we cater to in excess of one hundred million hotel guests annually, and every customer interaction, every breakfast and every room cleaning is undertaken by grassroot employees. Their level of professionalism and dedication determines our service standard.

In light of the characteristics of chain businesses and staff requirements, I propose the use of Legalist philosophy to manage basic level staff. The Legalists emphasized rules and regulations, and stressed precise execution. When I say 1.0 they should do it to 1.000 not 1.001. Han Fei (d. 223 BCE), the great Chinese Legalist philosopher put it well in 'Employing People':

> A task can be completed if a mediocre leader follows established rules and techniques, just like a mediocre artisan who follows prescribed methods and measurements. If a ruler avoids engaging in actions that even an intelligent individual cannot complete, and follows tested foolproof methods, then people will spare no effort in following him, and the ruler's mission will be accomplished.

This is an excellent summary of the importance of standardization and procedure, while emphasizing precise implementation.

At the same time the salaries of grassroot employees must be linked to operational performance. Work more, get more; work less, get less. We must not engage in egalitarianism to reward everyone equally from the proverbial big pot, because it would be impossible to continue the business, and employee turnover would inevitable.

We sincerely regard employees as family. A hotel or a department is just like a small family, members are united and mutually supportive. That is because the benefits are not fought over; benefits are the result of working hard together. The most successful hotels are the ones in which the employees are united and of one mind.

In addition to providing a relaxed and happy work ambience, we do our best to give our employees a sense of security. We have a H World fund to help families who are in difficulties. After the Wenchuan earthquake in 2008, we helped the staff who had lost their homes. If an immediate family member loses the ability to work, we provide financial assistance for their children to attend school, and other measures to make employees feel at ease.

H World is a large family. We are a group of industrious and dedicated people who work very hard at their jobs. We have achieved outstanding results for which we receive ample remuneration. In times of difficulty, we are much more inclined to help each other pass through crises.

Senior company officers and basic staff are identical in their need to support their families, so their primary need is a generous salary. But they have even more expectations for career advancement and education. High level staff want to have a sense of belonging, have a say inside the company, be trusted and be valued.

For mid-level managers, including hotel managers, the Confucian school is the most appropriate management philosophy. The famous Confucianists, like Zhuge Liang and Wang Yangming, were, like most of the imperial court councillors, followers of the Confucian school. Zhuge Liang famously said, "Spare no effort until your dying day."

The dedication and loyalty of the Confucianists stands out vividly.

Key words for mid-level managers are: compassion, loyalty, propriety, wisdom and integrity. Wang Yangming pushed Confucian thought to a higher plane, advocating a philosophy of action, integrating theory and practice. One must not just talk about military drills like an armchair strategist. Mid-level managers emphasize thinking about tactics: How do we run this hotel? How do we manage our teams? How do we defeat our competitors? Strategic questions require profound understanding to refine tactical objectives and actions, as mentioned in the Confucian classic and one of the Four Books, *The Golden Mean*: "Therefore, the superior man honours his virtuous nature, and maintains constant inquiry and study, seeking to carry it out to its breadth and greatness."

We need a large number of mid-level managers who can 'unify knowledge and action.'

The person in charge of the headquarters platform, the C-grade high level officers, the person in charge of brands are what we categorize as high-level officers. The management philosophy for high-level officers draws upon the Taoist school to look at problems from a strategic perspective, and not just stay on the tactical level. We must nurture outstanding leaders, not mere implementers, much less so-called professional managers – the sort of high-level employee who only pays attention to performance targets, duties and bonuses.

I have led this company for ten years but in the next ten years the company's scale will not be achieved by simple replication, and the pace of growth will not be attained by following convention. I cannot deal with the formidable issues facing the company, and the level of complexity, alone. These tasks will need a group of leaders – this is what I am referring to when I say, there is no leader among a host of dragons. We need innovators, leaders and managers with a master of the house spirit.

For leaders the first rule is the golden mean. The Taoists say: "Ruling a great nation is like cooking a small fish," that is, not too salty, not too bland, not too old, or too tender, prepared just right, following the golden mean. Like the ancient Taoist parable of the intuitive butchering of an ox, which teaches us to seek the key issues of a problem, take advantage of an opportunity and execute actions skilfully.

The second rule for leaders is, pay attention to being truthful, honest, and genuine. As the ancient Chinese text, the *Zhuangzi* suggests, "The sage seeks out the beauties of Heaven and Earth and masters the principles of the ten thousand things." and "Therefore the sage patterns himself on Heaven, prizes the Truth, and does not allow himself to be cramped by the vulgar." Being pretentious, affected and formalistic will only serve to waste our energy and interfere with wisdom. Only by returning to one's true nature, can we grasp the essence of an issue from the mass of chaotic information.

Leaders govern the heart not issues. "In ancient times the Yellow Emperor ruled the world by making the hearts of people one." Our high-level managers must find ways to make everyone to be of one mind. Master Zhuang taught us: "In an age of Perfect Virtue, the worthy are not honoured; the talented are not employed. Rulers are like the high branches of a tree; the people, like the deer of the fields." Ruling a country well does not only depend on a handful of wise and capable ministers. There are many examples throughout the history of China of wise and capable ministers being corrupt and running amok, weakening the dynasty and devastating the nation.

Leaders must be impartial. "Forget things, forget Heaven, and be called a forgetter of self. The man who has forgotten self may be said to have entered Heaven," according to Master Zhuang. "The Perfect Man has no self; the Holy Man has no merit; the Sage has no fame." Impartiality is essential to being true; impartiality is essential to the golden mean; impartiality is a prerequisite to winning hearts.

When leaders face complex problems, chaotic situations and mountains of work, they must be able to stand aloof. The proverbial, lift weights as if they were light, and be able to pick things up and put them down. Like the sage who "leans on the Sun and Moon, tucks the universe under his arm, merges himself with things," and "wanders beyond the dust and grime." "When the Sun comes up, I work; when the Sun goes down, I rest. I wander free and easy between Heaven and Earth, and my mind has found all that it could wish for." Zhuangzi spoke of this realm and we should reflect upon it. That kind of freedom, that free and unfettered transcendence is not just something that is required for work, it is even more appropriate for attitude to life and as a personal philosophy.

Income of management staff is connected to an enterprise's efficiency and scale of operations. Grassroot-level staff receive a stable income through lean management of the hotel; mid-level staff manage the scale of operations to increase their income; at the highest level increasing the scale of the entire operation and raising efficiency is their path to increased income. There is little difference between shares and cash in our remuneration packages, but at the higher levels the proportion of options is higher, and if the company grows, the individuals share value grows; when the company does well, their share will increase in value.

I have identified ten issues facing managers. Of course, these issues can constantly change with the times.

1. Team coordination. The regional offices and the platform offices complain about and find fault with each other: they don't acknowledge, coordinate or cooperate with each other.
2. Lack of maturity. Our staff cannot keep up with the company's development, they can't cope with their tasks – neither their state of mind, their capabilities nor their ability to lead. Occasionally they throw tantrums and create small hurdles for others. This is a lack of maturity.
3. Factionalism. The attitude is: My team, mine. My department, my region, and no one shall touch us, no

one shall offend against us. Shield your fiefdom and present a united front.

4. Departmental selfishness. Self-centred in thinking and action and never consider the big picture, or other departments and partners.
5. Bureaucratism. Holding a small position with the puffed-up bearing of a high official. Assumes bureaucratic airs and follows the rules inflexibly. Doesn't look for solutions to problems, rather seeks excuses to dodge problems; does not reflect upon their own problems, rather will skilfully pass the buck.
6. Refuse to change. Refuse to transfer to another hotel, refuse to accept price rises, refuse to work with new brands. Some have a conditioned reflex against any kind of change.
7. Inadequate leadership. Not able to manage people, not able to manage subordinates and team members. Unable to lead a team to work together on a project, instead personally does everything large and small. Lacks charisma and leadership skills.
8. Inadequate ability to learn. Unable to learn from mistakes and successes. Unable to learn from others, even less inclined to learn from rivals. Only capable of doing one particular task, but becomes disoriented when placed in another field.
9. Lack of dedication. Looks at working for H World as merely a job, not a career. Sees work at H World only in terms of a job and pay, not the development and the interests of the company. These colleagues must understand that even if what they do is only a vocation, to do it well, dedication is a must.
10. Lack of loyalty. Several years ago, the fashionable cachet 'professional managers' included a lot of this kind of person. They go wherever the salary is highest or the post is most impressive. This kind of person cannot be counted on when a problem is encountered.

Our requirements for staff are simple, just two words, 'red' and 'expert,' to use a political cliché. Staff have to be both red and expert.

Red covers four aspects: loyal to the company, responsible, devoted, deeply love the company.

Expert also has four aspects: efficient, team leadership, able to learn, innovative.

When selecting the best candidates for promotion using the red and expert criteria, it can be summarized by integrity and talent. A more comprehensive explanation is, demanding a triathlon of virtue, knowledge and stamina. Virtue, which refers to a system of values, is red. Knowledge, which relates to ability, is about being an expert. Stamina comes from fitness, health and energetic exuberance.

I have a metaphor to explain the selection process.

Farmers use a basket to rinse their rice; a basket of woven bamboo strips with very fine seams is used in rivers to rinse the rice. In the first pass, the basket is put into the water allowing the empty husks to float up to the surface and drift away with the bran. Empty husks and bran are the incompetent and useless people who we could definitely never use. The fine seams of the basket allow tiny grains of rice to slip through in the second phase, which are the people lacking ability. In the last phase, which is the hardest and most time consuming, stones, fragments and mud are scraped out. Sometimes these impurities are not easy to see clearly, like small white stones mixed in with the rice. That corresponds with people whose values do not match our company's.

When we are choosing candidates, we must discard people whose abilities are deficient or have incompatible values. It is difficult to cull people with incompatible values because they are difficult to discern.

People are usually motivated in two ways: rewards and fear.

When you do well, society, parents, teachers and companies provide a variety of benefits, such as commendations, affirmation, awards, promotions and money. This is what reward means, encouraging the determination of someone to continue to do more of what an organization or a society wants, to do more good deeds, and encourage others to do the same.

The most fundamental fear is the fear of death. Next comes fear for safety, fear of criticism, fear of being under pressure, fear of failure and so forth. All kinds of fear have the same effect of compelling people to do the job well.

I advocate that companies should use both rewards and punishments. Our company offers many rewards such as cash, stock, options, promotions, training and honours.

What sort of things should be punished? First of all, nonfeasance, just wasting time, punching the time clock as a token member of the team. Some managers know of a problem but don't try to solve it because that would entail trouble and conflicts. Next comes people who don't make an effort, are incompetent, or immoral. These people must be punished.

If people like this occupy a position they don't deserve, the company will become muddled, feeble, lack a sense of honour and lose its vital force.

However, we must be lenient toward mistakes or failures resulting from innovation. Otherwise no one will dare to do anything. Trying to do something, but not doing it well is making a mistake. We should be tolerant when people make mistakes in the course of doing their work and help them so they can learn lessons from the mistake. Innovation revolves around trying things out, experimentation that can lead to mistakes and result in failure. Failures in the course of innovating are a cost that organizations must bear to be able to achieve breakthroughs.

16 August, 2014

THE BIGGEST CHALLENGE WE ARE FACING

The principle underlying the design of H World's organizational structure is a solid foundation while being flexible. The foundation of frontline operations and our hotels must be sturdy and stable, while the headquarters must respond rapidly and adapt to change.

The H World group can be categorized under four functional modules: the platform, investment, new brands, hotel retail management. The different modules determine the organizational structures, salary structures, and appraisal and reward mechanisms.

Organizational principles: three acts of obedience and three priorities. Individuals obey the organization, small issues obey the general situation, lower levels obey higher levels. The team's interests have priority over an individual's, the interests of the whole company have priority over departments, long-term interests have priority over short-term interests.

"A nation's external rise is in fact an extension of its internal strength." (This is according to the Chinese political commentator Zheng Yongnian who was quoted in the 2006 documentary *The Rise of Great Nations*) Not only are nations like this, companies and families are too.

Therefore, H World's biggest challenge lies within us, in whether or not we are capable of building a great, world-class organization, and whether we are capable of balancing good management and leadership, quality of our products and speed of development, our standards and innovation. Our competitors are like surveyor's poles to arouse us to surpass. The accumulation of our power and strength is the key to our success, and this is the biggest challenge we are facing.

16 August, 2014

H WORLD'S FUTURE MANAGEMENT: COMMON SENSE MANAGEMENT

I have previously pointed out that H World's challenge is to build a great organization. We open six or seven hundred new hotels a year, which in international terms is the equivalent of a small hotel chain. How do we manage so many hotels? I once feared there would not be enough talent, so I paid a lot of attention to nurturing talent. Now I feel we don't need to depend on people. When the mechanisms are well-designed, we can deploy common sense management.

Our current organizational structure is: headquarters, regional, city and hotel. What would happen if we do away with the middle two levels of management and give retail outlets more autonomy and bigger incentives? Communication is very convenient nowadays. We know that information deteriorates as it is transmitted from one level to the next and becomes distorted, so will it be possible to flatten out the organization? If this can be achieved, nurturing talent will not be an issue. For retail outlets to use common sense management, the system has to be foolproof so that it can be simply switched on and be ready for use. For example, when we purchase rice and vegetables, the system will have statistics about the price and channels to make the purchases.

This is something like contemporary US military doctrine making officers and soldiers the same by using information systems, communications and big data to directly connect with all available resources in the rear, without the need for intermediaries. The headquarters can rely on common sense communication with the people on the ground. It just doesn't matter, for example, if two teeth or four are exposed when smiling at a guest, a smile is all that's needed. And even if there's no smiling, just be friendly to guests, because they can feel if they're being treated amicably. Shaking hands and taking luggage are not important, but making the guest feel welcome is important, and that's common sense. We only employ people who are friendly and polite to guests and diligent; we won't employ people who are sneaky, secretive and lazy. A person's character is easy to discern in a retail outlet with only a dozen employees.

Naturally, it's an enormous challenge to put this model into practice. But if it succeeds, it will be the start of a new era. In the past, important documents were transmitted downwards, layer by layer, but is there any need for that now? If we can actually use big data plus common sense, chain business will be rock steady.

16 August, 2014

THE FUTURE OF HOTELS

In the age of material shortages, people wanted to experience the extravagance of famous brands, gold and precious stones, and sumptuous houses; but these days people are looking inwards.

In the past, hotels at the basic level provided standard reliable lodgings; the more expensive ones provided a kind of luxurious lifestyle. Hotels in the future will continue in this manner, as all levels of hotels must satisfy the basic need of travellers for 'a reliable place to relax when they're on the road,' though the high end must now reflect the most advanced lifestyle.

As I see it, hotels of the future must be as secure as one's own home and calming, but also offer a lifestyle that cannot be experienced at home.

1. ARCHITECTURE AND APPEARANCE

In the past, only high end and luxury hotels had the ability to dazzle, but no longer, as more and more hotels, including mid-level and budget hotels, deploy flamboyant external appearances. As in developed countries, it is very difficult to judge a man's status and position by his clothes.

Actually, both the external architectural features, or interior decoration of rooms, are within the realm of art and the application of art. A good hotel design is a work of art in itself.

Art is the abstract synthesis of an era and a region's zeitgeist, a higher-level ideology. Integrated into a hotel, art can embody a hotel's aesthetic mood and preference of its values. Art is not made of a simple slapping together of ingredients – just as 'art hotels' are putting the cart before the horse. The primary function of hotels is lodging, not to house an art museum. Art works should be harmonious with, and naturally blend in with, the hotel, not be an ostentatious attention-grabbing display. Guests come first; the art is just a backdrop.

2. PUBLIC SPACES

In the past the open space in the majority of hotels tended toward grandiosity. It is an innovation when the first proponent does it, but when all hotels imitate or plagiarize the concept, it becomes a tired cliché, but a cliché that represents a huge waste of construction costs and space.

And so, hotels mostly have spacious and imposing lobbies with opulent crystal chandeliers. And no effort is spared to achieve the interior design effect. A standard high-class hotel in China usually has three or four restaurants (a breakfast room, an all-day restaurant, a Chinese restaurant, a Western restaurant, and so on), several conference rooms, a banquet hall, a gym, a sauna, a SPA, a swimming pool, a beauty salon, a shop, a bar and a business centre. The materials utilized are also the most ostentatious possible, with the generous use of marble, crystal lighting fixtures, solid wood furniture, the more expensive and high-class the better, and using imported rather than local materials. Two words encapsulate this phenomenon: pompous and grandiose.

Public spaces in hotels of the future will also be 'high-end, elegant and classy' but with a difference. First, there will be ample public spaces, but do they still need to use cathedral-like high ceilings and extravagant use of space to communicate the desired effect? In the Aman Tokyo, which is located in one of the most expensive districts in the world, a mind-boggling one thousand square meters, nine meters deep cuboid was excavated. The reception in the lobby has devolved to the smallest possible front desk, as most of the work, such as selecting rooms and making payments, can be accomplished on mobile terminals. The front desk is principally for checking of ID and servicing guests who are unfamiliar with the use of such terminals. As the front desk devolves to the equivalent of a human appendix, socializing, aesthetics and leisure activities can be moved to the front desk area. Amenities like the bar, a tearoom and comfortable outdoor furniture, can create a socializing space to facilitate meetings with friends who are also staying in the hotel, or to chat with other guests, or just to lose yourself in thought.

Sculptures, plants, furniture design and artistic ornaments play an important role in making public hotel spaces beautiful, sophisticated and stylish, without the need for the extravagant display of expensive materials. Mama Shelter is the ultimate in social interaction; Accor's MGallery uses designer furniture to make the public space on the ground floor feel like the living room of a luxury home; in contrast, the Oasia Hotel Downtown in Singapore deploys a large quantity of plants and lawns to convey the feeling of an oasis in the air; one Ace hotel lobby is like an internet bar, with guests crowded together surfing the internet drinking coffee, greeting people they know or don't know, just like a giant living room. Ji hotel lobbies are not large but sculptures, bookshelves, 'greeting pine trees' create a comfortable space with a hint of zen, a literary flavour and an artistic atmosphere, without resorting to overstatement.

3. SMALL GUEST ROOMS

The ideal guest room is refined and convenient, but not too large. Public spaces can be big, exteriors can be stylish, but guest rooms don't need to be, and ought not be too big.

Traditionally, bedrooms in China cannot be too big. The emperor's bedroom in the Qing dynasty imperial palace was tiny, which was said to agglomerate the vital chi energy. Excessively large bedrooms feel like a cold empty void, and for people traveling on business it's not a pleasant feeling to return to a desolate, empty hotel room.

Citizen M hotels are the ultimate in small rooms, with an average area of about 15 square meters with two metre by two metre beds. Large showers and toilets convey the appearance of luxury, together with designing the closet and the bar (or tea table) to be comfortable. Small guest rooms can also fully utilize space in a large metropolis with astronomical property values by cutting down the room size, while raising the quality to price ratio. And raising the overall aesthetics of spaces within the hotel can make up for other deficiencies and prevent this kind of hotel appearing ugly and sullen.

The traditional luxury hotel standard for rooms is outdated. The innovation age has new demands on aesthetics and function.

4. ART AND CULTURE

Cultural items are relatively abstract. The most important thing is to be attentive to the overall layout design, and not merely follow frosty and hoary old processes and rules. Some hotels, for example, have changed the atmosphere of their front desks to resemble coffee shops or tea houses, to reflect the designer's intention of providing a sense of cultured atmosphere for guests.

In addition to getting a good night's sleep in a hotel, people also need to spend a bit of time in a tranquil environment. Experiencing a slice of local culture, having a venue for some socializing, and encountering a certain amount of art are all added bonuses.

In hotels of the future, extravagant building materials and ostentatious public spaces will no longer be able to serve the purpose of manifesting modern aesthetics and lifestyles. Instead, that will be achieved on a spiritual level, with art and culture.

5. HIGH TECH

Information technology, especially mobile internet technology has made it easy, and indeed essential, for high tech to be taken up by hotels. Everyone who checks into a hotel room simply must connect to Wi-Fi to be connected with the world, and feel that family, friends and colleagues are close at hand. The Peninsula Group has stunning automation systems that operate the lighting, the curtains, the air conditioning, room service, the internet, the wakeup alarms and the TV, all from a single control panel. Citizen M, however, has done a better job with a touchpad that controls all the systems, and conveniently remembers your settings for the next visit to any hotel in the chain. That's considerate.

Technology can change many things. Once upon a time, the most complex task for hotels was guest registration at the front desk. Checking travel documents, signing credit card guarantees and the like do not really need human intervention. Why not select a room online with a mobile phone? A gold card member could choose the best room. Payment methods can also be done with a mobile phone, and machine facial verification of travel documents is possibly more accurate than manual checking. We are developing all of these technologies and have begun to deploy some. We are about to introduce unmanned front desks. Currently our technology leads the industry. H World has been called a 'technology' company, which I feel is apt.

All this automation will most likely flatten out our organizational structure. Five years ago, it was impossible to envisage. Five years from now, when automation and robotic technologies reach a certain level, it will all be possible. In the next five years, the division of labor between man and technology will be reorganized, and that will be an earth-shattering change for large chains. The service motto at Ritz-Carlton is, "We are Ladies and Gentlemen serving Ladies and Gentlemen." Is this traditional service credo suitable for all? People have different expectations of service, with some guests only concerned about price, while others expect to be treated with respect, and some are deeply impressed when someone brings towels and soap or cups of tea and leads the guest to the room. Some people just do not want to be disturbed. I am a high-end hotel guest who wants privacy and is not in the habit of socializing. I do not want to engage in chit-chat with some bell boy or room maid who I don't know, have him deliver my luggage to the room and then be obliged to give them a tip. Perhaps I have just been to a joyous event and want to savour the feeling a bit longer; or perhaps I have just experienced a tragedy and need to be sad alone for a moment; perhaps I'm exhausted from a flight and need a nap or just want to crash in the room. I should not have to change my mood for other people.

With the automated service of the future, or even a robotic hotel, the needs of a customer like me can be satisfied.

6. BIG DATA

The hotel industry is dealing with changing consumer needs on the one hand, and increasing labor costs on the other. Robots will do a better job than people because they are supported by big data. They can distinguish tone of voice and facial expressions and have a more reliable memory, and as a result will completely change the quality and methods of hotel service.

Technology does not have to be icy-cold, it can actually enhance human connection. Using WeChat, for example, the frequency of meetings with my friends can be reduced, but the quality of the interactions becomes so much more satisfying. The future of hotels is heading in a similar direction.

Our idea for the future is to refine the concept of 'sleep' by researching beds, music, incense, pillows, lighting, as well as oxygen levels, moisture content and temperature of the air in rooms, and using virtual reality and all sorts of tools to aid sleep. Our concept is to do a great job in these intrinsic tasks of a hotel.

In the past, sales required a salesman to make a personal visit, but this is no longer necessary. Now when I open a new hotel, it only takes sufficient data for me to be able to send news to let people know I've opened a new Ji Hotel, and if they've some spare time, come on over, and if you are a loyalty club member there's a discount waiting for you. We can also consider data exchanges – for example, exchange data with office buildings operators nearby to engage in more targeted advertising. There will be no need at all for sales staff, which means we can save a huge amount of labor expenses.

What, then, will people actually do? Well people will do what machines or data can't, like crafts that embody the unique quality of people. If the front desk doesn't need people to help you register, a friendly member of staff can brew you a cup of coffee. After guests have checked in, they will remember there's a very friendly person at the front desk who brewed a delicious cup of coffee. This sort of experience leaves a deep impression on people.

14 February, 2017

DEVIL IN THE DETAILS: THE HANTING STORY OF BUCKWHEAT PILLOWS, BATHROOMS AND BROADBAND

1. THE HANTING STORY: BUCKWHEAT PILLOWS

Hanting was the first budget hotel in the industry to use buckwheat pillows, which are beneficial for cervical spine health. The story behind this pillow's origin is also quite interesting.

Back in the Ctrip days, because the General Manager of the Beijing office, Wang Shengli, had a good relationship with Sunworld Dynasty Hotel, I often stayed there during business trips. It was convenient to get around and the atrium was particularly beautiful. I also found out that I slept like a baby at their hotel, feeling more refreshed the next day. I thought, it couldn't be because of the atrium, could it? So I carefully examined the room layout, finally discovering that their pillows were very special.

The standard king room setup included a long buckwheat pillow, which fit the cervical spine very well when sleeping on it. These pillows could also change shape and their heights could be adjusted. I had neck issues, and after sleeping on those soft, thick pillows common in other motels, I often found my neck experiencing discomfort the next day. It turned out that my reason for a good night's sleep at Sunworld was the pillow!

When I was checking out the next day, I wanted to take the pillow with me. My first thought was to call Wang Shengli to get the hotel to give me a new pillow. I had to rush for a flight, so I woke up particularly early. It would have been awkward for me to call him so early in the morning to get a pillow for me, so I shamelessly lugged a pillow downstairs to reception to pay my bill.

At the counter, I took the initiative to 'confess' that I was taking a pillow home with me. The guy at the front desk looked at me like I was the first person to make such a request, saying he had to make a call to confirm its price. This took ages, and I became really anxious, afraid that I would miss my flight. The matter was finally settled, with them saying that it would cost me 200 RMB – it was quite expensive. But I did not have time to hesitate, so I paid and rushed to the airport.

After sleeping with that pillow at home, my neck indeed felt much better, and I rarely experienced stiff necks again. Since then, I have always used buckwheat pillows.

When I started Hanting, I once again delved into hotel product research, considering that many of our guests frequently use computers and likely have cervical spine issues. It was then that I recalled that buckwheat pillow and asked the procurement department to inquire about its price. It turned out to be not very expensive, so I decided to introduce it to Hanting. Later, a supplier gave us a suggestion: one side could be buckwheat, and the other side could use a regular pillow filling. This would lower the cost while also giving guests an additional choice. We all thought this was a great idea. And so, one of Hanting's unique features – the dual-sided buckwheat pillow – was born.

Later, other budget hotel chains also followed Hanting's lead, and started using buckwheat pillows. I think this is a good thing; when something nice is shared with more people, the world gains a little more comfort and happiness.

2. THE HANTING STORY: BATHROOMS

The quality of life of a country, a region, a city, an organization, or a family, can be ascertained from its bathrooms. This observation has proven true time and again.

Visiting a company for the first time, to gauge its management quality, and its commitment to product requirements, one needs to use its restroom. Its renovation standards will tell you all about this company's capability. Its cleanliness speaks to its management capability. Of course, this is just a simple method and cannot be used for formal corporate investigations of due diligence.

A hotel's standard is directly correlated with its restrooms. Many high-end hotels will even have attendants specially stationed in their public restrooms to 'service' you. Even their hand towels will surpass those commonly used at home.

With this in mind, when designing Hanting's products, I was determined to ensure that our restrooms were top-notch.

After visiting numerous hotels, I noticed that in all modern, upscale hotels, restrooms were designed to be open and transparent, extensively using glass and stainless steel. It was as if the restroom was a transparent aesthetic display box, with functionality taking a backseat.

The advantage of transparency is that it makes the room appear more spacious, while the use of glass and stainless steel gives it a modern and upscale aesthetic. Since budget hotel rooms are inherently small, this open design seems perfectly suited for our space-conscious, 'miserly' budget hotel. Glass and stainless steel definitely look great, but they also increase costs, so I had to find ways to offset expenses elsewhere.

During a stay at a Holiday Inn Express near Hong Kong (PRC) Times Square, I discovered a brilliantly efficient restroom door design: a single door served both as the entrance to the restroom and as the shower door. It saved the cost of an extra door, while maintaining privacy. Apparently this design was also patented. Inspired by this concept,

I designed the idea of a shared door for the shower and toilet area, meanwhile incorporating separate wet/dry sections typically found in high-end hotels. We also patented this design.

To further reduce costs, I pored through a vast number of design books hoping to find solutions. While flipping through a book on boutique European apartment designs, I came across a modern micro-apartment in central Paris where the restroom had no wall separation at all. Its sink was placed right next to the bed, which initially shocked me, but then I got it!

As a result, the wall partition was eliminated in Hanting's restroom design and was integrated with the guest room that looked aesthetic and open. To address moisture and odor problems, we upgraded the ventilation system – this ensured that the open restroom would not affect room quality.

When this bathroom design first launched, it faced a great deal of skepticism, mainly with privacy concerns. But they had not thought through it carefully, or even personally experienced it – privacy would not be an issue at all.

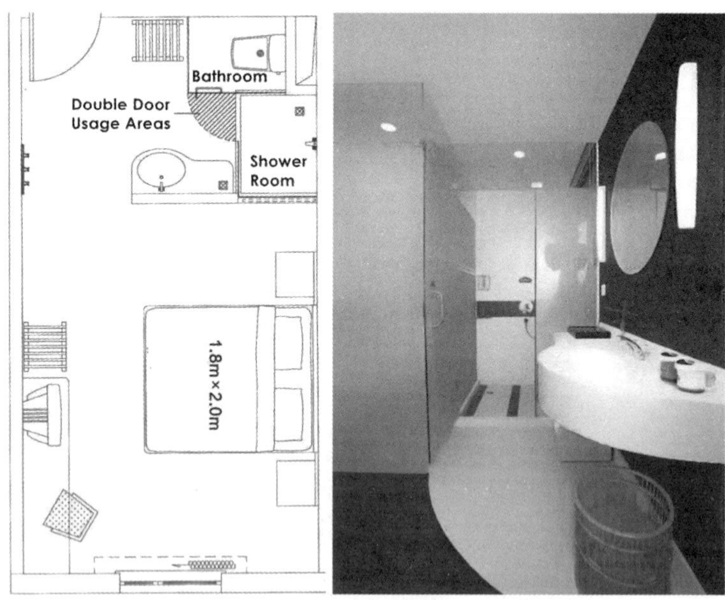

Shower and toilet single-door design

If a guest is staying alone, there will not be privacy issues. If that guest has visitors, the toilet is an isolated space with a door (frosted glass), and nothing can be seen either. Besides, we do not encourage visitors in the room. Hanting has specially-designated lounge areas for meetings that provide free coffee and other beverages (this is a story to be written about later).

If two guests are staying, they are often of the opposite sex. Even if there are privacy concerns, the person using the toilet cannot see the person showering when the shower door is closed. When the person done showering exits, the toilet door is also closed at that time. There are no privacy issues at all. If a person is showering, and the other one is in the room watching TV or using the internet, there are no worries about that either – a non-transparent curtain can be pulled over the glass pane between the bed and shower to prevent awkward mishaps. According to my observations, once the shower is being used, the steam itself turns the showering person into a hazy figure – you cannot see anything. To be honest, if two people are already staying in the same room, why is privacy even going to be an issue?

We can proudly say that Hanting's bathrooms are surely one of the most distinctive in the budget hotel industry (even though they have been imitated by others), and as close as they can get to high-end hotel bathrooms. We will continue to refine and enhance this aspect, to stay true to Hanting's core product philosophy of "Sleep Well, Shower Well, Work Well," to rival high-end hotels (3 and 4-star hotels) in these three areas.

3. THE HANTING STORY: BROADBAND

The broadband service in the entire budget hotel industry can be traced back to the time when I founded my first budget hotel. At that time, I was working alone in Beijing on integration efforts, leaving a large team behind in Shanghai, and mainly communicated via email. The hotel I stayed in had broadband access, but it was chargeable and cost a pretty penny.

During a management meeting, the issue of telephone expenses when analysing various room costs came up. At that time, this 120-room budget hotel had a monthly intracity telephone bill of around 5,000 RMB, but it was free for guests to use. The internet access fee was also around 5,000 RMB, which was chargeable for guests. I think it was 20 RMB per day. But the revenue collected was minimal and could not cover costs. Someone suggested cutting the broadband to reduce losses.

Since I had transitioned from IT to the hotel industry, I was particularly sensitive to new technology trends, especially IT-related ones. I not only relied on broadband for work, I also believed that more and more people would start using broadband in the future. The customer base for China's budget hotels was different from that of foreign hotels; they were primarily business travellers, not tourists.

So, I ran the numbers for them at that time. If we started charging for local calls, it could offset the 5,000 RMB monthly telephone cost. Offering free internet would increase guest satisfaction and repeat stays, lowering sales costs and increasing revenue. At the time, many people did not understand this logic, believing that there was an insignificant number of guests using the internet, and most of them used the hotel phone for intracity phone calls. But at my insistence, we still rolled out free broadband across the entire chain.

Responses from guests were natural, and many of them stayed with us precisely because of the free internet. We also received countless compliments.

Unexpectedly, our implementation set an industry standard. I have not heard of any budget hotel chain that does not offer free broadband.

In the early days of Hanting, I specifically observed broadband usage in international hotels during my research. Some hotel chains, like Marriott, offered free internet, but most still charged for it. The only exception I found was a hotel near Los Angeles Airport that provided free wireless broadband, but the signal was highly unstable.

When Hanting designed our own broadband services, we took it a step further.

First, we installed dual network ports in guest rooms – one at the desk, one by the bed. The table-side port is designed for easy laptop access, positioned above the table on the wall. We also used international power sockets, with an uninterrupted power supply, for guests visiting from outside the mainland to charge their laptops even when they left the room. The idea for a bedside broadband port also came from personal experience. One night, while staying at our own hotel in Beijing, I needed to reply to emails, but my feet were cold. I wanted to work from bed, but the network cable was not long enough. I had to request a longer one from the front desk. So I thought of a way to make it more convenient for 'lazy' guests like me – installing a broadband port near the bed. Hanting was the first – and still the only – budget hotel chain to implement this feature across their entire chain.

Second was providing wireless broadband coverage in public areas. To make it convenient for guests to hold meetings in the lobby and browse the internet in lounges or cafés, we installed wireless broadband throughout these public spaces. Initially, few people used it, so we placed wireless broadband signage in noticeable areas. Now, more and more guests rely on it. Seeing guests in the lobby enjoying coffee while working online makes me especially happy.

We also provided computers with broadband access in the lobby. Guests could browse the web, check emails and even print important documents. This was a great convenience for business travellers who did not carry laptops on their trips. If you are staying at Hanting on a business trip, there is zero need for you to lug a bulky laptop with you.

Hanting's internet service far surpasses that of most star-rated hotels. And prices aside, we are confident that our convenience and speed can compete with them. We currently use fiber-optic connections, ensuring no bandwidth bottlenecks.

I have not only had the unfortunate experiences of having to buy an internet card from the business center at 11 p.m. while staying at top luxury hotels, but have also had to pay for Wi-Fi in the lobby at a world-class hotel lobby. I find it hard to understand why high-end and luxury hotels still charge for broadband. I hope they learn from the strengths of budget hotels and put themselves more often in consumers' shoes. Non-guests have free access to lavish restrooms in luxury hotels. Why not do the same for the relatively low-cost broadband service?

I once had an even crazier idea: eliminating guest room telephones. The logic was simple – most people, including migrant workers, now own mobile phones. Local calls are also incredibly cheap, even more so for the more convenient cheaper text messages. Most people use their phones to stay connected to the outside world, while hotel phone charges have long had a notorious reputation for being expensive. Think about it: How often do you use a hotel room's telephone? Personally, I never do.

That is why I always say: A hotel can operate without a telephone, but it cannot function without broadband.

If you want to enjoy the best internet experience at a hotel, please come to Hanting!

From buckwheat pillows, bathrooms and broadband to lobbies, Hanting has amply deliberated the core needs of our guests and adhered to the principles of openness, freedom, comfort and complimentary services – giving guests a sense of being at home and in their personal studies. Hanting's design philosophy is simple: Every penny spent must add value for guests. Every inch of space must produce efficiency (or aid the production in efficiency).

4 February, 2009

MINIMUM EFFORT FOR THE BEST MOVEMENT

Compensation refers to a physiological behavior in which other parts of the body assist in completing a required task when a certain function is lacking. For example, when we do push-ups, if our arm strength is lacking, we will usually rely on moving our buttocks up and down or exerting our hips and back to help complete the task. When I first started practising Pilates, my core strength was weak and I often had to rely on my shoulders and neck to compensate. My coach, CK, told me, "If you're exerting too much effort to complete a movement, it must be because the other parts of your body are compensating." Then he calmly said, "Use minimum effort to achieve the best movement."

CK's full name is Kevin Chen. He comes from a dance background and was one of the earliest people to introduce Pilates to China. He opened a few Pilates studios out of sheer passion and has a profound understanding of Pilates. I have switched between several instructors, both male and female, but never quite found the right fit. Training with CK though, is an activity of pure enjoyment – like a form of meditation in motion that has greatly benefitted my mind and body. I would like to share this phrase of "using minimum effort to achieve the best movement" with you today.

H World's hotels pepper the country, having expanded further into lower-tier markets in recent years. China is vast, and there are many places I have not visited. Which is why conducting surveys on frontline and lower-tier markets has become one of our working methods. Each year, I undertake about six long-distance inspection trips, each lasting around five days, covering two to three prefecture-level cities daily. Firstly, it is to gain a firsthand understanding of lower-tier markets – to experience their economy, culture and environment, and to assess the industry landscape and competitors. More importantly, to understand the real conditions of our own hotels on the ground. Secondly, it is to interact with local teams personally, engaging them in face-to-face discussions, including direction, strategy, tactics and culture. This serves as both encouragement and accountability for the team. Thirdly, it is to liaise with franchisees, including meeting local partners, identifying and resolving issues, and understanding their businesses and daily lives.

From these recent visits, I have experienced the dedication and professionalism of regional and provincial managers. However, these efforts should not be overexerted. Just like when we exercise our bodies, if we force it all the time, our other body parts will compensate, resulting in incorrect movement.

Let me first talk about some 'overexertion' behaviours observed during my inspections:

Behaviour 1: As soon as employees see a superior arrive, they instantly drop everything they are doing, line up to greet them, and even start sweeping and mopping the floors on the spot.

Behaviour 2: Local managers really want to leave their superiors with a good impression, so they meticulously arrange visits to well-performing hotels while glossing over the underperforming ones or even skipping them entirely. Even invited franchisees only have good things to say about H World. Those with differing opinions or complaints are left out.

Behaviour 3: Local managers often over-service their superiors, helping them carry their bags, serving their food and pouring their drinks. Nicely put, this is them showing thoughtful care for their bosses. Bluntly said, it is blatant flattery and bootlicking. Our focus should not be catering to leadership, but on employees, franchisees and other key matters. If one's thoughts revolve around one's boss, one would have no room to spare a thought on anything else.

Behaviour 4: Meetings are long-winded and overly verbose. They start with a meaningless preamble and end with garrulous drivel. Discussions should be direct, brief and to the point. Flowery language and excessive embellishment indicate a lack of confidence. Concise speech reflects clear thinking.

H World's corporate culture strives for simplicity and directness – formalism has no place here! I am only left with a bad impression when I see such behaviour. I will doubt if actual work is being done during their day-to-day schedules, only capable of meeting deadlines at the last minute. Employees will also develop a negative impression of the company, feeling that its culture is insincere. If leadership visits are met with deception, how can employees be truly instilled with loyalty and dedication to the hotel and industry? Many competitors have been brought down by such unhealthy cultures, which is why we must remain vigilant.

For lower-tier market inspections, I recommend the following:

1. Plan routes logically to gain a comprehensive understanding of each city's situation throughout the journey.
2. Visit the top local competitors, whether they are chain hotels or local independent hotels.
3. Pay attention to both the best-performing and the worst-performing hotels. We must scrutinize our best and worst storefronts, then think about improving the worst, and using the best as case studies for best practices.
4. For meals, look for local specialty cuisine. Keep lunch simple, but evenings can be more casual for team bonding and franchisee engagement.

Four things to avoid:

1. No advance notice to hotels. The everyday state should be how it is – no need to make any unnecessary moves.
2. No flattery or fawning. That includes no toasting, serving food, carrying bags for superiors, among other acts. Because coworkers will follow suit and mimic your antics in a bid to compete.
3. No superficial lip service. No 'grand but empty' gestures, and do not stress or fatigue yourself and your team. Inspections should not disrupt normal operations. Use the least effort to be the best version of yourself.
4. No accepting perks from franchisees or local teams. All accommodation and meals should be properly paid for.

H World's culture is grounded in simplicity, sincerity and authenticity. Simplicity is the first of our core values. Its most fundamental aspect is to present reality as it is – only then can we progress toward pursuing higher truths, discern facts and distinguish between right and wrong. At the same time, the essentiality of lower-tier market inspections is to see the naked truth, then work together to improve and develop corresponding strategies. The team should demonstrate their real efforts, without embellishment, without a need to feel unnecessary tension – only a calm and steady approach is sustainable.

The best movement is always achieved with the least effort. A movement made with maximum effort is definitely not good or at least will not last long. Because this movement could be compensated for, there may be damage that you are not aware of. The course of nature is effortless; all in the natural world is harmonious, effortless and uncontrived. Therefore, it is perfect. So the best movements are effortless; good best management behaviour is simple and natural. Great achievements are built on ordinary consistent efforts; all excellence appears to be effortless and ordinary.

"Use minimum effort to achieve the best movement." I hope this becomes one of the guiding principles in everyone's daily work and a part of H World's culture.

15 January, 2024

LIFE IS ART

Life is art. We must transform our lives into the most unique, most important, most valuable, most elegant work of creation.

THE BEAUTY OF SIMPLICITY

At school when I was young, whether it was because the teachers were too busy to be bothered or it had simply always been the case, I noticed that solutions to examination questions were always simple and elegant. If you struggled to produce a complex result you were bound to be wrong. After doing a large number of maths problems I gradually came to the realization that there is beauty in mathematics. Not simply the beauty of logic, but formulas are also extremely beautiful. In an analytic geometry class, a teacher set a question to see who could solve it the fastest. Like all such problems it would take a very long time to solve. But I glanced at the question and blurted out the answer. The teacher and my classmates were astonished and asked how I did it. I explained that my intuition was that only one kind of formula could produce an accurate result, so I tried it and it worked.

That is what I mean by the beauty of formulas. From mathematics to physics and on to the laws of the natural world, all embody the beauty of formulas. An interesting example is the forces of attraction, and these two well-known formulae.

The equation for universal gravitation: $F=G\frac{m_1 m_2}{r_2}$, where F is the force of attraction between the two bodies, G is the universal gravitational constant, m is the mass of the first object, and r is the distance between the centres of each object.

Coulomb's law: $F=k\frac{q_1 q_2}{r_2}$,where k is a proportionality constant known as the Coulomb's constant, q_1 and q_2 are the magnitudes of the charges, and r is the distance of separation.

One is a large attractive force of heavenly bodies, while the other is the force of attraction between the smallest of particles, yet their formulas are remarkably similar.

And now consider the force of attraction between people, which is also quite similar: $F=L\frac{c_1 c_2}{r_2}$,where L is the constant of attraction, c_1 and c_2 are measures of charisma, which relate to a person's qualities like appearance, intellect, personality, wealth, status, etc., and r is the distance of separation.

Albert Einstein attempted to unify Coulomb's law and the law of gravitational force using the concept of gravitational fields to explain it but he never completed the work. Nonetheless, I strongly believe that this unity exists, and a simple formula is just awaiting someone as great as Einstein to discover it. If there is an active force between the smallest particles then there ought to be a comparable active force between humans, matter and heavenly bodies which, after all, are all made of these particles.

God created all living things in accordance with just a few simple rules, otherwise God would not be omnipotent.

God created the exquisite patterns and lines on flowers and animals in the natural world. In mathematics they are called differentiable functions. Always graceful, sleek and symmetrical – nothing in the natural world ever exhibits disharmonious lines or disordered patterns.

Needless to say, God created as exquisite an organism as homo sapiens. When we are unwell, we can see just how truly marvellous the human body is. If any part of us is just a little out of balance, we can feel very uncomfortable. But the genes of this exquisite creation are just a small distance from monkeys, pigs or sheep. The difference between men and women, a beautiful woman and an ugly woman, life and death, is an even smaller change in the genetic code.

Such a vibrant world, such exquisite creations, stem entirely from variations of just a few simple rules.

As part of the universe, an infinitesimally small part, humans must follow rules: use the least amount of resources to achieve the desired end and express it in a simple and unadorned style. This is the beauty of simplicity, that is to say, Simplicity is the Ultimate Sophistication.

The entire universe is comprised of a tiny number of basic components that can be applied in different dimensions. Thus, both the organization of humankind and the design of products must adhere to the laws of nature to attain the beauty of simplicity.

26 March, 2009

MY MINIMALIST TAKE

My work desk, PC and iPad, even my mobile phone screen, are neat and clean, not an unnecessary object in sight. When I buy clothes, it is basically a dozen suitable pants and T-shirts. I do not stop to consider what I need to wear every day. My hair is also cut into a flat-top with an electric hair clipper. Naturally, the space I use is also extremely plain, open, with no unnecessary ornaments. Such an attitude toward life influences all aspects of your life: your interpersonal relationships, business management and even H World's product design. I believe this is a more interesting way of living, so I will organize the threads of this philosophy to share with everyone.

1. BAUHAUS

When I first entered the hotel industry, I read some books on architecture. The one that had a deep impact on me was the Bauhaus style.

The Bauhaus spirit's particularity is that it is highly rational, functional, simplified, minimalist and geometric. Form follows function, with focus on function; no frills, removing all unneeded embellishments.

"Less is more" was proposed by Bauhaus' Mies Van der Rohe (in office 1930 to 1933). Here, 'less' is not about emptiness, but simplicity. 'More' is not about being crowded, but perfection. His architectural designs, from interior decoration to furniture, were to be simplified to the point where no further modifications could be made. As he said, "I don't want to be interesting. I want to be good."

My criticism of the traditional hotel industry stems from here. Traditional hotel products are flashy yet impractical, overly embellished, form is greater than function, superficially imitating styles, dogmatic, a living example of 'Rococo.'

From an outsider's perspective, I reconsidered the functions and facilities that a hotel should have, focusing on the core needs of the main customer groups, and pushed those to their extremes. This guiding principle not only saved money in construction costs, it also reduced management complexity. Staff count was reduced, role requirements were lowered, guests enjoyed greater convenience, and it was environmentally friendly. Spearheaded by the designer Mr Zhou Guangming, Ji Hotel was one of the earliest and most representative products to embody this thought. Other H World brands continue this tradition.

The other important idea of Bauhaus is this: Design serves the public, not the select few. This idea is similar to Schumpeter's statement: "The capitalist achievement does not typically consist in providing more silk stockings for queens but in bringing them within the reach of factory girls in return for steadily decreasing amounts of effort." This is the result of the modern industrial revolution, which has created a better life for the greatest number of people.

The hotel industry is similar. Many hotels we know all too well, like the Ritz, Waldorf, St Regis and Four Seasons, are extremely luxurious – they originally served royalty and nobles. Even today, they primarily serve a small elite group.

H World started with budget hotels, gradually grew, and is still now focusing on budget and mid-range hotels, serving a few hundred million people annually, the majority of whom are ordinary people. I am extremely proud of this!

Industrialization and informatization have made society freer and more equal. Many affordable yet high-quality products have benefitted countless ordinary people. Products that once only served the few have gradually been marginalized, replaced by brands like Tesla, Apple, Lululemon, Starbucks and Ji Hotels. It is no exaggeration to say that ordinary workers, university professors and even queens would not be out of place at all using these brands.

2. OCCAM'S RAZOR

I started practising Pilates a few years ago, and had a chance encounter with an incredible trainer – the founder of Body Concept Pilates, Kevin Chen, also known as 'CK.' He was both my mentor and friend. He taught me Pilates, and I sometimes shared business insights with him.

In the beginning, I was lacking core strength, often using other body parts to compensate for movement. He told me to use the least effort to make the best movement. Only in exerting the least effort, can you perform the best move. If you spared no effort in doing a movement, the result would be distorted.

I later happened to come across the term 'Occam's Razor.' It states that one should not introduce unnecessary complexity. Occam went further to explain: Do not waste more resources when fewer can achieve the same result. This principle is almost identical to the one that CK told me about for Pilates.

This principle applies just as well in business. If someone spends the longest time introducing their business model, launching into a slew of esoteric jargon, but you still cannot understand them, it means that this person is either bluffing or trying to pull the wool over your eyes. This is the feeling I get when I hear someone talk about Bitcoin or the metaverse.

Good entrepreneurs follow the principle of simplest, greatest truths. It strikes at the heart of the matter with no embellishments, focusing on human nature, the core requirement, using the least resources to achieve the goal.

This is also true in business management: few management tiers (typically three), a lean staff count (quality before quantity), simple work processes (based on sensibilities rather than SOPs), clear, concise evaluations (not too many KPIs, typically not more than five), crisp, direct strategies (three points are optimal; understood at a glance, easy-to-remember taglines).

Occam's Razor is widely applied in the scientific community; Newton and Einstein were its staunchest advocates. Newton once said: If a certain cause is both true and sufficiently explains a natural phenomenon, then we should not accept more causes than necessary. Einstein summarized it this way: Everything should be made as simple as possible, but not simpler. From universal gravitation to relativity, they are influenced by this principle. These two absolutely important formulae in the natural world are so astonishingly simple, and simply beautiful. Even more so in the world of business, which is much simpler!

In software and product design, there is a famous 'KISS' principle (Keep It Simple, Stupid, meaning that the simpler and more idiot-proof a product is, the better) that perfectly embodies the principle of Occam's Razor.

One of the most interesting applications of this principle is light switches. I have to spend some time figuring out where and how to turn off all the lights in a hotel room before I go to bed. H World's design requirement is that all lights are turned off with one switch. This applies to the other facilities in the room as well. It is bad design practice to have a user learn and figure out your product. The entire room should be designed around the basis of common sense. Even if it is high technology, it needs to be idiot-proof.

3. ZEN SPIRIT

"Since all is void from the very start, on what could dust be bound?" When I saw this Zen poem by the Sixth Patriarch Huineng for the first time, it was literally as if I had attained enlightenment. Our many worries and struggles crumble in the face of this poem! Those unnecessary obligations, people you do not wish to see, those distractions that you can bat away, all shattered by a simple line from Huineng!

Perhaps I have a connection to Buddhism. A long time ago, I dared not visit the Tiger Spring Temple where Master Hongyi had taken his vows, afraid that I might accidentally get lost on the path.

Later, in a fortuitous encounter, Master Yangren led me in meditation. To think 20 minutes of quiet sitting could bring about such clarity, like a computer rebooting, clearing my memory and cache. With a zero-load CPU, I had become a new me!

I later gradually practised meditation by myself. The benefits were many, allowing me to become calmer, composed, and able to shift effortlessly between different emotional states. I could very quietly take my time brewing tea, very meticulously savour each tasteful sip of the tea, and focus on every step during a walk. The physical cultivation that led to my great change in spirit helped me understand Huineng's Zen poem.

I have always believed that consciousness determines matter, and that practice leads to concepts. This is a world of the heart, not of matter. The latter is just a projection of the heart.

The Western philosophers I read in university, like Nietzsche, Schopenhauer and Spinoza, all came to the same conclusion. Reading the Heart Sūtra, "Form is emptiness, emptiness is form," I seemingly understood many things as well. I also seemed to understand the phrase "a single grain of sand is a world, a single leaf is a Buddha." Yes, the part contains the whole, and the whole contains the part (an excellent master acupuncturist, Zuo Changbo, also bases his acupuncture method on this principle), which is why the Avatamsaka Sūtra says, "One is all, all is one."

People are always in pursuit of the infinite 'many,' often neglecting the easily attainable 'few,' and therefore find it hard to understand the state of "when looking back, that person is there, in the dim light of the lantern."

What we commonly refer to as the 'Zen Spirit' is the application of Zen Buddhism in daily life, characterized by 'Emptiness, Tranquility and Simplicity,' not clinging to the material, removing unnecessary elements from reality to reach this supposed state of 'Zen.'

Applied to our daily lives, it is to subtract rather than add, to be simple rather than ostentatious. Applied to product design, it is to practise restraint rather than flaunt, to simplify rather than convolute.

Of course, Zen is not 'withered Zen;' it is not decaying wood. Only when you are quiet, when you empty your mind, can you more subtly experience the various aspects of life. And then life will truly become more refreshing.

From life to design, from products to the way we live, I advocate a minimalist approach while continuing to apply these principles in our product design, corporate management and various aspects of life.

Everyone seems to have an inherent resonance with certain music, novels or cultures. When you encounter it, you just know: That's right! This is it!

It is the same for aesthetics and values. What styles you like, what values you accept, they are apparently inherent. Just like me having read many books on architectural design, yet I only love the Bauhaus style. Through Russell's *History of Western Philosophy,* only the idealist philosophers have charmed me.

My admiration for minimalism is decided by my own channel. It may not be for everyone, but I am not forcing it on others. Neither is there judgment, only sharing. It is good enough if it can inspire anyone.

12 August, 2022

LIFE IS ART

A few years ago, as I was trying to maintain the standards of our mid-range hotels and planning to venture into the high-end market, I felt I should upgrade myself – no more T-shirts and jeans. I put on a learned air. I went to various art shows, mingled with arty types and I started to collect art.

At the beginning, I didn't have a clue. Luckily, I was not totally reckless, so I did not waste too much money. Then I made purchasing decisions based on expert advice from my circle of friends in the art world. I made fewer mistakes, but still, those artworks that cost me a considerable amount did not excite me. I later realized that if people have different definitions of female beauty, why should I collect art based on other people's tastes? I had spent money to buy things other people like. Even if these people were experts and celebrities, the taste is theirs, not mine. Collecting art is like marrying a wife – you have to face her every day and it will be awkward if you don't really like her.

I don't know much about art and am not particularly good at estimating the price of artworks. Price differences are huge – from tens of thousands to tens of millions. What could I do? Gradually, I came to realize that art collectors are in fact the patrons of artists. When we collect artworks, we are helping artists maintain their lifestyle to ensure they can focus on their creative utopia.

Since then, my prerequisites for collecting artworks have become: I have to like the work, I have to like the artist, and the price has to be affordable. I make the decision to purchase only when all three conditions are met. And to achieve that, I need to have a deep understanding of the artist's life, views and values.

Artists are fascinating and have much in common. For example, they are all extremely narcissistic, whether in fact or in fantasy, and they are first of all moved by their own lives. Their lives swing between their dreams and their reality, but obviously they prefer to live in dreams, and are not good at handling the chores of everyday life. Their artworks reflect their inner world and they express themselves through their art.

One renowned artist is famous for powerful large-scale paintings characterized by his utilization of black tones and tragic themes. Once we were on the same flight and I learned that out of safety concerns his family was on a different flight. His worldview is so pessimistic but isn't that exactly what inspires him to create his works of art?

Then there is a sculptor who has strong views and a powerful personality. I had purchased some of his small-scale works but only when a piece of his larger work was installed in my yard, did I truly appreciate the power of his work: Proud, powerful, resolute, and confident, but at the same time humble and sincere, and filled with a reverence for nature.

There is also a famous Rock & Roll singer who occasionally sculpts and even paints in oils. I purchased one of his large oil paintings. But when it was delivered, I realized it is hard to find a place to hang the painting because it is just like his music – a strong personality with some bad boy characteristics, gaudy yet critical, reckless yet innocent, but the painting does not fit with its surroundings. This is his way of expressing himself, through either his music or his paintings.

One day, a celebrated art critic sent me an essay by Michel Foucault about living art. I found one sentence in the essay enlightening: "But couldn't everyone's life become a work of art?" It was like an awakening from a dream.

He's right. Techniques are no longer important, and neither are the art forms. Artworks are simply the material expression of an artist's metaphysical ideas. Only an artist with intelligence can create intelligent artworks. Only great souls can produce great works.

And their lives are also their art.

If the French-American artist Marcel Duchamp can turn an ordinary porcelain urinal into a piece of art by signing it, then everyone's life is even more deserving of being treated as a piece of art. "From the idea that the self is not given to us, I think there is only one practical consequence: we have to create ourselves as a work of art."

This is what I accidently learned on my journey into cultural pretensions, which then led to changes in my life.

Our office in Shanghai is a rental property. It was a dilapidated house with a short-term lease. We had made some improvements when we moved in a few years ago but more needed to be done. For example, there was a door between my study and the balcony, as well as French windows. I felt the space was too open, so we walled off the door. Now the space in my study is tidier, privacy on the balcony is increased and there's one extra wall to hang paintings. Despite the short lease, I meticulously made improvements to perfect the space.

Our attitude to life is not about eternity. If we want to treat life as a piece of art, then we should focus on every present possibility and do our best to make them perfect. This is not about business strategies or social skills. It is about making our lives better to the best of our ability. This is not about waiting or dreaming. It is about living the present.

My work requires a lot of business travelling. As the saying goes, "It's good to stay at home for one thousand days, and it's hard to be away from home for just one day." That is to say, "There's no place like home." Business trips are exhausting. To make my life on the road less boring, I put together an essential travel kit for myself.

A pair of wireless headphones designed by Philippe Starck. Apart from being able to listen to music on an airplane, I can use them when answering phone calls. Sometimes I use an iPad Pro to watch a TV series and listen to the soundtrack on the headphones. The Bluetooth range is enough to avoid interruption even if I go to the toilet.

Small packs of my favourite loose-leaf tea or tea bags. Simply add hot water and I can enjoy good quality tea on a plane or on the road. My favourite tea bags are Chazu Old Tree Tea which contain good quality tea leaves and are easy to brew.

Apart from tea, I also bring a small incense holder and a box of short agarwood incense sticks. No matter where I stay, the scent of agarwood incense instantly disperses my exhaustion and brightens my day. I also bring my favourite shampoo and body wash. The aroma from a blend of pure essential oils invigorates the senses and makes me feel revitalized.

Although these things seem trivial, they are affordable and bring joy to my life. They make me appreciate life even more, work harder and be a better person.

It does not need to be a task. I turn my life into my own work of art and put my personal aesthetics into practice.

As far as business is concerned, I have already built – alone or with others – three companies listed on Nasdaq, each valued at over a billion US dollars, so starting a new business is no real challenge to me. But if I can make each of my businesses the best of its kind in the world, now that would be meaningful.

I no longer need to prove myself in business, much less to accumulate wealth. My raison d'être in business is to do things I have not done before and continuously improve myself when facing an uncertain future. I cannot do without business in my life because it allows me to continuously learn and think. Doing business always challenges my intellect and allows me to apply my values to real situations. It also improves the lives of a large number of people. Business enriches my life experience.

When I came to the realization that life is art, I then wanted to keep on doing things that I had never done before.

I know what I already know, but what I want to know is what I don't yet know. To quote Foucault again: "The main interest in life and work is to become someone else that you were not in the beginning."

The Buddha said, "Buddhahood is within you, and all can achieve Buddhahood."

I took a circuitous route to find art and artists, but ultimately, I discovered that we are all artists and everyone's life is art.

Life is art. We must make our own lives unique, indispensable, priceless and beautiful original works of art.

15 February, 2016

TWO POINTS OF VIEW ON LIFE

Our eyes are constantly observing people or looking at things. We rarely get to see ourselves, except when looking in a mirror. Now remove the mirror, close your eyes and look inwards. Observe yourself and see what you can learn.

First draw an x-axis. The point of origin is the you of today.

Look to the left. That points to you in the past. But it does not extend to infinity. The furthest point is you as an infant. Look to the right, the axis points toward your future. But that is not infinite either. The very end is you facing death, perhaps as a frail old person, or in some other condition.

This is your life presented in two dimensions – simple, clear and straightforward.

Draw an x-axis in your heart and look to the left and right often. You might feel that life is short and precious, or feel dispirited, or helpless. And this will give us a sense of reverence and compassion. It will make us be grateful.

This self-examination method is called a two-dimensional viewpoint.

Another method is a three-dimensional viewpoint.

Sit up straight or stand up. Imagine running a centre axis through your body and past your head and continue up infinitely. Leave your body behind. Bring your eyes and soul with you and follow the axis, up, up and up.

You will see your body become smaller and smaller. You will become a point on the Earth. Then the point fades and the Earth will become a small point. Continue the journey up. The solar system becomes a star cloud. Stop here for now, for the imagination cannot reach any further once this axis goes beyond the solar system.

This is the three-dimensional illustration of our lives. It's like our souls have left our bodies. It is surreal and desolate.

When you look down at yourself from outer space, you will perceive your insignificance. Will the universe be any different with you or without you? Maybe, maybe not.

Perhaps this will make us humbler and more tolerant.

When we bring our viewpoint back from the infinite universe, we resume 'internal examination.' Imagine entering your body. First enter an organ, then the tissue and cells of the organ, then, finally, the smallest unit – the quantum.

Through cloning technology, we humans can replicate ourselves. Quantum entanglement might be coded with karma. The rules regulating the human body in Tibetan medicine are identical to the laws regulating celestial bodies. Every person possesses the same potential for Buddhahood, the purity and sincerity of which is at one with all living things in the cosmos.

The universe is comprised of all things yet every single one of the smallest units includes all information in the universe.

Every person is unique and important. We are small universes. We possess the potential for Buddhahood. This enables us to feel complete and happy.

If we change perspectives to look at our lives, our lives will be different.

31 December, 2009

A UNIFIED FIELD THEORY OF SOCIETY

Specialization of labor is making differentiations between occupations increasingly obvious. People with different occupations have different work habits, some ingrained in their personalities which in turn become hallmarks of these occupations. For example, accountants and lawyers tend to be conservative, politicians are supposed to be rational, a pastor is kind and old-fashioned, artists are sensitive, businesspeople are adaptable, scientists tend to be otherworldly, and soldiers boorish.

But when you closely observe the best performers in different occupations, you will discover some obvious similarities. Their views are similar. Their attitudes and values are similar, too.

Their similarities, mathematically speaking, are a case of combining like terms which can be identified as follows:

1. Persistence, commitment and focus. Anyone who makes a name for themselves in any field possesses a stubborn headstrong quality. They refuse to give up before achieving their goals. Apart from dedication and love for what they do, their resoluteness enables them to achieve their goals.
2. Oblivious to wealth and fame. Artists are unlikely to create works that withstand the test of time if they are calculating how much money they can get for each square inch of a painting. It is the purity of attitude that frees them from restraints and maximizes their creativity to achieve what others cannot.

3. Inclusive and boundary free. Successful people will not allow themselves to be tied down by dogmas or be restrained by existing practice. They learn from people in different fields and absorb the wisdom of the past to create something new.
4. Keep humanity in mind and cultivate compassion. These individuals also think with most people's interests in mind, instead of solely their own interests. This kind of resource allocation will maximize return, as the resource consumption will generate energy in the most effective way which supports the system and forms a stable virtuous cycle.
5. Luck. All great achievers benefit from one factor: good luck. Many people ignore this factor and instead reflect solely upon themselves, which leads them to believe they are capable and exceptional. Many think the word 'luck' is 'idealistic' and superstitious. In fact, 'luck' is simply a result of us intentionally, or unintentionally, following the trajectory of the cosmos. It has nothing to do with superstition.

I think of hiking whenever I observe successful people in different fields.

When the world was created, there was only one primordial mountain with no path. At the dawn of civilization some curious and ingenious people explored and opened up many paths. Those paths did not have clear boundaries. Take the paths opened up by geniuses like Leonardo da Vinci as examples: painting, sculpting, invention, philosophy, music, medicine, biology, geology, architecture and military engineering. Gradually, more and more people trudged along the paths. The paths circled the mountain and eventually the many paths created reached the summit. The summit is the goal people want to reach. Our ancestors called it the Tao, or the Way. Regardless of which path they take, people who reach the summit share the same vista.

The Tao is the finishing point for knowledge of all kinds. All cultures, after all, are the Tao. The Tao is hard to define. According to Taoists, "The Tao that can be told is not the True Tao." And Zen Buddhism also has the concept of 'sudden enlightenment,' which is not about the immediacy of time but about a breakthrough in logic and space. All high achievers in different fields will experience a similar stage of awakening.

While the concept of the Tao is hard to explain, "the Tao models itself on nature." which means the Tao and all things in the universe follow the same order.

In fact, the great scientists, Isaac Newton, Albert Einstein and Stephen Hawking all tried to find a 'unified field,' which not only embodies the order of everyday objects but also reflects the order of particles and celestial bodies. Of course, they did not succeed. Newton and Einstein turned to religion, but Hawking in principle did not believe in the existence of a god in man's form. But I think this is slipping toward Baruch Spinoza's God[3] on his journey of exploration.

The workings of a seemingly chaotic universe are actually precise and harmonious. And to draw an elegant and simple line on what appears to be a random boundary will earn the admiration of innumerable great people for all time.

Humanity is part of the universe and societies that are formed by people are also part of the universe. The unified field theory of the universe has not been solved. Does the world of humanity also consist of a similar unified field? The journey to discover more similarities and intrinsic qualities is the path to reach closer to the truth.

6 October, 2010

---

3 Spinoza believed there was a single kind of substance in the universe and that God and the universe were the same thing. His conclusion is based on a series of definitions and axioms and deduced logically. Spinoza's God not only includes the material world, it also incorporates the spiritual world. He believed human wisdom is a constituent part of God's wisdom. Spinoza also believed that God was the 'internal factor' of everything, that God used natural laws to rule the world and, therefore, every material occurrence in the world was necessary; only God is completely free, while people may attempt to remove external constraints, they can never achieve free will. If we are able to see the inevitability of things it will be easier for us to one with God. Thus, Spinoza held that we should look at the inherent nature of things.

STEVE JOBS' INSPIRATION

In 2005 Steve Jobs delivered the Stanford University Commencement address. It is a very famous speech and I'd like to share my perspective.

In his speech, Jobs told three stories from his life.

The first story is about connecting the dots in life.

He began the story with his birth. His biological mother was a young, unwed college graduate student who decided to put him up for adoption. But there was a condition – his adoptive parents must be university graduates.

One day, Steve Jobs' future adoptive parents received a phone call in the middle of the night asking if they were willing to adopt an unexpected baby boy. They happily agreed. But Jobs' biological mother refused to sign the adoption papers because she later discovered that the adopting mother had never graduated from college and the adopting father had not even graduated from high school. Some months later, she reluctantly consented to the adoption, but only after the couple promised her that they would send Steve to college.

Jobs went to university when he was 17 years old. Tuition at Reed College was exorbitant. His blue-collar adoptive parents were spending almost all of their savings on his college tuition. Six months later, Jobs thought it was not worth it. He said, "I had no idea what I wanted to do with my life, and no idea how college was going to help me figure it out. And here I was, spending all of the money my parents had saved their entire life." He dropped out of the college after the first six months. At the time this decision was scary for him but looking back, Jobs thought that had been one of the best decisions he had ever made.

It wasn't a romantic decision. He did not have a dorm room, so he camped on the floor in friends' rooms. He collected Coca Cola bottles for the five cent deposits to pay for food. On Sunday nights, he had to walk seven miles across the town to go to the Hare Krishna Temple to get a decent meal. Following his curiosity and intuition, he stumbled into things that later turned out to be priceless.

At the time, Reed College offered perhaps the best calligraphy classes in America. Everywhere on campus, every poster, every label on every drawer, was beautifully executed. Because he had dropped out and did not have to take normal classes, he could attend a calligraphy class. He learned about serif and san serif typefaces, about varying the amount of space between different letter combinations. None of this appeared to be useful for him at the time but ten years later, when Jobs and his partners were designing the first Macintosh computer, he applied all he had learned in the calligraphy class into the Mac. He said, "If I had never dropped in on that single course in college, the Mac would have never had multiple typefaces or proportionally spaced fonts."

Looking back ten years later, it was very clear that all dots are connected.

To conclude his story, he said, "So you have to trust that the dots will somehow connect in your future. You have to trust in something – your gut, destiny, life, karma, whatever. This approach has never let me down, and it has made all the difference in my life."

This story tells us true gold shines no matter where it is. Do not lay the blame upon fate or others. It is up to us ourselves. We sometimes blame our fate, family backgrounds, the times we live in, the company we work for, the industry we are involved in, or our superiors. But in fact, perhaps something in your life today could be the cause of one thing in your future. The apparent hardships we face might just be the force to help us rise in the future.

I was born in the countryside. The hardships of childhood in a village provided ample training for my body and soul, making the difficulties and disappointments encountered later in life easier to shrug off. A village child who has wrestled in the mud is better equipped to work under pressure and persevere in the face of challenges, and that child's desire to succeed is much stronger. Many successful entrepreneurs, politicians and artists have endured difficult childhoods. If difficulties don't overwhelm us, they will make us stronger. Past privations inspire initiative and determination. If I had grown up in comfortable circumstances, I doubt that I would have had sufficient impetuousness and tenacity to survive the hardships I endured over the ten years of building my business.

After graduating from university, I could not work for P & G's joint venture company due to restrictions of China's household registration regulations. My only choice was to work in a state-owned company – the Shanghai Changjiang Computer Group. The experience of working in a state-owned company for some years taught me a lot about society and human nature. And because I could not adapt to the working environment in this state-owned company, I forced myself to quit my job and 'jump into the ocean,' to use the term for exiting the government workforce in those days, and started my own business. This led to the establishment of Ctrip.com, an influential online travel agency in China, and Hanting Hotels. Had I entered P & G, China would have had one more business manager, but one less entrepreneur.

I entered university in 1985. That year, many of my high school classmates got into university through recommendations. Some went to Nanjing University, and others went to the Southeast University. I was not included in the recommendation quota probably because I had been rather mischievous, and my teachers did not think my character and academic performance were good enough. I had to sit the competitive university entrance exam. My first preference was to enter Shanghai Jiao Tong University. When I was attending that university, I met Wan Hui who was in another class. Through him, I met James Liang, who had returned to China from overseas and was looking for opportunities, and Neil Shen who was working for Deutsche Bank. The three of us (later joined by Fan Min) were all involved in founding Ctrip.com.

The story of Ctrip.com would not have been written, had I been recommended to enter Nanjing University.

Regardless of the road before our eyes, sometimes life just does not give us choices. But as long as we hold on to our faith and aspirations, every situation in life, every person we meet could be an important dot in our lives. These dots will somehow connect and form our unique lives, be it ordinary or extraordinary, rich or poor, a success or a failure, lucky or unlucky. They are trajectories connected by those dots in our lives.

The second story in Jobs' speech is about love and how a loss may turn out to be a blessing in disguise.

When he was 20 years old Steve Jobs started Apple Computer Company with Steve Wozniak in his parents' garage. Ten years later, Apple had grown into a large company with 4,000 employees and was worth over US$ 2 billion. A year earlier, the company had released the Macintosh – its best product. But in the same year, Jobs was fired from the very company he had founded. The reason was that Apple had hired a very talented person to run the company with Jobs. Their collaboration went well at first but then they had different visions of the company's future. The board of directors sided against Jobs.

When he was 30 years old, Jobs was forced out of the company. It was devastating for him. He did not know what to do in the first few months. He even thought about leaving Silicon Valley and leaving behind everything associated with it. But later he realized that he still loved what he did and what had happened in Apple had not changed his love in the slightest. He decided to start again.

It turned out that being fired by Apple was the best thing that could have happened to Jobs: the burden of being successful had been replaced by the lightness of being a starter. He felt relieved and entered the most creative stage of his life. He set up a software company called NeXT, and also set up Pixar Animation Studios, and met his future wife. Apple later bought NeXT so Jobs returned to Apple. The technology they developed at NeXT later played a key role in Apple's renaissance.

These events would not have happened had Jobs not been fired by Apple. "Sometimes life hits you in the head with a brick," said Jobs.

> Don't lose faith. I'm convinced that the only thing that kept me going was that I loved what I did. You've got to find what you love. And that is as true for your work as it is for your lovers. Your work is going to fill a large part of your life, and the only way to be truly satisfied is to do what you believe is great work. And the only way to do great work is to love what you do. If you haven't found it yet, keep looking. Don't settle. As with all matters of the heart, you'll know when you find it.

Many of us may encounter similar situations. Life brings us ups and downs. You might lose hope and not know what to do when you are down. But an ancient Chinese story teaches us something similar: When an old man on the frontier lost his mare, who could have guessed it was a blessing – sometime later, the horse returned and with another horse.

For true winners, setbacks are simply boosters or even rebound drivers. If Steve Jobs had not experienced being fired, he would not have achieved his later success, and his character would not have become as well-rounded.

Humans have always pondered this question: How should we live our lives? Many people do not even think about it, while others are too fixated with things such as power, wealth, fame and advantage, and cannot think clearly. Jobs' answer is: Find your love and spend all your time on things you love. Don't live for others. Live for yourself. In the final days of his life, he followed this principle. He devoted his final moments to his family and met with only a few outsiders.

The luckiest thing in the world is to be able to combine what you do with what you love. Warren Buffett said he "tap dances to work" every morning – this is what loving what you do looks like. Of course, not everyone is as lucky as Buffett. You either fall in love with your job or switch to a job you love. Even if it's just for making a living, you should find a field you like and a company you like.

There are many ways to live your life: strategizing enrolment into a prestigious university as soon as you get into a kindergarten, hunting for a well-paid job as soon as you graduate from university, dreaming of luxury houses and cars as soon as you find a job. Another cycle starts as soon as you have your own child. There is nothing wrong with chasing these things if they are your true love. But can we find a meaning to life that is deeper, greater and more spiritual?

It is alright to have a love that is straightforward and materialistic. As long as we can find it, as long as that's what we truly need and truly love, it's worth spending our lives on it.

The third story in Steve Jobs' speech was about death.

A year before delivering the speech, he was diagnosed with pancreatic cancer. He had a scan at 7.30 in the morning. The report clearly showed a malignant tumour on his pancreas. The doctor told him that this type of cancer was incurable, and that he might only have three to six months to live. The doctor told him to go home and sort out his affairs. This meant he had just a few months to tell his children everything he had wanted to say to them in the following ten years; it meant he had to make arrangements for his death and to make it as easy as possible for his family; it meant it was time to say his goodbyes. Then he had surgery and was told he was 'cured.'

That was the closest Jobs had come to facing death and it brought him a deeper understanding of mortality. He said:

> No one has ever escaped it. And that is as it should be, because Death is very likely the single best invention of Life ... Your time is limited, so don't waste it living someone else's life. Don't be trapped by dogma – which is living with the results of other people's thinking. Don't let the noise of others' opinions drown out your own inner voice. And most important, have the courage to follow your heart and intuition. They somehow already know what you truly want to become. Everything else is secondary.

When I studied English at university, a saying caught my eye, and to this day I have not forgotten it: "Listen to the sound of your heart." We don't know what the future holds and we don't know which path will lead to success, let alone what we will encounter along the way. Instead of throwing the dice, listen to the sound of your heart. There will be no regrets if you lose because you have gone where your heart wanted to go. If you succeed, the sound of your heart will be clearer and more resolute and your life will be even more wonderful.

In 2004 Jobs was diagnosed with pancreatic cancer, had surgery and thought he was cured. And yet seven years later he was gone. In those seven years Steve Jobs brought so much wonder to the world and Apple's stock soared from $17 a share to over $230 (in fact, that was when the meteoric rise in Apple shares began). It was as if Jobs was racing against life, innovating non-stop, continuously introducing new products and always surprising the world. After Jobs was diagnosed with cancer he could easily have retired from day-to-day work at Apple and turned his mind to convalescence, taking his time to recuperate. Perhaps his cancer would not have relapsed or at least not worsen. Perhaps he would have had another ten or twenty years to watch his children grow up. But that is not the path Steve Jobs chose. He chose to dive headlong into the things he loved most. He knew, more than at any time before, just how precious life is, and for that reason he made even more effort. That intensity is not something that most people can sustain, much less a cancer patient. The many great Apple products we have today are the fruit of Jobs' life of painstaking labor.

Death is the same for everyone; it's fair, no more, no less. It doesn't matter how capable a person is, how successful, how smart, or even how great, high, mighty or powerful; no one can avoid death. It is the shared destination of every single person – the great or the ordinary, the rich or the poor, the noble or the dishonourable.

No matter if we feel helpless and empty when we think about death, while we're alive we must, "Stay hungry. Stay foolish."

9 October, 2011

EVERY DAY IS A GOOD DAY

Holidays often cause a lot of headaches.

Congratulatory messages, for example. I am not in the habit of sending greetings by SMS, but I'm constantly receiving SMS and WeChat messages. I'm embarrassed to not reply, but to do so takes a lot of time. It's a headache. And ever since the arrival of digital red envelopes, it's become an even bigger headache. If people ask me for a red envelope, I can't very well refuse them because, after all, I'm the boss of a company. Apart from fattening the coffers of the telephone company and Tencent, SMS and WeChat greetings are superfluous. Most of the people who send greetings on public holidays are people you hardly know, people who you are rarely in contact with, or people who are trying to worm their way into being friends and slide into some kind of connection with you. Close friends don't need to send greetings on public holidays; it's pointless for strangers to send greetings. How many points do you get for receiving a mountain of greetings? How many more close friendships are made?

Another headache is due to my being constantly busy and working at a hectic pace. As soon as I slow down on a holiday, it feels abnormal. My body is unable to adapt, and I get sick.

Social engagements tend to be excessive during holidays. Giving mooncakes before the mid-Autumn festival, giving Zongzi – glutinous rice wrapped in bamboo leaves –

before the Dragon Boat Festival, and going to various parties on Christmas are more than I can cope with, let alone having to participate in important Lunar New Year activities, such as giving red envelopes, joining family banquets and attending various dinner parties. Many other social engagements entail even more burdens.

There are other downsides of holidays that we are all too familiar with: highway congestion caused by temporary toll waivers, the annual ritual of massive human migrations across the country during Chinese New Year, and the air and noise pollution caused by fireworks.

A few years ago, I started to spend Chinese New Year overseas. I even gave it a name: New Year Escape. It worked well. But these days spending Chinese New Year abroad is the latest trend which is followed by social engagements. There is nowhere to flee.

There is one way to solve the problem: Mind cultivation.

A while ago, there was a popular motto: Work hard, play hard. It suggests an ideal lifestyle is to switch between the two extremes. I disagree. High-intensity work causes mental and physical exhaustion. That is to say, when constantly switching between the two extremes, the nervous and sympathetic nervous systems just won't be able to adjust, and over time will become vegetative.

If we sit down and think about it, we will realize that all festivals have been defined by people. Festivals were once just another day. And people gave them a name for such purposes as remembrance, celebration, succession, or preaching a certain kind of virtue, or even simply as an excuse to have fun.

Therefore, if we see every day as just another day, and treasure and enjoy it, then no matter whether we are at work or on holiday, if we have great hopes for life, if we have great aspirations for life, if we can shoulder group responsibilities, if we have dreams to fulfil, we will be happy every day. Then what's the difference between a workday and a holiday?

For me, there is now no longer any difference between going to work and going on holidays.

I get up every morning full of desire to make our company better. I think my work is meaningful because it plays a role in the lives of many Chinese people when they travel (nearly one hundred million a year). We provide personable and reliable products and services to them when they are away from home. H World's many hotels give them a place where they can relax while they are on the road.

When I finish work every day, my heart is filled with joy – I feel happy for the many achievements I made that day, I feel ecstatic about the great ideas I formed and learned, I am delighted for having met interesting people.

I do not stop thinking about my company during holidays. I feel even more excited about my work because during holidays we have even more customers to serve. Much of my important strategic thinking, and many articles I have written, were conceived while I was on a plane or in the middle of boisterous holiday activities. Where I am does not make much difference.

When I was a little boy, I divided movie characters into opposing camps: Chinese vs Americans; the Eighth Route Army under the Communist Party vs Japanese devils; and good people vs bad people. I later realized that there are many ways to categorize people in this world (and in movies, too). Simply dividing people into two kinds does not reflect the real world. In a complex society, we are used to labelling everyone out of convenience, based on factors such as family background, level of education and occupation. Other types of labelling include fashions, morals and customs. Language and written texts are the most common labels. These labels restrict people's thinking and create artificial boundaries in people's minds. When you are still applying the binary classification (right vs wrong, good vs bad) on people and things, if you could just stop labelling, then all boundaries are removed and all possibilities are opened up, and you will see the world is a wonderful place!

As I am writing this essay, my heart is filled with joy. A Zen poem by Wumen Hui Kai comes to my mind:

spring flowers autumn moons
summer breezes winters snow
now no worries cloud the mind
it's the best time to be alive I find

If you watch time and days go by with this attitude, you will see the light. Every day is a good day, and every night a good night.

'Every day is a good day' is an attitude of not differentiating things, a Zen attitude. In this materialistic world, in this fragmented time, it is very important to keep a non-differentiating Zen attitude.

14 February, 2016

THE TRUE MEANING OF LIFE

Slow down for a moment, try to visualize this scene with me: outside the window, a range of mountains, rolling clouds, falling leaves, flowering chrysanthemums, a hazy mist, trees, the scent of rosemary, a stone house, reflections on a window pane, lights in the distance, smoke rising from a fireplace ...

Such scenes have existed for who knows how many centuries. I gaze at this vista lost in thought, absent-minded, not knowing what day it is, or what year. All the complications of life, the struggles, the fighting, the manoeuvring for advantage, the scrambling for fame, the quest for wealth, the pursuit of achievements, the love, the hate, the jealousy, the passion, the revenge, the suspicions, the callings of life and social interactions, they all dissipate and float away, as if illusions, or could it be that at that moment ...

People have lived like this for many years. Before me, many people have lived like this and after I've gone so too will many more.

In this absent-minded moment, I ask myself, can there really be incarnation, or is there only this one life? My life is limited, so how can I spend what little time I have on the most important things?

In my childhood, I had an orthodox education – materialism, infused with lots of ideological preaching. While I was growing up, I had an unstoppable drive for survival, never for a moment believing in anything idealistic because

I felt that was just pure ignorance. But after exhausting all the possibilities of materialism, after seeing so much of life, after experiencing so many difficulties and successes in business, after reviewing the experiences of many other people, I had to ask myself: Am I also lost in the ignorance of materialism?

In recent years I have read widely the idealistic writings of Wang Yangming on the School of Mind, the Buddhist methods of enlightenment, Lao Tzu's *Tao Te Ching*, as well as Nietzsche on power and consciousness, Arthur Schopenhauer on metaphysical will, Heidegger on existentialism, Foucault on life and aesthetics. What appears to be a constant thread is idealism. Moreover, my heart became more and more in step with these idealistic points of view.

Opening the window of idealism, I found myself growing and evolving in that direction, and began to read more Buddhist works, especially Zen Buddhist works. I began to meditate, and I reread Wang Yangming's *Record of Practicing What Has been Transmitted*.

But I still don't understand reincarnation, so I can't be certain about it. At first, I understood absolutely nothing, and now after strenuous searching, perhaps more than 60%, but I can't be sure. But that's alright; it's along the lines of an essay I wrote long ago – Two Assumptions About Life – I can make the assumption that life has two possibilities: one has reincarnation, and one does not.

If one has a next life, regardless of whether it comes about according to the laws of karma or quantum entanglement, in this life we should strive to be good people and spend the limited time of our lives with that which we love. We must not harm other people and other beings for our momentary indulgence. On the contrary, we must do our best to create beauty to benefit all beings. All of the manoeuvring and striving for fame are in fact worthless, meaningless and unnecessary. All of the struggles, the fighting, are in fact self-imposed problems. The

Tao models itself on nature, we shall follow the order of nature. Avoid selfishness and cruelty, be not hypocritical and boastful, live a life of simplicity and avoid becoming obsessively materialistic.

If there is no such thing as reincarnation, and all we have is this life, then we should be even more committed to being better people, to not waste our lives. We should follow our hearts and be ourselves. We should spend our limited time on worthy matters, and share our time, wisdom and wealth with people we love, and those we are blessed to meet.

Looking back, I wasted so much time on meaningless matters, on unnecessary social engagements, and on those irrelevant people. I could have used the wasted time with people I love ...

My life will one day come to an end, but beauty has no end. When I leave this world, I must not have regrets and feel I have wasted my life. Things that are worth treasuring the most and about which I will have no regrets over certainly will not be fame, wealth, vanity, success or failure. The most meaningful things will definitely be, I followed my heart, I lived a full life, I loved and I created.

When I was young, I used to ponder the meaning of life. (For individuals, life has nothing to do with meanings, it's merely about the process and the present.) A few years ago, I began to ruminate on the meaning of Truth, Compassion and Beauty. Now I have realized that regardless of whether or not there is a next life, in this life we must strive to be honest, kind and refined. (This is similar to Wang Yangming's ideas on the innate knowledge.)

I am merely a passer-by in this world. Regardless of my return or otherwise, I have no reason to be haughty or feel inferior. I have no fear of losing, nor glee at gaining. I do not recklessly clutch at sensual pleasures, nor will I indulge in self-imposed trouble and let myself be consumed by circuitous thoughts. A life with no return is how life should be. A life with return is how life is predestined.

Everyone is thus, all are thus, eternally thus. All things have Mind and Mind follows all things, and all things return to unity.

17 January, 2017

LOOKING TO THE HEAVENS WHILE KEEPING YOUR FEET FIRMLY ON THE GROUND

When I was young, I was very fond of Somerset Maugham's novel *The Moon and Sixpence*. The protagonist was "so busy yearning for the Moon that he never saw the sixpence at his feet." The Moon symbolizes a marvellous spiritual realm while a sixpenny is a low value coin that represents the paltry benefits chased by mercenary individuals.

In those days, I too was infatuated with the Moon and interested in everything idealistic: reciting poetry on lawns, reading Romain Rolland's novel *Jean-Christophe*, as well as Nietzsche's philosophy and Sartre's existentialism ... We had minimal material things and no desires for them, but a spiritual richness was our counterbalance to a paucity of material possessions.

I entered the workforce and then took the plunge into business. I established several enterprises and found myself drifting further and further away from the idealism of my youth. Occasionally, after a few drinks, I'd look up to the sky, and recalling my earlier idealism, deeply sigh with regret at the current reality. At heart, idealists are gentle and delicate, who have no advantages in the cold reality of the world, and can be hurt easily.

In middle age I became calmer and gentler. My idealism resurfaced just like the Moon which, though blocked out by dark clouds, had always been there. Looking back at where I had come from and how I now live, what I have done is precisely real-world experimentation and the realization of the idealism of my university days. Without that lofty idealism, perhaps I wouldn't have been able to come this far and just fallen into the quagmire of materialism, unable to pull myself out. Perhaps I would succumb to the tender temptations of the secular world and become comfortably numb. Or perhaps be hoodwinked by my own ego and vanity and waste my entire life.

In recent years I have become friends with artists and writers. They are idealists and their idealistic spirit resembles that of my university days. In their daily lives, some have adhered to pure idealism, some have become cynical and some have become extreme. When idealism lacks an outlet, intense passion and extremism become a kind of self-harm. I am quite ordinary and relatively lucky because the years of surviving challenges made me more moderate. At the moment, while many of our ideals have no outlet, I still believe that we should strive toward hope, and not just be sarcastic, critical and negative. In the past our courage and strength unshackled China and brought the nation out of a long period in the shadows. There are still many areas in need of reform and breaking through, but this era is most in need of constructiveness and creativity to improve the livelihoods of the people even more.

In *Conversations with Kafka*, Franz Kafka says: "If one wishes to live, one must believe. In what? In the significant interrelation of all things and all moments, in the external existence of life as a single whole, in what is nearest and what is farthest."

Without a doubt, it is better to believe in something than to believe in nothing.

What is believed is relatively unimportant. All religions parade themselves as the font of absolute truth. Perhaps they possess only one aspect of absolute truth; perhaps to believers they are the absolute truth. In any event, religion gives people serenity, tranquillity, peace and kind-heartedness, and indeed soothes many people by freeing them of their worldly worries, enabling ordinary people to catch a glimpse of a dazzling spiritual light in their everyday lives.

But not only religion, belief in entrepreneurial ideals, belief in one's dreams, as Kafka said, "[to believe] in what is nearest and what is farthest" is still a belief.

Ideals and beliefs are the Maugham's Moon. A life of yearning for the Moon and ignoring the sixpence at his feet cannot be beautiful. In fact, the adherence of Eastern philosophy to the middle way is identical to the dialectic, the Socratic method of debate, in which everything must find balance and all extremes are bigotry. Poetry and novels can powerfully express idealism, but real-life needs both. Without ideals and beliefs, heights will not be attained, we will not travel far, and we will not be visionary enough; without taking reality and economic considerations into account, the wings of idealism are easily broken and the chances of descending into bitter misanthropy are great.

Regardless of whether you are looking to the heavens with your feet firmly planted on the ground or if it is the 'Moon and sixpence,' there's a Chinese phrase that much more vividly encapsulates the concept: "You can ascend to the nine heavens to grasp the Moon and descend to the five oceans to snare a turtle." This line from a poem by Mao Zedong means, you can do both the idealistic, and the practical. That's because in China a turtle is a euphemism for a bastard. It might be a little hard on the ear but here the truth behind the vulgarity is not vulgar.

If you are determined to make great achievements in business, you must be able to grab the Moon as well as snare the turtle. Attending to the tedious, meticulous details, and the computations of daily life are the snaring the turtle part, while the dedication to ideals and beliefs belong to the grasp-the-Moon category.

The late Joseph Schumpeter said, "The capitalist achievement does not typically consist in providing more silk stockings for queens but in bringing them within the reach of factory girls in return for steadily decreasing amounts of effort." Weaving silk stockings equals 'snaring the turtle' because a love of silk stockings is no longer the monopoly of queens when every female worker will be able to afford them. Looking at a business from this perspective, that is grasping the Moon.

The act of manufacturing stockings is the same, but the point of view is different, and the significance is also different. It is as the Buddhists say, intention for enlightenment is the most important. Original intentions to achieve something are what Buddhists mean by intention.

With a correct intention you can see true meaning and acquire more strength on the road forward. You will be more empowered on your journey and will receive more recognition and help. This will be more likely to bring out the goodness in your intentions.

This is why a person, or an enterprise, must aspire to the heavens to grasp the Moon and be able to descend to the depths to snare the turtle, and why the Moon and sixpence are equally important.

4 February, 2018

THREE STAGES OF LIFE

Wang Guowei once divided life into three realms: Those who achieve great accomplishments and attain great knowledge, must pass through three realms:

> 'Last night's west wind withers the lush trees. Ascending the high tower alone, gazing into the endless horizon.' This is the first realm. 'Clothes gradually loosening, but never regretting, for her I have grown gaunt and worn.' This is the second realm. 'Searching for him thousands of times in the crowd, only to see him when I turned back, standing in the dim light.' This is the third realm.

From another perspective, I will also roughly divide life into three stages: knowledge inheritance, professional training and elevating wisdom.

KNOWLEDGE INHERITANCE

The first stage begins when we enter elementary school, then through to middle school and ending at university, with inheriting humanity's most basic, most important knowledge as the main goal.

Language, mathematics, physics, chemistry, geography, history and various methods such as memorization, problem-solving and exams are all aimed at learning, passing down the essence of the various knowledge accumulated by humanity. Due to limited educational resources, and because not all future careers will utilize university knowledge, after the once-over in the college entrance exam, for most people and most jobs, the knowledge learned in high school is already sufficient.

Artificial intelligence and machine learning far exceed humans in learning knowledge and logical reasoning. The reality of powerful computing power, immense storage capacity and vast networks of information will allow computers to possess far more knowledge than an ordinary person.

How to better adjust the education system in the future, and how to shorten or increase the efficiency to fulfil the inheritance of human knowledge is an important issue we face. Can a person borrow the power of computers to shorten this stage of learning? We spend about 12+4 years learning knowledge, which is about 1/5 of our lives – that seems like such a waste. Can we more easily acquire richer, more detailed knowledge? If everyone were highly knowledgeable and luminaries of their field without the existence of knowledge gaps, that would create a more equal world.

PROFESSIONAL TRAINING

The second stage is professional training.

After graduation, we enter the employment stage, going along the so-called career path. Some become accountants, some engineers, some teachers, some till the fields, some work in retail, some in politics. We will notice that, over the years, the personalities and habits of people in different professions will differ, while people within the same profession will develop similar traits. This is the result of professional training. For example, accountants and lawyers tend to be conservative and think in terms of bottom-line logic. Business people are talkative. Engineers are meticulous, and so on.

It is most obvious when there is a middle school or university gathering. Impressions still linger from the school days, but after many years, everyone develops differences because of our varied professions. Sometimes it feels like the person has changed into someone completely different.

I am an example of this. I liked reading in school and was considered a bookworm. I did not enjoy socializing or talking. After entering the IT industry and doing a sales job, I became more chatty, loved persuading people, was less concerned with appearances and was less nitpicky about life's details. Later, because I entered the hotel industry, there was an even bigger shift in my habits. I became more detail-oriented, meticulous and organized. My desk was neat, everything was in order, and sometimes it felt like I had obsessive-compulsive tendencies. This is the result of professional training. Although this was a later development, because it happened during the most crucial decades of my life, and was basically my livelihood, the impact it had on me was still quite significant.

AI scores almost perfectly in this aspect. As long as the best practices and most perfect methods are taught to computers, they can perform more accurately and consistently than humans. Humans have emotions and bodily fatigue, but machines do not.

Still, there are some professions which are not easy to consolidate for machines to learn, such as entrepreneurs, artists, therapists, chefs and others in more creative or personalized fields.

ELEVATING WISDOM

When a person reaches middle age, their job and income are stable. It is times like these when they run into a development bottleneck in their lives. Compared to a younger person, their influx of information lacks volume, their learning ability lacks strength, and they lack sufficient mental and physical fortitude. Those familiar methods and experiences of theirs will plateau. To surpass their own limits, knowledge and professional training will not be of much help. At this time, the path to resolution is to elevate their wisdom.

Confucius said: "At 15, I set my heart on learning; at 30, I stood firm; at 40, I had no doubts; at 50, I understood the will of Heaven; at 60, I was at peace with the world; at 70, I could follow my heart's desire, without overstepping the bounds." "Had no doubts," "understanding the will of Heaven," "peace with the world," and "following one's heart's desire" are all aspects of wisdom. These four stages are also a continuous, progressional process. In terms of time, they also take twice as long as 'learning' (knowledge inheritance) and 'standing firm' (professional training).

The pursuit of wisdom is enlightenment in its highest form.

Throughout history, the founders of major religions were all enlightened beings: Jesus, Moses, Sakyamuni, Muhammad, Lao Tzu, Zhuangzi, Wang Yangming and Confucius were those who "nearly attained the Way."

Ordinary people can also elevate their wisdom through various methods. After Sakyamuni attained enlightenment, he saw that all beings are 'capable of possessing wisdom.' Moses, on Mount Sinai, realized that God is 'omnipresent and eternal.' Anyone can attain Buddhahood, and anyone can receive divine salvation (believe and you will be saved). The Buddha spoke of 84,000 paths. Each person's pursuit of the path of wisdom is different. Some read books, some visit wise masters, some run marathons, some climb mountains, some meditate, some survive calamities, some drift apart like rivers flowing to the sea, some stand solitary among crowds, some receive an epiphany in enlightenment ...

AI cannot score any points in this stage of wisdom.

If humans and the universe are advanced simulators and our world is a game played by higher beings, our attempt to elevate our wisdom is just an attempt to understand the inklings of our creators' intent – even if we get infinitely close, we will never reach it.

AI is a creation of humans. In the same vein, a created entity cannot attain the level of wisdom of its creator. Creation, intimate relationships and wisdom are boundaries that AI cannot reach. Just as the speed of light and time are the boundaries of humanity, AI also has its own boundaries. Like love: AI can simulate it, perhaps even highly convincingly, but it cannot produce those sort of heart-wrenching, soul-stirring emotions that humans have. At least not to my knowledge, or with currently known technology.

Let us just earnestly focus on being a person, singing the tune to suit the mountain you have climbed, seizing every present moment with gusto, making the most of each stage. Whether it is pursuing knowledge, working or cultivating wisdom, it is all a form of spiritual sojourn, a journey to enrich the soul.

20 August, 2024

THE FINISH AND STARTING POINTS

We are inherently a part of the universe.
When worldly desires become heavy, distractions
become many, making it impossible to know
what the universe is. When desire is shed,
and one becomes one with the universe,
one will naturally perceive the way of the universe.

SEARCHING AND SETTLING DOWN

Since going into business, everything I have done has been connected with hotels. I am often asked, was the choice of this line of business by chance or inevitable? Often when we are faced with choices, it seems at the time it is by chance, but looking back later, it seems that it was indeed inevitable.

Why did I choose hotels and, moreover, high-end hotels?

My childhood was miserable. I can't say the stars were visible through the ceiling of where we lived, but it's not far from the truth. When it rained outside, it would also rain inside our home. I was always cold at night in winter and had to pile lots of clothes on my thin blanket to keep warm. On top of that, my parents were constantly quarrelling. Nothing gave me the feeling of home. Because I had such a bitter childhood, I made every effort to make my hotels feel like home for people who had to be away from home, a home that was safe and secure like a home should be. I've always harbored this hope, or more accurately, ideal.

I believe most Chinese entrepreneurs have hopes too, though their ways of expressing them differ. Perhaps their hopes exceed those of most people. We all hope to escape from inner torments but in the course of escaping our torments we must overcome weaknesses to be able to realize our ideals.

Time is the touchstone of ideals. Different people might initially do the same thing at the same time. But with the passage of time, you will be able to tell the difference.

For example, there was a time when many companies withdrew from the US stock market and took their companies private. The value of our company's stock was also very low, and the Chinese stock market was doing well. But I did not follow the trend because I entered the business world not solely to accumulate wealth. In addition, withdrawing from the market then re-entering the market would have taken up a lot of my time. If I had time to spare, why not spend the time on developing new products? Or on team building? I prefer that investors, not speculators, buy our company's stock. This is the test that reveals whether or not a businessman has passion for the business. At the time, I did not hesitate for a moment – I did not need to take the company private. I did not move when American Depositary Shares (ADSs) and American Depositary Receipts (ADRs) were being hyped, either.

But I am not always as calm as that. Maintaining inner peace is a process that requires a long period of consideration. Some say young people these days stay up late and drink. I use the time to think: Will my hotels survive? Should I operate bars? Or, if there is a well-managed hotel in the market, I will try to understand their products and understand why they are good. Changes in trends and clients are the things I care about.

We are all ordinary people who enjoy having a sip of fine wine, a cup of good tea and other indulgences in everyday life. But we should have loftier ambitions. The different levels of desire determine the differences among people and among companies.

But perhaps the most significant difference is an invisible one: whether or not one maintains inner peace.

20 March, 2018

EVERYTHING IN THE WORLD IS A REFLECTION OF OUR OWN HEARTS

This year at the Qing Ming Festival I returned to sweep graves at my ancestral home in Rudong county, Jiangsu Province. Everything appeared the same, yet people had changed.

I saw many childhood friends. Some should have been close, but I felt estranged and distant. We were once innocent, but the sense of guileless childhood playmates had completely disappeared. Thinking back to childhood days, I recalled how adorable they were but looking at them now it was hard to connect them to the memories. I recalled that my neighbors were kind and friendly. And now? Had they changed or was it me? They appeared distant and their greetings were perfunctory. Anything joyous had disappeared.

I rarely venture back home nowadays precisely because I can't bear for these encounters in real life to ruin my beautiful memories of childhood.

The way we view humanity, places and other people is actually a reflection of our own hearts. Then isn't the me today no longer the same as the me from my childhood? When we are innocent and pure, we can see people as innocent and view the world as pure and cheerful. As we age, we seem to better understand the world, and the way we look at the world also becomes more like that of a calculating, world-wise adult and, naturally, the world we see is no longer the same.

Through which eyes do you see the real world? Perhaps both are true. If one day you transcend worldliness, and perhaps leave home to become a Buddhist monk, the way you view the world will be different again. When you harbor desire, embrace the ambition to succeed, succumb to the urge to make money, your view of the world will see opportunities everywhere, goals and successes everywhere.

That's the road I travelled. The inside of your heart will determine the way you see the outside. The more enriched your heart is, the more you can see.

On this spring day as I write my essay in a courtyard, I feel a gentle breeze, I observe swaying trees, I look at the just sprouted luscious green grass and small red buds about to blossom on the cherry trees. In the past, I could not see such beautiful things even when they were in front of my eyes. Now I can see them and take joy in the vibrant natural world.

15 April, 2018

THE ART OF MEDITATION

Meditation is now a part of my life and there is a reason I started this practice.

When Home Inns was privatizing, I was conflicted as to whether I should compete with another group to snatch it up. Home Inns was intertwined with my life: I was the founder, but it was also my competitor. But the leaders of the Beijing Travel Group (BTG) were all there – initially Home Inns was a joint venture with the BTG, and Home Inns was very important to them. I faced a sentimental dilemma.

I rarely hesitate when it comes to business decisions. It's usually simple and straightforward for me. But when it comes to sentimentality, I am often conflicted. And this internal conflict made me feel terrible. Around that time a friend told me I should see an abbot who happened to be in Shanghai. I didn't really want to meet him because I don't know how to talk to abbots, but I was vexed and agreed without thinking much about it. When we met, we didn't really talk about anything. He just said, "Let's meditate for a while." And so, we meditated.

That was the first time I genuinely meditated. It didn't last long, maybe 20 minutes. But in a moment, my mind became simple, pure and clear, and all my troubles were swept away. I once read a book by the spiritual teacher Nan Huaijin and tried the 'seven supportings' sitting meditation method described in the appendix. I sat on a mat and tried the breathing method, but I never achieved this kind of feeling.

I don't know if Abbot Nan's teaching method resonated with me or whether his aura affected me, but he did help me reach a wonderful place.

My headache about Home Inns vanished because of meditation. Thinking back, the matter was not in fact complicated. Not competing for Home Inns would not have affected me too much. But I would have lost all my friends had I done so. A full-scale war between the two companies would have erupted because the management team of Home Inns certainly did not want the company to be purchased by us. The decision-making was quick once my mind was clear.

I prefer the seven supportings sitting meditation method to the more common cross-legged sitting posture which is not comfortable, and the discomfort can be distracting. The sitting posture for meditation should make you feel comfortable. Do not let your body distract you. The meditation will not be beneficial if the discomfort in your legs distracts you. Therefore, it is important to first train your legs to ensure you can focus on meditation.

Now I can last for about one hour when I employ single leg meditation. Cross-legged I can last about a quarter of an hour. First concentrate on your abdomen to regulate your breathing, and then you will no longer need to pay attention to breathing. Gently direct your attention toward your abdomen. If there are too many thoughts on your mind, let them drift away. Do not try to fight them but do not follow them either.

I try to meditate every day. Usually I meditate in my bedroom for about 40 minutes before going to sleep. This has been part of my daily routine, as is exercising. If I am too tired, I sometimes doze off while meditating, although it happens rarely, in which case I just go to sleep. When I am on business trips, I may go out with friends to have a few drinks until around midnight. It is not wise to meditate after consuming alcohol because the mind may be muddled.

When I'm not too busy during the day I'll meditate for 20 minutes or so to help me relax.

After emptying the mind and entering a peaceful state the thoughts of daily irritations can be guided in: Should I marry that person? Should I acquire that company? At that time your first intuition is invariably the right answer. It's possible that when meditating the brain approaches its natural state, a state where desires are at a minimum. Now when you weigh up desires you can arrive at the correct weighting. Wang Yangming said, "When desire is banished, that is where the natural order of things resides." I understand this to mean, people are one part of Heaven, but when desire and distractions are excessive, it is impossible to know what Heaven is. When desire is banished, unity with Heaven is achieved and then it is natural to become aware of Heaven's law. Tranquillity may allow you to hear a real kind of existence – some say, that's God, some say, it's nature, some say, it's truth.

10 April, 2018

THE PINNACLE OF AESTHETICS IS EQUILIBRIUM

The H World Group has a globalization strategy and that is bound to lead to collisions of Eastern and Western aesthetics. Aesthetics is the manifestation of a value system in the arena of the visual and the experiential. Both Eastern and Western aesthetics have their own distinctive characteristics, and yet share some core values, which is an example of sharing a close affinity.

Everyone, Eastern or Western, likes my bamboo garden: its style is acknowledged to satisfy both Eastern and Western aesthetics. I have a house in France. Chinese guests like it just as much as French people do, and for the same reason. I have always attempted to present harmonious aesthetics with both Eastern and Western elements, yet not completely employing Eastern or Western practice.

Our Singapore headquarters is in a black and white house, which is a unique colonial adoption in the tropics of local architecture and English Tudor style. I may install one of sculptor Sui Jianguo's Sun Yat-sen tunics and a work by English sculptor Tony Cragg, whose art is very abstract and beautifully balanced. It will create a dialogue between East and West: the Eastern in this instance quite concrete and the Western abstract, which makes the setting interesting. Indoors, I will hang one of Zhou Chunya's green dogs. This series of Zhou's paintings are quintessentially Chinese; either the dogs are adorable, or they are brimming with desire – Chinese style desire, the kind of desire that Chinese artists, businessmen or ordinary people display ostentatiously. I will also choose some Western paintings like an abstract or a distorted piece of figural art by Harrison Fisher. I also would like to find some works by Singaporean artists. This is the sort of environment I want, one that is neither Eastern, nor Western, in form and aesthetics an environment that is global, in which each element is expressing a unique point of view yet none dominating.

Beauty makes us happy and feel comfortable, yet this feeling of comfort is not desire. Desire is materialistic and beauty is metaphysical. Aesthetics allows you to observe something that transcends where you are situated. When we look at the beauty of cherry blossoms we will sigh, "Oh my, that's so beautiful!" because such things are not part of our daily lives, but cherry blossoms express something that will strike your heart.

All beauty is an expression that transcends everyday experience, and aesthetics is what connects the expression. If you have desire there can be no aesthetics, it is just an experience, a pleasure of the senses. Of course, there is no distinction of right or wrong, or one better than the other. People exist right between gods and animals, with a portion of godliness and a portion of beastliness. Many believe that godliness is best and that becomes their only pursuit. I believe that as people the best attitude is to enjoy both. On the godly side you can enjoy the spiritual, such as philosophy, art and music; on the beast side we can enjoy the worldly pleasures of drinking, eating and lovemaking. Is that not also a kind of equilibrium?

5 April, 2018

THE GRACE AND LUXURY OF THE SONG DYNASTY

In my mind's eye there are innumerable forms of beauty, but grace comes first. Grace is not the flirtatious style of a Bean-curd Queen, nor is it the delicate romantic style of Lin Daiyu of the classic Chinese novel, *The Story of the Stone*; it is a balance between the two. Excess is not graceful. That is the case for people just as it is for designs. A designer who overemphasizes his own personality will not produce a graceful design; only careful deliberation and weighing up options will achieve grace. Grace delicately transcends reality, it is hidden and reserved. In *The Story of the Stone* Xue Baochai is very graceful and finely balanced.

I have recently been studying the history and culture of the Song dynasty (960–1279) because in my quest to create a truly top-class hotel I have found nourishment in the aesthetics of the Song dynasty lifestyle. This is one story I came across: in the Northern Song era a powerful eunuch called Tong Guan had a strict division of labor in his home for making buns. The filling for the buns was made by people who specialized in different ingredients. A girl was responsible for the julienne strip of spring onions and no one else could do that job. She then married and her husband asked her to make some buns. She said she couldn't because she only knew how to make strips of spring onions. You could say this is a sign of dissipation, but we can also see through this that the Song were most meticulous about life.

Look at the painting titled 'Listening to a Zither' by Zhao Ji of the Northern Song and you will see the emperor and a high official listening to a zither with incense burning on the side, a graceful scene indeed. In the Song dynasty, interactions between people were also very graceful. Even in a brothel the media of interactions were verse and music, and the four arts (zither, the boardgame Go, calligraphy and painting). If you had no money, then like Qin Shaoyou you could write a poem; if you had money you still had to conform with poetic grace. Although the Song dynasty was constantly at war, the urban population was relatively well off and spent their lives in the pursuit of pleasure, ultimately refining their lives to live elegantly.

The Song dynasty reached great heights in almost every aspect of our traditional culture. Now we are more familiar with the elegance of Ming dynasty furniture, but paintings show that the aesthetics of Song dynasty furniture was supreme. In fact, Ming dynasty furniture represents a continuation of the minimalism in Song dynasty aesthetics. But this minimalization does not change the spirit of the aesthetic that matured in the Song dynasty. Apart from furniture, calligraphic art and paintings created in the Song dynasty are also superb. For example, Fan Kuan's paintings, and the calligraphy of Mi Fu and Cai Jing.

Unfortunately, the Song dynasty was conquered by an ethnic group that was culturally and aesthetically less sophisticated, and economically less advanced. China's many problems stem from a lack of consideration of the external environment. This is fine for a totally isolated and entirely independent economy. However, this is not how the world operates. Both culture and the military are vital. This logic applies to a country, a company and all individuals. Without military strength, an advanced culture will not be enough for a country. For example, with an advanced economy, the Song dynasty should have had a strong army. However, the Song court did not strengthen its military due to inadequate policies and this led to the dynasty's destruction.

Sometimes aesthetics is a luxury and even linked to death. The exquisite aesthetic created in the Song dynasty was too fragile, and in the end, it led to the dynasty's destruction. This prompts me to think: Maintaining a good balance is vital for individuals and businesses. The foundation of the H World group is economy hotels like Hanting and Ji Hotels, and our crown will only have one or two dazzling diamonds, which I consider a good balance. If we paved our road to the future with gold and precious stone, this enterprise of ours would be in danger of becoming as fragile as the Song dynasty.

12 April, 2018

TIME IS HUMANITY'S ILLUSION

Time is a concept mankind invented. When you were a child, did you have a concept of time? No. It was second nature to cry or babble or sleep, but your awareness of time was inchoate. During meditation my awareness of time is also weak. When I meditate for 40 minutes or an hour it feels like ten minutes to me.

The relation of time to reality resembles that of language to thought. Just as language limits human thought, time also limits our understanding of the true nature of the universe. Ignore time and you can perceive information outside the realm of time and decode time.

Space is also relative – space is easy to understand; Einstein's theory of relativity tells us that when mass has rapid motion, as fast as the speed of light, space will undergo change. When the timeline is smashed and compressed to zero, expanding distance to infinity, with sufficiently sensitive instruments, we can witness everything.

Meditation in terms of physics is negative entropy or entropic stability. The concept of entropy is that in a closed system, a vessel has many particles, which are initially ordered, perhaps into a straight line, but even without outside interference the straight line can bend and become disorganized. When we children were asked to line up, we did. As soon as the teacher walked away, we'd begin to talk among ourselves and then run around, and the neat line became completely disorganized – that's increased entropy.

As infants we are very ordered and our limited bodies possess unlimited possibilities of knowledge, bodily strength or appearance – when we grow up, we might look like you, like me or like someone else. And the process of growing up, getting old and dying is a process of progressing from order to disorder. Death brings complete disorder: cremation turns us into water molecules and carbon dioxide; burial changes us in a different way to disperse us into the universe.

The ideas of reincarnation expounded by Sakyamuni, the founder of Buddhism, can be viewed as the reincarnation of quanta, that different levels of information cause us to take on different forms. Information organized in one way will become you, and information organized another way will become me, or a rock, or a tree. Buddhist reincarnation is not merely one person's reincarnation, it involves the reincarnation of everything, in compliance with the principal of increased entropy. Meditation is a process of negative entropy or entropy stability. When meditating you look inward and in order to shut out external distractions you concentrate all your thoughts on breathing. Then you will not think about the things that scatter your thoughts, enabling you to concentrate your spirit a little more, and as you pay close attention to that alone, your body, undistracted, will enter a state of nothingness. If your thoughts distract you, you cannot meditate. Human thoughts can impact the outside world, but when your thoughts are zero, or more precisely, approach zero, when they are infinitesimally small, that is more or less when you can enter a meditative state, and that state is the least increase in entropy.

If you try meditation and reach this level, you will feel that time is relative, and space is non-existent. When I meditate, I have no idea where I am, and I forget about time. I'm yet to achieve true selflessness, but I can indeed forget about space and time. When you feel this change your sense of time will change, too.

The last time I was in Yunnan Province I heard the artist Luo Xu speak of his experience entering a meditative state. This free-spirited artist once went fishing and spent a whole month away just fishing. One day snow began to fall. He sat by the water's edge and quickly entered a state in which the world around him ceased to exist. He was aware of snowflakes fluttering down onto his head and then heard a voice in the distance say in the Sichuan dialect, "Is that fool dead?" The sound was distant, but he heard it distinctly. He had achieved the state of Samadhi meditative consciousness but didn't realize it.

Meditation allows us to enter another world, which has a different mode of communication. But this communication is connected with the world, and this connection is extremely acute. He had been sitting there for over two hours, but it felt like a brief moment. The person who thought he was dead had come over from a great distance to see if he was alright, a distance that usually takes 20 minutes to walk, but from the moment the person made the utterance until he arrived, it felt to Luo as if just an instant had passed. I have never achieved that level.

Follow the natural course and engage in nothingness; that, perhaps, is the essence of meditation.

12 April, 2018

SEEKING ANSWERS ABOVE AND BELOW

1. THE METAPHYSICAL IS THE GUIDING PRINCIPLE

From 2008 to 2018, over these ten years, I recorded my observations and reflections from different identities and perspectives – as an individual, an entrepreneur and a friend. These writings became the *Founder's Notes*.

Among entrepreneurs, I consider myself relatively competent at writing – I can at least faithfully document events that happened. But the hardest thing to capture accurately is my thoughts. Human thought is myriad. It is a full-spectrum, living thing, yet once put into language and text, it becomes rigid, distorted; much of the important information is lost. Those who write well lose less in the process.

We live in an era of 'dramatic change.' Entrepreneurs in these times will face countless challenges – contradictions, dilemmas, conflicts, anxieties, temptations, inspirations. Though the *Founder's Notes* is a personal journey of my thoughts, because it was personally experienced and written, it at least depicts a more accurate snapshot, hence it is still something worth sharing.

When I am giving away these books and signing them, I often write this line: "The metaphysical is the principle; the physical is its manifestation. Apprehend the principle, and the details will unfold."

This is also the inspiration behind this article's title. 'Above' and 'Below' refer to the metaphysical and physical. A person's career, life, actions and even their entire existence are, first and foremost, matters of the metaphysical. Without the metaphysical, nothing physical will manifest. The metaphysical is the most important, for it is the criterion, the principle, the guiding precept.

Which is why I will start with my values.

My values can be summed up in six words: Seek truth, ultimate goodness, beautiful perfection.

2. SEEK TRUTH

I believe there is no absolute truth that exists in this world. Humanity can only attain relative or superficial truth. Creation is the only thing that is absolutely true. But, for a person to establish themselves in their pursuits, they must seek the truth that they can accept, or they will have no way forward.

Such as, where do we come from? Where are we going? What is the meaning of life? What is the purpose of life? Does God exist? Is there reincarnation? Which is closer to the truth, science or religion? Hang on, there are many facets to absolute truth.

The first time that I encountered these ultimate questions, I was on my way to class in my second year of university. I woke up late that day, and had to rush to class. As I walked past the sign that had Shanghai Jiao Tong University's motto, "When you drink water, never shall you forget its source," most of my peers were already in class, and the vicinity was quiet. Sunlight filtered through sycamore tree branches onto the empty path, devoid of life. As I hurried along, I suddenly stopped and asked myself: Why am I in such a hurry to get to class? Why am I even going to class? Why do we need to learn? I even thought about: Why do humans eat or sleep? What is the meaning of all of this?

That day, I sat under a tree, ruminating, and skipped class.

That dazed moment of existential inquiries brought me into deep contemplation on the ultimate meaning of life: What is the meaning of it? This notion tormented me for about a month. I could barely eat or drink, and I was disinterested in everything else.

The event conclusion was surprisingly simple. I thought: For an entity to contemplate meaning is in itself a paradox. Meaning is not something an entity can seek or define for itself. If a duck could think like a human and ponder its own meaning, do you think it could arrive at an answer? Meaning is defined by objects – the one who raises ducks, the duck's offspring, family, companions. It is defined by all external aspects besides the duck.

If an entity cannot find meaning, it can only be a process. This process is the entire meaning to the entity. The 'present moment' stated in Buddhist teaching is such a concept born from acceptance. The Diamond Sūtra states: "The past mind is unattainable, the present mind is unattainable, the future mind is unattainable." Only the 'present moment' is left.

If this concept of the 'present' is established, there will be profound changes to how one lives, such as having a meal.

Everyone has to eat every day, but how often do we empty our minds and really focus on eating? Breakfast has to be eaten in a rush, and lunch and dinner are spent talking shop with clients and coworkers. There may never have been a time when you earnestly devoted your attention to a meal. When you eat, if you focus your entire attention on chewing, and the rice grains in your mouth, you will find that that meal is particularly sweet and fragrant. Most of us have become slaves to time. We are either lamenting the past, or yearning for the future, yet we have overlooked the most bountiful, exciting 'present.'

When you focus on the 'present,' all your senses, and your heart and mind become incredibly sensitive. Details will reveal themselves, and everything becomes more abundant, more meaningful.

You can try it. Eat a meal, drink water and do something with this notion of the 'present' in mind – things will not be quite the same.

When the search for ultimate meaning is in vain, life becomes more of a journey – one composed of countless 'present moments.' We do not know the destination, nor the final outcome, but we can walk this path well using the concept of the 'present.' There may be wild thunderstorms, but also fine blue skies. There may be rugged mountain paths, but also vast expanses of plains. There may be moments of hardship, as well as moments of jubilant cheer. We do not complain, fantasize, wallow in regret, or even hope. Let your inner self become calm and composed, ready for everything, and embrace each and every 'present' now.

I once wrote a short poem, "Shooting Stars and Dust":

If I were but a shooting star,
in my final moments,
I still would blaze across the plain night.
Even if all I left behind
was a glimmering trail unnoticed by all.

Even if I were but a speck of cosmic dust,
I still would meld into something grand.
Foolish dreams, the universe,
merging dust and light.

Though we are but dust in the cosmos, we still long to be part of something grand and eternal. We work, write, propagate ... all in an effort to leave something behind, hoping to merge with the light and settle in the dust.

Absolute truth is an entire perspective on the universe, the world, life, others, all things. The establishment of this faith confirms the foundation of existence.

As Kafka once said: To live, one must have faith. Faith in what? Faith in the reasonable intrinsic connection between all things and all moments, faith that life, as a whole, will continue forever, faith in what is nearest, and what is farthest.

3. ULTIMATE GOODNESS

When we realize that our original essence cannot define our own meaning, but is defined by external factors, the second core value naturally comes into play – goodness.

Our existence has different connotations to different people: To a child, it is the mother who gives life and raises them. To a wife, it is a husband who can be relied on for companionship. To coworkers, it is their other peers who contribute to their work efforts. To guests, the meaning of H World lies in providing accommodation.

This supposed goodness is an individual's reflection onto the external world. When light shines upon us, do we light up or remain in darkness? Are we creators or destroyers? Are we exploiters or contributors? Over the course of finding the truth we believe in, and after establishing our own faith, we will be guided in our actions toward goodness, reaching the realm of virtue.

Something that Joseph Schumpeter said very succinctly summarizes my understanding of business: "The capitalist achievement does not typically consist in providing more silk stockings for queens but in bringing them within the reach of factory girls in return for steadily decreasing amounts of effort." This is how I perceive goodness in business, which has also become my guiding principle in business activities. It naturally has become the guiding principle in running H World as well.

H World is not averse to profit or public listing. In fact, many investors have profited from the rise in our stock prices, and numerous employees have been able to buy cars and homes and improve their quality of life because of stock options. But the greater impact is that our guests had to choose between filthy, rundown guesthouses and overpriced hotels back then. Because of our hotels, they now enjoy clean, safe, affordable and convenient accommodation. Our hotels have improved the travel experience for these people. Each year, we serve nearly 100 million people – it could be 200 million, or even 300 million in future. We have realistically influenced the quality of travel for the entire Chinese population in a more convenient, reliable and safe way. "Staying home is best, for the journey outside is tough." We may yet be able to revise this old saying. The goal of a business is not in stock prices or market values, nor is it about extravagance and vanity. Our core objective lies in value creation and, in turn, contributing to the improvement of many lives, and influencing the progress of human civilization.

4. BEAUTIFUL PERFECTION

When we decided that H World's mission was "Better H World, Better Life," we were moving into the third realm of pursuing 'perfection' on the foundation of 'truth' and 'goodness.'

Jeep once had a slogan that encapsulated this idea: "Experience the Width of Life." Life is not just long, it is wide as well. And that width is abundance and diversity, an aesthetic process. Since life is a journey, can it be made more interesting, beautiful and different? Within a limited length, there can be infinite width. In the pursuit of beauty, there can be endless joy!

Before founding H World, my partners and I built two companies. The first was Ctrip, now the world's second-largest OTA. We did not have much money back then and simply wanted to start a business to make a living. Our thinking was simple and modest. The second company we founded was Home Inn. At that time, I wanted to prove myself, because Ctrip was built by four people. Home Inn was something

I started from scratch, raised little by little. I later left Home Inn and founded Hanting, which is now called H World.

Why did I start H World back then? Was it to take another company public, to prove myself again? I felt there was no need – I had already been there, done that. What I wanted was a different kind of journey. Building another company was no longer simply about financial considerations, but about 'width' and 'aesthetics.' So, from the very start of H World's founding, I proposed the idea of "a group of like-minded friends happily working together to achieve something great." Words like 'like-minded,' 'happiness,' and 'greatness' all belong to the aesthetic stage, already unrelated to financing, public listings, wealth and other facets of material success.

H World cannot become a money-making tool, or a means of profit-seeking, or even a platform for speculation. I want it to be a community who shares the same values, working together to build something great. It is not just something I require of my partners and staff, but also of my franchisees and guests. Some franchisees see things differently with misaligned values and goals. I can decline to do business with them. Some guests berate our staff at our storefronts – they are instantly going on our blacklist. If you cannot even show basic respect, we have the choice to refuse your business. We understand that guests are friends and family, not superior individuals, not God.

H World has been around for over a decade. It is no longer a small company, but it is still far from being great, let alone influencing the course of human civilization. But we have an ambition – for the opportunity to expand our business to greater heights. Only after that, will you get the chance to affect the course of human civilization.

That is my understanding of 'beautiful perfection.'

I have adopted 'seeking truth, ultimate goodness, beautiful perfection' as my personal values, and made these acts H World's values as well.

5. ENTREPRENEURSHIP REQUIRES FAITH

Many people have asked me why I keep founding startups, and how I keep up with every one of them. In reality, starting a business is extremely tiring and very difficult. It massively affects your moods, values, health and many other aspects of your life, even your family. It is already hard enough to have done it once and brought it to the stage of being publicly listed. When you do it a second, third time, you need support from a certain something. It must not be material, but a certain mental factor that is strong enough to keep you going.

For example, many lives were lost when SARS was rampant during my time at Home Inn. Beijing was a ghost town when I was walking along its streets during that time. Braving the risk of being infected, I went to one of our hotels that catered to Beijing's medical staff. This profession is most vulnerable to crowds. It was quite scary just thinking back on it, since I could have been infected.

So, to me, is this not what life is all about? The things I want to do are not to prolong my lifespan. What I want is to build a startup, and to build it well. And this period of SARS could best illustrate what sort of company we wanted to be. I went to visit staff, encourage them, and told them to work without worry. I did not even know if I was safe, but I at least instilled confidence in them.

Tens of thousands of people died in the Wenchuan earthquake; many of our staff members feared for their lives, some had lost family members or their houses had collapsed. I flew to Chengdu the first day airlines resumed operations and invited the employees to dine with me. Coincidentally, there were reports that there was an earthquake in Chengdu that same day. I was the only hotel CEO to fly to Chengdu to check in on my staff. Was it dangerous? Honestly, it probably was. The hotel I stayed in was located in Chengdu's western development area, close to Dujiangyan

– probably the riskiest area to be in. I placed my bottle of mineral water upside down, planning to run at the first sign of it toppling. I was lucky that night – no earthquake occurred, the bottle did not topple and I slept like a baby. After the earthquake, our Chengdu operations' performance led all our other competitors.

In the face of danger and challenges, even disasters that could threaten your life, the founder cannot flee. They have no choice but to charge into the fray, because that is the position where you are needed the most.

Which is why startups are not for everyone. They can just as easily uplift or crush an individual. If you do not have tenacity of will, ambition nor unwavering values, you will find it hard to last till the finish line. As a serial entrepreneur, the very elements that propped me up were not so-called cash flow, wealth, ego or success stories that everyone assumes – it was conviction in my unshakable faith, a spiritual pursuit that transcends the material, a commitment to metaphysical ideals.

6. ACHIEVING GREATNESS REQUIRES A VISIONARY METAPHYSICAL

Today, I would like to share with everyone my own values, the process of how the metaphysical formed, in a bid to arrive at this conclusion: Each and every one of us has to have our own reflections on the metaphysical, including the universe, the world, people, society, and where we came from, where we are going. If you wish to achieve greatness, your metaphysics must be both ambitious and unwavering. Only then can the metaphysical seeds grow into a towering tree on a plot of fertile soil.

China is one such plot. China is the world's largest homogenous market. Of the approximately 300 million population in the USA, there are about 200 million who are actual, effective consumers. China has around 1.4 billion people, with our effective consumers numbering about 600 million – triple the size of the USA. Faced with such a huge market, one must think big and go big from a macro-perspective, otherwise you will fail to capitalize on such a massive business opportunity.

This fertile land will inevitably nurture many world-class enterprises – because its platform is massive enough, its competition is intense enough, and its development is rapid enough. Be it technological capability, company scale, profitability, among many other systematic factors, it will surely reach world-class status.

Such a large market presents a rare golden opportunity for Singaporeans. Singaporean entrepreneurs and young people will find it easier to enter the Chinese market. Singapore is a city-state nation with a small population and no geographical depth. It must tread beyond its borders to achieve great achievements.

Brush up on your Chinese, understand China's history and culture better, and take the chance to come to China to work, learn and live. In the next 30 to 50 years, even if China and the USA are locked in another trade war, Singapore's best bet might just be in China. Look at Temasek, CapitaLand, Ascott and other Singaporean companies that have worked hard in China for so many years – their investments and market shares in China are plenty, and they have thrived very well.

This world will not always be tranquil. I have experienced the dot-com bubble burst, SARS, earthquakes, financial crises and the recent trade wars. In the face of these problems, I would like to borrow what Mr Fu Lei said in his dedication in *Jean-Christophe*: "True light is never a time without darkness; it is just that darkness can never put it out!"

Whether it is trade disputes between China and the USA, or past tribulations, other hardships and setbacks will surely arise in the future; the time of darkness will surely come.

Only those who have established a grand metaphysical structure will stoically be able to face the unknown world of the future.

7. HUMANITY'S FUTURE LIES IN SPIRITUAL ELEVATION

Where exactly is the future heading? What will be the next leap in humanity's evolution? Is it the Internet of Things, or AI, or genetic engineering? It could be none of them. Humanity's next leap should be on the spiritual level.

Life is a journey, as well as a practice of cultivation for us. The goal of this practice is clearly to elevate all of humanity, perhaps even the entire biosphere to a more advanced, better plane. Just like Ksitigarbha Bodhisattva said: "I vow not to attain Buddhahood until Hell is emptied; liberation of all beings is proof of my enlightenment." Why do many conflicts, problems and contradictions occur in this world? The reason people scheme and fight endlessly over ego, profit, vanity and power, is because we fundamentally lack a higher spiritual perspective.

The dot-com bubble was driven by greed, and the financial crisis was caused by excessive leverage, leading to the American credit system crashing ... Thus, technological advancement will only inflate human desire. Only through spiritual elevation can people become wiser and temper the balance of desire.

The ground is littered with sixpence, but some still look up and see the Moon. When the masses are preoccupied with the pursuit of survival, consumed by material concerns, to be able to gaze at the stars and find that idealistic Moon – that is truly rare. The Moon represents the metaphysical, and the theme of today's speech is this: The metaphysical is the principle; the physical is its manifestation. Apprehend the principle, and the details will unfold.

Socrates said: "The unexamined life is not worth living." You must have an overview of your own life. This overview must not be material, but spiritual. Not concrete, but abstract. Not short-term, but long-term. Not individual, but worldly, universally. This metaphysical pursuit should never cease, because if you do, then you will find it difficult to gain macro-perspective in your life.

22 June, 2019

UNITY OF CONDITION AND CAUSE

Each time I climbed a mountain, I would reward myself with a peach when I reached its top.

On this day, atop the same mountain, eating the same peach, I toss the pit into the valley below (biodegradable, so it is not littering). At this moment, I recall a phrase from the Buddhist scriptures: All things arise from the "coming together of causes and conditions." I am hit by an epiphany ...

That's it! Each time I arrive at the mountaintop, I eat a peach and throw the pit into the valley without fail. If there is no problem with the seed, if the soil, amount of sunlight, surrounding environment and terrain are suitable, it may take root and grow into a young peach tree. If it is not trampled by passers-by or wild animals, or suffocated by surrounding twining weeds and vines, washed away by a mountain flood, chewed up or uprooted by wild boars mistaking it for a weed, maybe it will gradually grow bigger and taller. If it manages to grow, receiving enough sunlight and rain in the forest, it might one day escape the law of the jungle and mature into a peach tree. Spring brings its blooms, and autumn brings its fruit ...

Is not a person's life the same? Setting aside how our parents met, fell in love and got married (or whether it was arranged), just the fact that out of billions of sperm, it was this one that fused with the egg to create the you and me now. The odds alone are one in a billion! After birth, through childhood, youth and middle age, how many trials and tribulations, how much turbulence have we endured to become you and me today? Our distant childhood aside, focusing solely on the fact that if not for Deng Xiaoping's economic reforms and the reinstatement of college entrance exams, I would likely still be plowing the fields in my hometown of Rudong (a town in Nantong City, Jiangsu Province). If I had not met James Liang, I would not have embarked on my entrepreneurial journey in the travel industry. If there were no SARS and clashes with investors, there would be no H World today.

Just like that peach pit, whether it grows into a tree relies on countless factors. Everything in this world truly comes together from the intertwining of causes and conditions! Even the slightest difference cannot be tolerated.

The world is so unpredictable! Even the slightest shift or change may result in very different outcomes. Is this fate? Human will? I do not assume to know the machinations of destiny. What we can do is, in fact, very little.

Thus, as Buddha said, live in the present. Everything is in flux, and everything starts from their origins; the only thing to do is live in the present. Cherish every minute, every second of life, every person we meet, and devote yourself in earnest to every task at hand. Eat every mouthful of your meal and savour every sip of soup, focusing on the 'present,' and experience the myriad flavours of life in the consciousness of the present ...

One day, we will all return to dust. We came together through causes and conditions, and will end through it, spawning from the boundless specks of the vast cosmos, and returning to it.

I think, from the perspective of quantum theory, particles are infinitely divisible and capable of carrying information. The famous quantum entanglement phenomenon and its 'spooky action at a distance' also invoke plenty of imagination. If human beings are formed from these quantum particles, from the convergence of causes and conditions, then what is the meaning of these quantum manifestations of ours? To elevate ourselves one step at a time, thereby allowing the entire universe to ascend to a higher plane?

The currently popular Big Bang theory suggests that the universe began from a singularity. This singularity suddenly exploded, releasing immense energy, thus creating time and space, which evolved into the universe. This singularity is neither something nor nothing, similar to the infinitesimal concept in mathematics. This hypothesis is similar to the Buddhist concept of 'emptiness,' as well as the Taoist saying of "One begets Two; Two begets Three; Three begets all things." Even in Ecclesiastes, Solomon also preached: "Vanity of vanities, saith the Preacher, vanity of vanities; all is vanity."

The universe originated from emptiness, from the infinitesimal. Quantum particles may be incredibly small, but they are not infinitesimal, just an infinitesimal manifestation. I think that everything can be seen as oscillating quantum waves, where their characteristics possess uncertainty. This means that the idea that all things come together through causes and conditions seems to make sense ...

The universe, existence and life are abyssal and unfathomable. Zhuangzi lamented: "My life is finite, and knowledge is infinite. To pursue the infinite with the finite, what folly! He who knows, yet insists, is doomed to futility!" If someone as wise as Zhuangzi said this, what can we average mortals do about it? Perhaps it is best if we can 'cultivate goodness in solitude.' If we followed the 'Buddhist way,' it would be to 'live in the present.' Or be like Zhuangzi – forget the boundaries between the self and the world, reaching a state without ego, achievements, fame, to wander the world, free and easy.

17 July, 2019

DEPTH IS MORE IMPORTANT THAN BREADTH

1. ADVOCATION OF DEPTH

In our era, social media and mobile devices have made information exchange incredibly easy. We have shifted far away from the nerve-wracking days of writing love letters and waiting for replies. Everything is so fast, so direct. Instant messaging, WeChat, Toutiao, Kuaishou, Douyin, danmaku ... One can tell the characteristics of current communication modes just by looking at these terms. Fewer people read magazines and novels, and even fewer read the classics.

I am not opposed to the trend, nor am I advocating for a return to the past, but this fragmented way of communication will just not do. By scrutinizing the development of human history, what has truly influenced us? It is the classical texts, profound thoughts and the deep thinking and communication of academic sages. Whether it is China's Confucius or Lao Tzu, or Plato and Socrates from the West, whether it is Sakyamuni from the East or Jesus from the West, all of them have had an immense impact on the progress of human civilization. I believe that the banter at aristocratic banquets, those casual conversations beneath spring nights, even if they were recorded in writing, they would probably have been long forgotten and lost to time, let alone having any impact on future generations.

Humanity is experiencing information transfer at an immediate rate for the first time – like children with a new toy, still unsure of how to use it properly. The fragmentation of information and superficiality of communication are one of the gravest errors of this era. We cannot simply jump on the bandwagon or be swept away by its tide. As a group of people striving to forge grand achievements, as a person resolving to impact the course of human civilization, we should calmly return to our common senses and return to our natures.

Therefore, I advocate: deep reading, deep thinking, deep exchanges.

2. DEEP READING

I have a particular quirk – I do not read on electronic devices. Instead, I print everything out to read. I even specially got an HP OfficeJet Pro (a high-end HP inkjet printer) and 120–140g printing paper (has a nice texture) just for this. The benefit of doing this is aside from protecting my eyes, is that anything worth reading must also be worth printing, or I will just read the title, not the content. This helps me avoid a lot of boring, meaningless gossip and motivational fluff.

Also, I insist on reading magazines and classics, and even take notes. When reading books and printed materials, I will have pens in different colors to highlight important or essential passages and label them.

I basically do not read novels anymore, focusing more on history, philosophy, political commentary, religion, art, poetry. Apart from art and poetry, the other subjects have to be read by engaging your brain. I will sometimes pause to think about what I just read, sometimes realization will hit me, and sometimes I have to wrack my brain.

We were filled with curiosity in our youth, and reading was one of the avenues in which we could better understand the world. One should read all of humanity's classics once. If there are religious or philosophical materials that you do not understand at that moment, you can skim through them, at least for a general understanding.

As we grow older, our patience for reading may decline, and our eyesight may deteriorate, but the habit of reading must not be abandoned. In fact, we should engage in deeper reading on metaphysical fields like philosophy, religion and aesthetics, instead of glossing over them.

3. DEEP THINKING

To prevent myself from being harassed and interrupted by social media, I use the iPad version of WeChat. I have turned off almost all app notifications. This way, when I run the app, I will obtain the information I need, not be sent all sorts of notifications. I need undisrupted blocks of time and, more importantly, need to be able to assign time to myself for self-reflection.

I named many of H World's brands, and they have been lauded for their coinage, as if complimenting my quick wit. This could not be further from the truth – they are the fruits of deep contemplation and thoughtful struggle.

Most of us are not geniuses, but ordinary people. Only by working harder, putting in more effort, engaging in deeper thought than other people, can we both surpass the musings and achievements of the average person.

Many of the world's greatest achievements are not random – like Sakyamuni's enlightenment, Wang Wangming's realization, Newton's universal gravitation and Einstein's theory of relativity. We can also imagine that Lao Tzu was fishing along the Yun-meng Lakes and ruminating on his *Tao Te Ching*. The world's greatest ideas can influence humanity's imagination and are the result of deep thinking. Only poetry and music are possible in drunken inspiration, but they are beautiful, not great.

The internet and social media have intensified everyone's anxiety, as if they are being pushed along by a pair of invisible hands, hurrying forward, leaving not a sliver of time to quiet down, to self-reflect. The Apple Watch has a very useful app that reminds you to compose yourself and take deep breaths for a minute. I recommend everyone give it a try. It is great!

I have started businesses several times and been fortunate enough to find success. It is not because I am a genius; rather it is the result of constant iteration, elimination, validation and deep thinking.

I am one of those types who will stand at the foot of a mountain and look into the distance. I am one who climbs a mountain one step at a time, so that I can see even farther, even clearer, and work toward the next peak. Every time I ascend a peak, that is our journey of iteration and progress. At such heights, our thoughts will also gain elevation and depth. Each time you successfully conquer a peak, that is the result of meticulous planning, not a chance encounter!

How can a brand stand above its peers? How can a membership plan be differentiated? How can a guest's experience be improved? How can a breakfast be inexpensive, yet delicious? How can organizational and brand strengths be ensured at the lower tiers? There are many layers of strategy and tactics that require our constant deep thinking.

4. DEEP EXCHANGES

Do you remember the last time you held a pen to write something? Or the last time you slipped a letter in an envelope, stuck a stamp on it, then dropped it in the mail?

We mostly use the so-called 'instant messaging' software – short and fast, cannot be too long, since many apps have character limits. Even voice notes have time limits. Our feeds are littered with selfies and flexes – not a drop of true emotion. Plenty of filters, check-ins, influencers, all ephemeral, all unrealistic.

We use PowerPoint or Keynote during meetings, focusing on main points, concise and lucid, just like the sayings and aphorisms we loved to recite as kids. Few write longform essays; even fewer produce deep, insightful articles.

During this pandemic, many became accustomed to video conferences. Some thought this was a good thing; they could make fewer business trips in future, or even not at all. Of course, the voice is mightier than text, and video is better than voice, but true meaningful communication is face-to-face. The temperature, smell, surrounding ambience in the present moment – they all become a part of the exchange. Video conferences will not and should not replace interpersonal exchanges and communication.

From a human perspective, as lonely individuals, we all thirst for communication with our own species. The advancement of technology has made superficial communication more convenient, but it cannot replace deep exchanges. Like the opportunity to clinch a partnership – if you do not look into the other party's eyes, the partnership will never transpire.

Humanity's communication methods have been twisted by technology. "A new toilet smells fresh for three days" – we are overusing new-fangled technology.

Instant messages are appropriate for simple communications and interactions. Email is more suited for formal occasions, when the need for documentation arises. Videos are great for simple communications between familiar coworkers. Discussions and debates, engaging in deep exchanges – these need to be face-to-face. Even a casual bump into a coworker along the hallway is important for developing relationships.

Thus, I advocate face-to-face communication, whether it is a colleague or a loved one. I advocate using words to describe deep thoughts and major topics, whether it concerns an enterprise's critical decisions or life's reflections.

28 August, 2020

PLUG-AND-PLAY, USE-AND-DISCARD

'Plug and play' was originally a computer term – the average person could turn on the PC and use something, without requiring professional assistance. It embodies the KISS principle. IT devices and civilian appliances today are all 'plug and play.' For example, to listen to Hi-Fi music in the past, you had to buy a pile of gear: amplifiers, tube amps, speakers and dedicated players like CD players or vinyl turntables. They were expensive, cumbersome and required a certain level of specialized knowledge.

The quality of streaming service players now is really good. A song's size is under 30 megabytes, and ordinary people's ears cannot even tell its audio difference from a CD's. Songs can be downloaded to your local device or stored in the cloud to be listened to at any time (requires an internet connection). It is nothing like back then, when you had to carry a CD pouch on your travels. There is a French speaker called Devialet that came with its own amplifier; no need for complicated and expensive devices. Its audio quality is nearly comparable to Hi-Fi (especially vocals). That is a true plug and play music system, perfectly suited for streaming! Always online, no need to turn your machine on or off.

Cloud technology has made the plug and play feature even more convenient: portable and exportable at any time. Almost all collaterals can be conveniently stored in the cloud: documents, music, videos. A specific file can be shared with as many mobile phones, tablets and laptops as you like at the same time. If you change your phone or any end device, you can just restore it from the cloud within minutes. 'Use-and-discard' can also be called 'use and separate' – instantly separate or split it up when you are done using. It sounds environmentally wasteful and irresponsible, but is actually aligned with 'plug and play.' 'Use-and-discard' is not monopolistic nor possessive; it makes the most efficient use of resources. Many areas with low usage frequency, higher purchase and maintenance costs can adopt this concept.

I will give a few examples of 'plug-and-play, use-and-discard.'

Almost all public resources, like public transport – airplanes, high-speed trains, buses – are examples of this. Private planes are very costly. A plane costs tens, maybe even hundreds of millions, with annual maintenance and operation costs running up millions more. For the majority of people, civilian airlines are more economical. A flight from Beijing to Shanghai can be settled from a few hundred to a few thousand RMB. Even if you make a one-way trip from Shanghai to Paris, first class only costs tens of thousands of RMB, and is still cheaper than flying private. And plane fuel combustion emits heavy pollution. A few hundred passengers on one airplane is far more environmentally friendly. Highways, public libraries, hospitals, theaters, museums – they all follow this concept.

In the business field, a prime example is the meteoric rise of the sharing economy in recent years. This is the classic 'plug-and-play, use-and-discard' model, like shared bicycles, ride-hailing services and coworking spaces. You do not need to own one, and there are no regular maintenance fees involved. Pay a fixed fee every time you use it, and you can forget about it after you are done using it. Sharing is usually more intensive than ownership or exclusivity, with lower costs and higher usage efficiency. Another example: items used only once in a lifetime, including but not limited to weddings, textbooks and even library books. Some hotels specialize in the wedding business, sometimes hosting several weddings simultaneously in a single day. Weddings typically require a grand and spacious venue to highlight their splendor and sense of ceremony. Wedding guests require banquet tables and a large kitchen to support catering. These are not things an ordinary household possesses, so dedicated wedding venues have emerged. Some are hotels, and some are large holiday resorts or restaurants. Most people marry only once in their lifetime, and wedding halls are a classic example of a 'plug-and-play, use-and-discard' venue.

I still remember, after my college entrance exam was over, I disposed of all my textbooks as waste paper. It felt like I finally escaped from the endless exams and assignments – it was really cathartic. Besides keeping them as memorabilia, there would be no reason to use textbooks again, which is why universities have a tradition where upperclassmen sell their textbooks to lowerclassmen. Second-hand textbooks are cheaper and can save money through circulated reuse. Most people have a study with a bookshelf full of read or unread books, for both decoration and convenience. When online bookstores and the Kindle popped up, I realized that any book could be instantly and very conveniently obtained. There could be any number of books, the quantity of which far exceeds what any private study could store. From then on, bookshelves became optional for me. Whatever I wanted to read, I could buy it from Dangdang or download it on my Kindle any time.

Of course, hotels are the most typical example of a 'plug-and-play, use-and-discard' product. We only use hotels a few times a year, and most of the time, not in the same place. Hotels are maintained by professional managers and are available whenever guests need them. The hotel industry is an ancient one, but it perfectly matches the most contemporary way of thinking.

In the future, when renewable energy gradually replaces fossil fuels, energy costs will continue to decrease. With the development of modern industrial manufacturing capabilities, 3D printing, recycled materials, synthetic food, AI and other technologies, a combination of these advancements could possibly change our way of life completely. This new way of life is highly likely to develop in the direction of 'plug-and-play, use-and-discard.'

For example, cars. There would be no private vehicles, nor would drivers be needed. Just export whatever car model you need from the cloud, store it in its original place after use, ready for the next passenger.

Clothing can be selected from the cloud based on what you want to wear that day according to style, material and color, 3D-printed on demand, used, then discarded and recycled. Furniture would employ the same logic.

If you want to eat beef, you can just print it. If it does not taste good enough, you can also use a drone to deliver a meal to your doorstep. It would just cost more than printing it. (By then, human labor will be a valuable commodity!)

Under such circumstances, the form of 'home' may change as well. The preference for certain interior designs, a vibrant wardrobe full of clothes, and a kitchen for cooking would no longer be needed. With videos and music being streamed media, we can completely call any location 'home.' Long-term rental apartments and hotels would replace developers in providing residential services. We would no longer need to spend our life savings to purchase expensive housing, no longer becoming 'mortgage slaves,' instead becoming our own masters – living wherever we want, however we want. The concept of travel would cease to exist, because we would always be on the road, always in the cloud, truly achieving freedom in life!

The possibility of such an imagined vision becoming reality is very high. It is said that the maverick Elon Musk agrees to this concept: 'for freedom.' He sold nearly all of his tangible assets under his name and will no longer own a house! He usually stays in a simple mobile home or a friend's place and, of course, in hotels.

With the advancement of information technology, along with the revolution of energy acquisition methods, human society will undergo massive changes, and 'plug-and-play, use-and-discard' will become an extremely important mindset of thought.

25 August, 2022

LIGHT OF SPIRITUALITY

1. KNOWLEDGE AND COMPUTING POWER

The internet has changed the traditional methods of storing, acquiring and transmitting knowledge.

It used to be that when you complimented someone for being knowledgeable and erudite, it was considered remarkable. Typically, people with great memories would have the upper hand in intellectual competitions, such as those quiz shows on TV asking their contestants questions on world population, the size of New Zealand and the number of races in Singapore.

With the advent of the internet though, such knowledge has become readily accessible, and possessing a strong memory has become a less significant advantage.

Most of us acquire knowledge through reading, interacting with others and learning from teachers, among other channels. The internet currently accounts for the majority of these channels. Academic education mainly builds on the structural framework for knowledge; its primary directive is not necessarily to impart information itself. The rote memorization exams we hated can now be largely reduced.

Due to advancements in information technology, the dissemination of knowledge has also become more diverse. It is no longer limited between people or through books. Knowledge can also be stored and shared in the form of text, audio, images and videos. Many people listen to history while driving, watch documentaries while working out, and learn to cook through social media. Online courses and remote training have also become commonplace.

Computers have also changed traditional approaches in people's calculations and logical reasoning. When we learn mathematics, calculation and logic are crucial, but no matter how fast we perform mental or written calculations, it does not even compare to the computing power of machines. Artificial intelligence AlphaGo defeating the best human Go players also demonstrates that computers have neared or even surpassed humanity in logical reasoning.

With technological advancements, increasing computing power and improvements in storage and communication technology, it is only natural for computers to replace humans in most tasks requiring calculation and logical reasoning, such as driving, pricing and weather forecasting.

2. CREATION AND SPIRITUALITY

When knowledge and computation make human beings seem less important, we will once again plunge into the existential dilemma of life's meaning. When humans have lost part of their supposed superiority, confusion and uncertainty will inevitably ensue. Then, what is the true value of human beings? Where are our unique qualities and higher nature now? We consider ourselves the wisest life form, the highest order of species – then where is our wisdom? And how exactly is it of a higher nature?

Gödel's 'Incompleteness Theorems' tell us: All man-made systems are inherently flawed. Which also means that artificial computational systems, including the internet, are flawed and incomplete. Only an existence higher than humanity could have created us humans as complete and flawless entities. This is, in fact, the fundamental distinction between humans and machines.

Humanity's unique creativity and spirituality cannot be replaced and replicated by machines. These so-called computer creations of music and poetry are, in reality, a series of computations made according to human calculations, and then arrangements produced based on computational combinations. They have nothing to do with true creation. True creation arises from nothing.

Lao Tzu said: "The Tao begets One; One begets Two; Two begets Three; Three begets all things." This can be understood as knowledge and computing power. It is a process of reproduction and iteration. However, "The Tao begets One" is about creation itself, the transition from 0 to 1. This process is something that no man-made system can accomplish – only the Tao can. And this 'Tao' is essentially the same as what the West calls the 'Creator' – an ultimate existence beyond human description, grasp or even imagination. As the *Tao Te Ching* states: "The Tao that can be spoken of is not the constant Tao ... The nameless was the beginning of Heaven and Earth."

As we are part of the existence of Heaven and Earth's essences, humans have inherited the creativity of the Tao, retaining vestiges of the Creator's spirituality. We can create things that never existed in nature, such as Mozart's Symphony No. 41 in C Major, Michelangelo's David, and China's *Classic of Poetry*. We have also created writing, language, computers and the internet. The great intellectual explosion of the Axial Age has further paved the way for humanity toward the reflection and exploration of spirituality. Whether in Zen Buddhism or Christianity, they all teach us to let go of the 'self' and 'return to One,' to reunite with the 'Tao.'

Thus, I have always believed humanity's progress is not just industrial, technological or scientific, but more fundamentally an elevation in the spiritual – the so-called 'returning to our original nature,' forming humanity's 'unified will.'

It is precisely so that the internet, Internet of Things, brain-computer interfaces and other technologies provide potential methods and means for humans to achieve this unified will. But at its most fundamental, it is still meditation, spiritual cultivation and religious beliefs that are the best practices to reach the Tao.

At this point of writing, I realize that this essay itself is a creation that has 'arisen from nothing.' I completed this piece on my computer, and will later use the internet's TCP/IP protocol to distribute it to everyone. My thoughts shimmer with the light of spirituality. This is a classic example of a creation about computing power, knowledge, creativity and spirituality.

16 November, 2022

THE CLOUD AND TEMPLES

1. THE CLOUD

In the past, monks and Taoist priests would travel far and wide, seeking immortal enlightenment, also called *yún yóu* (云游).

Since 2020, people have grown accustomed to working from home, attending video conferences and working together across the globe. This has led to the realization that working in a physical location is not the only option – people can be scattered across different parts of the world, working in different venues, such as at home, cafés or airport lounges to participate in various meetings and handle business affairs.

And so, the mode of working in the cloud began to take shape.

Our photos, music, emails and documents are mostly stored in the cloud. Not on a certain device, but in a different end terminal, a different location. You just need to connect to the cloud, and all your work and data will be consistently presented, ready for shared use or subsequent work. There will not be different versions because of a change in location.

2. THE TEMPLES

Religious sites, such as churches and temples are grand architectural feats. Various statues and inscriptions can be seen within, casting a solemn atmosphere with a sense of ceremony. This is the original meaning of a temple (*dào chǎng*（道场）in Chinese).

Since 2023, many tech companies in the USA have once again mandated that employees return to the office to increase face-to-face interactions, maintain a competitive edge and boost productivity. These tech companies have impressive headquarters, free coffee and meals, and stylish, gorgeous communal spaces – a high-tech version of the modern temple.

3. H WORLD'S BEST PRACTICES

Businesses like H World have thousands of chain locations, tens of thousands of staff members and franchisee partners scattered across the globe running daily operations across hundreds, if not thousands of different cities. The platform (formerly known as HQ) serves these storefronts and partners, and our daily work revolves around these thousands of physical addresses. It is unrealistic to be constantly shuttling between such a vast number of locations, but acquiring a deep understanding of these frontline sites is absolutely essential. H World advocates for frontline management and hands-on involvement, rather than issuing orders and holding decision-making meetings while sitting in some supposed headquarters. Even the smartest person will never be able to experience or imagine frontline challenges in such a situation.

Of course, investigative research requires careful planning. Many matters also require in-depth communication and interaction through face-to-face meetings. Many roles also require fixed workplaces, such as programmers and finance personnel.

If we exclude those employees who need a fixed workspace, our traditional work model could realistically evolve into a new approach of 'temple + cloud.' Not only would this save significant office space, it would also bring us closer to our customers and users. What is of greater value is that it would transform our lifestyle. This is a revolution of epochal change. Jiangqiao HQ is our largest and most important 'temple.' Each flagship store serves as our 'brand temple,' while the Aesthetics Living Hall is our 'aesthetic temple.'

And our platform – especially for mid-to-senior management in the group – allows for seamless access to H World's cloud from anywhere in the world, connecting everyone to the H World Shared Community. Through emails, H-Tone, WeChat and phone calls, managers can stay connected to every sliver of communication within the organization. We could be in Beijing, Shenzhen, Chengdu, Xi'an, Wuhan, Harbin, Singapore or Frankfurt, and be connected to the H World Cloud. Of course, even while surveying lower-tier markets, we could work from the lobby of a Ji Hotel in Dazhu County or on the road through the Gobi Desert. With the concept of cloud-based work, any place we settle can become our workspace. Just as the company wishes to stay asset light, we as individuals should also embrace an 'asset-light' lifestyle – free from cumbersome burden, so that we can better enjoy life's most precious things and improve our quality of life. Let us establish the concept of cloud-based work to lighten our offices, and meticulously furbish our temples, to strengthen our brand and culture. The integration of light and heavy couples with the interweaving of Yin and Yang, maintaining balance after reaching the pinnacle, achieving greatness in turn!

10 November, 2022

QUALITY OF LIFE

After 2020, I was quarantined twice. Although it was somewhat boring, I had time to reflect on some matters. If the meaning of life lies in the journey, then the length and richness of life are equally important. Cherishing the present and creating more interactions with the world's elements, that is what makes life worthwhile!

First, I went to Singapore, during which I experienced two to three weeks of quasi-quarantined life. After returning to Shanghai, I went through another two weeks of quarantine. Quarantine was not boring; if I wanted to eat something, I could order takeout. If I needed to have a meeting, I could use the video conferencing system. WeChat and other communication tools kept me in basic contact with the people around me, so it did not impede my work.

When I had free time, I would daydream or meditate to keep boredom at bay. Sometimes I had sudden thoughts, which I recorded to share with everyone.

In our everyday lives, we have plenty of freedom. With high-speed trains, cars and airplanes, we can easily travel to anywhere we want, meeting different people and experiencing many different things – a truly three-dimensional life. Usually, we go to work and go home; a linear route with two points – more like a two-dimensional existence. And when we stay at home, we are limited in space to a single point, like a one-dimensional creature – our dimensional freedom is reduced to one. We still have the appearance of a life, but our connection to the world has degraded, rendering the quality of life completely different!

An extreme form of life would be living an entire life at a single physical point, being a one-dimensional person. We can imagine how bland and boring that would be. Most of us are not like this, but there are still quite a few people who follow the two-point or three-point routine.

People always hope for immortality, but have they ever thought: How does one live a rich, interesting, quality life when it has a time limit?

If the meaning of life lies in the process, in the experience, then undoubtedly, the length and richness of life are equally important. It is the integral of a function over time. Connection is the function, the y-axis. Length is time, the x-axis. If we could measure the meaning, essence or quality of our life, it would be the integral of a function:

$$\text{Life} = \int_0^T f(t)\,dt$$

It is the shaded area in the following diagram:

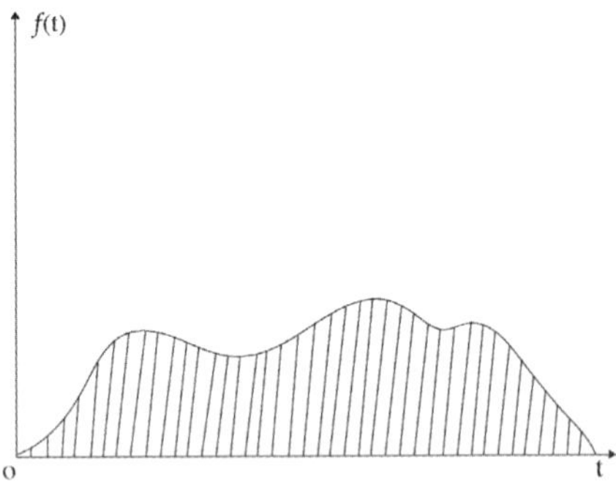

Life is finite, and an afterlife is uncertain. If there is a next life, what emerges from the convergence of causes and conditions will be a different life, another form of existence. So we must cherish the present and use this life to the fullest, allowing its function to bloom in full splendour and soar through the skies.

To live a rich and quality life, the key is to interact with this world and build more connections. This includes, but is not limited to, travelling, starting a business, working, school, giving speeches, publishing books, falling in love, dating, marriage, having children, visiting exhibitions, meeting friends and family ... Or basking in the sunlight, wandering through a meadow of flowers, strolling along the beach, hiking, marathons, enjoying fine wine, lighting aromatic incense, brewing a fresh pot of Ming Qian Dragon Well tea, taking a cab to eat your favorite noodles, flying to London to feed the pigeons ... The essence of life is in its connections, in interactions with this world, and the most interesting lives, then, entail creation and changing this world.

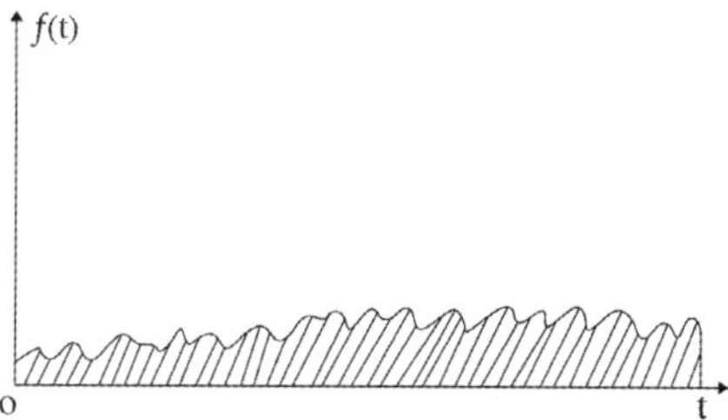

The mediocrity between two extremes

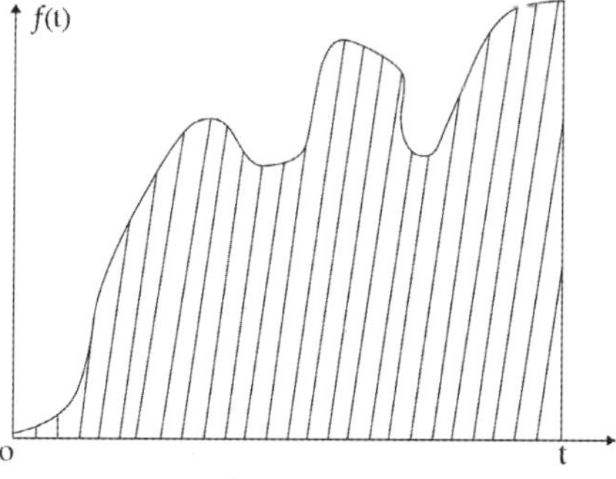

The vibrancy between two extremes

This is the insight and reflection that sparked during my time in quarantine, allowing me to gain a deeper understanding of life itself, confirming the path I should take on my life's journey. It seems like the quarantine and boredom were not so bad after all.

24 April, 2021

FROM AFAR TO HOME

I can work my days away in a vineyard,
living the life of a wanderer, just like Gauguin,
severing ties with my past and starting anew.

LOST IN PROVENCE

Provence is a dream destination for many, thanks to works by Impressionist masters such as Vincent van Gogh, Paul Gauguin and Paul Cézanne, as well as the British author Peter Mayle who wrote *A Year in Provence*.

Provence was my dream destination too.

When Accor's co-founder Paul Dubrule came to China, we talked about joining him on a bicycle ride near his home in Provence. This time I was to be his guest. To keep his promise, he arranged for a cycling tour. The over-100-kilometre cycling route is very well designed. It goes through the best part of Provence, with flat terrain and hilly sections.

The scenery was indeed captivating in the first part of the journey – we rode past vineyards, cycling up and down hills, and through charming small towns. Fifty kilometers passed without us realizing it. By the time we had cycled 60 kilometers, my knees started to hurt because I had pushed too hard when we were riding uphill. Luckily, we were not far from the picnic spot by the river, so I had to drop my pride and let the 'rescue van' take me there.

I was not willing to quit as the only Chinese rider. Although my endurance and strength could not compare with my French friends (cycling in France is as common as table tennis in China), I could not allow myself to lose the contest of willpower. I decided to continue the ride after lunch, but gradually I fell behind. I did not panic since I had a map with me. I continued.

The pain was excruciating for me by the time I reached the 80-kilometre point. I decided to find a place to wait and be 'rescued' again. I went into a small village by the main road to rest while waiting. The last vehicle of my team drove past and left me behind, a stranger, in a beautiful but strange village in Provence.

I did not have any money on me, not even a mobile phone. I did not speak much French, either. Although I was not exhausted, my knees were too painful for me to continue the ride. I had to trudge toward the destination.

Sunlight in Provence is still burning hot at 4 pm. I was drenched in sweat. The last drop of water in my bottle had been consumed and no roadside water taps were in sight.

The hilly road added more pain to my knees and by now I could hardly walk.

The few French farmers working in the field spoke limited English. I had to ask a number of them to figure out the direction.

Hitchhiking was not easy either. My bicycle was too big for a sedan. A truck or a van would be good, but I did not see any. There were very few vans. Eventually, one van stopped. The driver appeared to be a worker on a construction site. He could not understand me. Another van stopped. The driver was a mother. and there were a few children on board. We could not communicate either. They waved apologetically and left.

I had not anticipated the 'pitiable' situation I found myself in. Apart from the sweat-drenched clothes I was wearing and the borrowed bicycle, I had nothing. Nonetheless, I could think, and I could breathe. Here are my random thoughts:

1. REGRESSION

After living in cities for decades, I have become so helpless and vulnerable in the wilds, without the support of modern technology. Having no drinking water for a short while was already unbearable. Having no access to a mobile phone and a few banknotes meant great inconvenience for me. I reminisced for these things.

The progress of modern technology is making people regress by various modern conveniences. Our physical abilities are slowly regressing. Many generations later, will humans like me become strange creatures with weak limbs and large bodies?

This reminds me of the importance of physical exercise. Overall, people in developed countries are more engaged in physical exercise than people in China. I must do that, too.

2. APPRECIATING NATURAL BEAUTY

Provence has abundant sunlight. It is not far from the coast. Most of the rain falls in the late autumn when nameless flowers and plants, grape vines and lavender fields blanket the entire area. Along the route, I saw the undulating hills and houses in the distance. The scenery was delightful indeed. After six o'clock, historical small towns were bathed in a now gentler sunlight. It was stunningly beautiful.

But as exhaustion, pain and thirst built up, my appreciation of the picturesque scenery began to fade. In the backdrop of my physical agony, the natural beauty became unexciting. And the faraway ancient town reminded me of more challenges ahead.

I thought about the hard-working farmers in Provence and the grape harvesters who work under the blistering Sun every day. I guess just like me at the moment, they have become indifferent to the breath-taking natural beauty that people around the world want to celebrate.

Appreciation of beauty is subjective and personal. In terms of basic needs in life, appreciation of beauty is on another level. It is a luxury. In terms of quality of life, it is an advancement, a sign of progress. The basis of appreciation of this advancement has to be a strong body and mind.

3. ON RETIRING IN SECLUSION

I did not bring my passport. A crazy thought came to my mind: What if I change the route and walk to the more remote part of Provence? What happens if I wander to other EU countries where there is no national border? I can work in vineyards as a laborer. I can live like a drifter. I can live like Paul Gauguin. I can cut ties with my past and start all over again.

Now is my chance!

Perhaps my cycling friends will call the police to report my disappearance. Perhaps they will try to look for me. Someone will probably be blamed for what happens. But I will be as free as fish jumping in the ocean. I will have a new start in this foreign land. Perhaps I can be a farmer, or maybe even a famous writer. Launching another entrepreneurial undertaking is probably too hard, but it is not entirely impossible to become a shop clerk in a small roadside store or a winemaker, even a relatively famous one.

My thoughts drifted, becoming wilder and wilder, and more confused. Perhaps it was due to exhaustion. Fortunately, I found the people who were driving around searching for me. It was as if I found my long-lost relatives! Apologies and adventure stories were exchanged but for a long moment, my mind was stuck in the wild thoughts I had along the journey. There was a sense of loss ...

This is the story about how I got lost in Provence. I got lost because of the beauty of Provence and my own vulnerability.

20 August, 2010

POETRY AND GROWING UP

Misty poetry, greatly influenced by modern Western poets, was popular in my university days in the 1980s.

Sitting on the grass next to the Chairman Mao statue on the campus of Jiao Tong University in Shanghai, we recited works by Bei Dao, Gu Cheng and Shu Ting. The famous poem "To an Oak" by Shu Ting goes like this:

If I love you—
I won't be like the trumpet creeper
Flaunting itself on your tall branches,
If I love you—
I won't be like the love-sick bird,
Repeating to the green shade its monotonous song;
Nor like a brook,
Bringing cool solace the year round;
Nor like a perilous peak,
Add to your height, complementing your grandeur;
Nor even sunlight,
Nor even spring rain ...

Bei Dao's "The Answer":
Debasement is the password of the base,
Nobility the epitaph of the noble.
See how the gilded sky is covered
With the drifting twisted shadows of the dead ...

Poetry was the dominant color of my youth, the backdrop that cannot be avoided when I recall those days.

The years of youth and innocence suddenly came back to me when I later read the Chinese writer and aesthetician Zong Baihua's essay, "Poetry and I" in his essay collection A *Stroll in Aesthetics*. There are many wonderful articles in this collection, especially the ones written before 1950. The later ones contain heavy political overtones, which eroded his independence and the expression of his true emotions.

The essay "Poetry and I" was written in 1923. The author, who had returned to China a year earlier, was 26 years old at the time. Brimming with the beauty and charm of youth, the essay in fact is not about poetry and him, but is more about looking back at his adolescent years.

Writing poetry and reciting poetry comes when a person has strong feelings to express. The feelings can be about sadness of farewells, despair of separation, about love, about melancholy, marvelling at natural beauty, or the helplessness of life. Poems cannot be 'composed' or 'written.' They 'burst out' or 'stream out.' It is an indispensable channel to express strong feelings.

Just like the peak of classical music has faded with its time, the popularity of poetry has also dimmed, along with a bygone era. Poetry and ideals have largely been painted over by motifs of our present time of money and wealth, fame and vanity, designer brands and clothes, wealth and power, and political dogma. Today, perhaps moving images and high tech have replaced written texts to become the new backdrop of life for the younger generation.

But there are still plenty of people who need poetry. It is still close to my heart. In my intimate circles, there have always been people who write poetry and recite poetry.

To me, poetry represents the truthfulness and purity of our early days. It is the idealism that has yet to be eroded away, the beauty that refuses to be compromised, the monologue of our true feelings.

The times that embrace wealth and fame but not poetry are the times of misery.

These words are in memory of the long-gone time of poetry.

25 June, 2011

A TRIP TO THE SOUTH POLE

The South Pole has always been my dream destination.

At the 'instigation' of Li Shuanke, director of the popular monthly magazine *Chinese National Geography* and one of the first Chinese research team members to set foot on the South Pole, I persuaded a few friends to join the first expedition organized by the magazine.

It was a long journey. We departed from Beijing and took 11 hours to fly to Paris. After waiting for nine hours in transit, we flew to Buenos Aires. Thirteen hours later, we landed. We stayed there overnight and flew for three and a half hours to Ushuaia in Tierra del Fuego, Argentina. From Ushuaia we boarded the French cruise ship L'Austral. We sailed for two and a half days, crossed the Drake Passage and finally arrived in Antarctica. We spent eight days of the trip in air or on sea and our time spent on the Antarctic Peninsula was only five days.

Ushuaia, the southernmost city in the world, is an economic hub. I learned that the city has a thriving manufacturing industry thanks to preferential tax policies. Agriculture and animal husbandry in Argentina are well-developed, especially for cattle and sheep.

Before boarding the cruise ship, we had Argentinian-style roasted lamb at a restaurant outside of Ushuaia. A circle of lamb, beef and pork was placed around a campfire and roasted for four to five hours. The meat was truly crusty on the outside and tender on the inside.

We left Ushuaia, crossed the Drake Passage and arrived at the Antarctic Peninsula. We spent most of the time on this trip near the Peninsula, instead of going to the Antarctic mainland or the Antarctic Circle.

Visiting Antarctica requires a lot of luck. The sea route is subject to floating icebergs. The route may change if there are too many icebergs. Landing is subject to weather conditions. Windy and rainy weather will increase difficulties for landing and even prevent landing.

I heard we were exceptionally lucky. The captain said he had been sailing for nine years and never had as perfect weather as this. In the following five days, we visited nine islands and cruised twice at sea. It was sunny every day, and the sea was calm. This was nothing like what we had anticipated for the trip, because there was none of the hardship that is often associated with expeditions. Before embarking on the journey, we did a lot of preparation, both psychological and physical, in order to survive the extreme cold weather and possible hardship. Not much was put in use.

Another wonderful experience on this trip was that I had the good fortune to visit the engine room on the lowest deck and look closely at the machinery. This is a technically advanced vessel. All the electricity needed is supplied by diesel generators. Cruise ships sailing in Antarctic waters use light refined fuels with minimum polluting emissions. We were told to use water economically. Initially, we thought the water we used onboard was delivered from the port. Later, I learned that it is supplied by an onboard sea water desalination system. By saving water, we reduced energy consumption. As long as there was enough diesel fuel, our water supply was plentiful. The cabins were like hotel rooms – 24-hour hot water, air-conditioning, satellite TV, and even satellite telephone and internet services. However, many of my fellow travellers were heavy Weibo and WeChat users, but the speed of the internet on the boat was so slow that they were hardly accessible.

Most crew members were French, but the food was not French, just ordinary Western-style meals. We could order à la carte dishes or have buffet meals. I lost my appetite after two days. Luckily, my friend Zhang Chaoying shared some shredded chillies with me. The Xinjiang Snow Lotus brand of shredded chillies became the best food in my memory.

There is a Chinese saying about being grateful: a drop of water in need shall be returned with a burst of spring. I later thanked my friend with a bottle of 15-year-old Maotai liquor. I also asked my assistant to find the same brand of shredded chillies. They are delicious indeed. When I was in Urumqi a few days ago, I discovered that these chillies are a famous local delicacy. Nowadays, that brand of shredded chillies is my favourite choice to go with pancakes. It often reminds me of the trip to the South Pole.

It was not too cold on the first day when we visited one of the islands. We brothers in arms bravely took off our coats and staged a shirtless show at the South Pole. The famous photographer Zhang Chaoying took a snapshot of us from the distance. We all look pretty handsome in the photo.

The islands we visited looked rather similar, except for the shapes of the glacier and the islands. Glaciers, penguins and pristine snow are the three main attractions of the Antarctic Peninsula. Everything was exciting at the beginning of our trip but a couple of days later we developed 'beauty fatigue.' The magic of travelling is about novelty and searching for the unknown, about the feeling of 'being somewhere else' and 'on the road.' When we are tired of our mundane existence in everyday life, we step out of our familiar environment, travel to different places and meet different people. We feel refreshed, and even experience the thrill of exploration. This is the appeal of travelling.

It is a human tendency to be fond of the new and tired of the old, when it comes to sensory pleasures, just as we miss simple dishes after having many elaborate meals.

We long for the simple pleasures of life in the countryside after living in the city for a long time.

On the vessel there were many white-collar travellers. Most were singles. They used their long service leave to go to the South Pole. Feeling exhausted from working in an office, a brief outing like this is an escape, and an adjustment. They must feel much refreshed on their return, I thought, and will start to dream about their next adventure.

Antarctica has an annual precipitation of only 5 mm, but as the snow accumulates, little by little, continuously over tens of thousands of years, or even hundreds of thousands of years, the build-up of forces is truly enormous. Temperatures in the South Pole are low, so it is pressure that melts snow, not the temperature. As the layer of snow becomes thicker, the pressure at the bottom becomes greater, and the snow grains at the bottom melt – ablation – and freeze again in this low temperature environment – regelation. With the passage of time, and under its own weight, snowflakes are transformed into ice sheets. Ice sheets flow along topographical lines of Antarctica toward the edges of the continent, and sections end up floating above the ocean to form the ice shelf; parts of the ice shelf break off and fall into the ocean to become icebergs. The accumulation of snow over hundreds of thousands of years creates huge forces and high densities, so high, in fact, that some ice does not reflect all of the light that falls on it, while the parts that do reflect light are called blue ice; the ice with a density so high that it reflects almost no light is black ice.

I once was fortunate enough to receive a block of ice from the South Pole. The blue-hued ice must be tens of thousands of years old. When I put the ice in whiskey or brandy, tiny bubbles appeared as the ice melted – I was drinking air that was tens of thousands of years old! It was magical!

Shuanke's story about penguins is also fascinating.

People often assume mandarin ducks are the most 'faithful' birds to their partners. But this is not true. Penguins are the truly faithful ones. When male penguins go out to look for rocks, female penguin stay behind to build their nest. In the world of humans, men court women with diamonds and other jewellery. In the penguin world, they use rocks to show their commitment. A penguin family's status is measured by the amount of rocks they have. The more rocks, the higher the status they enjoy, and the wealthier the family is.

If one partner disappears and dies, the remaining partner will follow the law of the penguin world and remain single. It will eventually die of grief.

Some experts challenge this theory. But Shuanke was so passionate when he was telling the story, I am inclined to believe what he said.

Shuanke also challenged the theory of global warming. He believes humanity is insignificant compared with nature, and human activity cannot possibly change natural processes on the Earth that are tens of millions of years in the making. The global warming hoax is actually a sensational lie manufactured by a group of Americans to scare people.

Atmospheric temperature is principally sourced from sunlight. Radiation from the Sun penetrates the atmosphere to reach the surface of the Earth, where objects on the surface, especially the large mirror-like areas of ice on the North and South Poles, reflect the radiation which becomes long wave radiation that can be absorbed by the atmosphere and allow the earth to retain the Sun's heat energy. As the temperature of the Earth rises, the accumulated snow at the poles as well as the polar ice caps melts, meaning the area of white reflective ice is reduced, and the amount of solar energy in the form of heat is also reduced causing the temperature to fall. The two poles actually play the role of the Earth's air conditioner.

As far as China is concerned, being in a monsoonal weather zone, global warming would benefit us. Atmospheric warming would prolong and extend the summer monsoon westward, enlarging the range of rainfall precipitation; the area of land under cultivation in northern China will greatly increase, the period of cultivation will lengthen, and productivity per unit of land will increase. The quality of China's land will greatly improve and the cost of enduring the winter months when there can be no cultivation will be reduced. Grain production will increase, reproduction of flora and fauna will accelerate, increasing the availability of food for people. For these reasons, regardless of whether global warming is conjecture or fact, as far as China's natural environment is concerned, the benefits outweigh the damage. It is in the nature of people to concentrate on making profits and avoid calamity, just as a skinny person must not blindly follow the diet of an obese person.

As a scientist by training, Shuanke is a knowledgeable man, rigorous in his argument. I thought what he said makes sense. People too easily accept the words of others at face value, they are too ready to believe in the latest fad. Just as during the Middle Ages, people believed that the Earth was fixed and the heavens rotated around it, people now believe in the theory of global warming.

Our everyday life transpires within a radius of a few dozen kilometers. Even if we are on business trips, that boundary extends to a few thousand kilometers. Our experience in life, love and hatred, joy and sorrow, wealth and fame, riches and poverty, all took place in this geographic area which is insignificant compared to the seemingly boundless ocean waters and the snowy land in the South Pole. Compared to the millions-of-years-old snow in the South Pole, the few dozen years of human life is also insignificant.

We humans are too arrogant and too self-assured in our abilities. In the face of the vast ocean and tens of millions-of-years-old glaciers, we must be humble. In the hundreds of millions of years of the history of the Earth, we too are insignificant.

I gazed at the ocean and the glaciers, remembering Shuanke's stories about the South Pole. For a moment, I felt the life I had temporarily left behind, the money and fame, the clamour, day in and day out, mean little.

Perhaps this is the real attraction of travelling – a chance to live in a different time and space, live in a different life, and adopt a different way of thinking. By doing so, do we become different selves? Or perhaps our true selves. I don't know.

We returned to Ushuaia. For dinner we had delicious deep-water crabs and a few drinks at a small restaurant. I remember there was a sculpture at the door. After dinner, I returned to the ship, a little bit tipsy. That night, in my dream I became a penguin searching for rocks (diamonds for penguins). Just like in the ancient Taoist tale "The Butterfly Dream," Zhuang Zhou dreams of being a butterfly but wakes up dazed to realize he is Zhuang Zhou, I too woke up astonished to be Ji Qi. Did I really become a penguin in my dream? Or am I just an image in a penguin's dreams? I don't know, either.

30 January, 2013

GOING ON A LONG JOURNEY

In the Autumn of 2014, a few friends and I planned to drive from Chengdu along the Sichuan-Tibet Highway all the way to Lhasa. Part of China's 318 National Road, the treacherous journey offers plenty of reasons to feel anxious. Landslides, rock avalanches, perilous cliffs, traffic accidents, altitude sickness due to lack of oxygen, collapsed bridge ... it feels like taking a gamble with life.

According to the Chinese zodiac, that was the recurrent year of my year of birth in the 12-year cycle. Many things happened in my life that year and I had the urge to escape. Driving along the 318 National Road to Tibet certainly was a good chance.

With this sentiment in mind, as I was packing, I felt the need to write something. I sat down in front of the computer and let my emotions flow and turn them into a poem titled "Going on a Long Journey."

Every journey is a goodbye
Perhaps it's a brief parting
Perhaps it's everlasting,
Life and death, yin and yang.
We don't know this time,
We will be parted in life? Or separated by death?

Every journey is an act of atonement
Perhaps, it is a trip of rescue,
Perhaps, it is a trip for self-redemption.
But, in the end, hardly anyone is saved, not others, not oneself.

Every journey is a rebirth
Perhaps we will be entirely new people,
But, in the end, it is more likely we are the same, except for the mud on our shoes
But, at least, a journey gives us more reasons to live

Every journey is an unknown
Perhaps, at the next corner, I will meet the flower in my dream
But, most times, I see bored strangers and boring scenes.
What awaits in the distance, is like the future, like ourselves,
Longing, but not knowing.

The poem records how I felt at the time.

Reading literary works is a process that allows people to be emotionally engaged. It lets readers bring their own life experiences, feelings and imagination into the world of the author's pen and create their own works. I think others' feelings may be different from mine when they read the poem.

In it, I mused on travel and life, from an unknown future to human nature, and from bleak darkness in life to the power of rebirth. It reflects how I felt during this period.

Poetry is private. I have written many poems, but I am reluctant to publish them or share with others, since I have passed the age of seeking the appreciation of others.

Misty poetry was popular in my university days. We sat on the grass on the campus of Jiao Tong University and recited works by Bei Dao, Gu Cheng and Shu Ting. We were vehement and our words were filled with vigour. To this day I still vaguely remember the scent of youth. Traces of culture we encountered in those days fermented over the course of our life experience. Like a bottle of red wine that matures and improves as the years pass. The feigned sentiment of our youth withers as we reach a wiser middle age. Love and jealousies, once as clear as a scarlet mark on my chest, to use a metaphor in a novel by the Chinese writer Eileen Chang, has become merely a mosquito-blood streak smeared on the wall. Poetry, however, comes back from my dormant memory. It is natural and sincere, and a perfect way to express feelings. Even the poetic form is secondary.

As the development of social media advances, poetry is becoming popular again. This reminds us: Our times need poetry. Our times need something that touches upon humanity. In an age of information explosion, and when material desires trump everything else, people still yearn for something more enriching for their souls. Cultural activities such as poetry appreciation are now an option for elites.

Our Ji Hotels emerged and grow against this backdrop. And we introduced the Ji Culture program to respond to the needs of our loyal followers. If my poetry can resonate slightly with the poetic feelings of others, if my efforts can help make our country a better place, I will be more than happy to contribute. My poems may not be good, but I am sincere.

People are not born good or evil, and life is not sweet, nor bitter. The key is how it is reflected in our hearts. A life with poetry, with song and dance, must be a life of joy. We should write poetry and recite poetry. We not only should be our own poets but also should live poetic lives.

2 November, 2016

AMAZING BURGUNDY

A friend invited me to visit a vineyard in Burgundy. He had arranged a tour for us to visit the famous Romanée-Conti estate. But that Saturday we were told the owner was in a bad mood and did not want to see us. Alas, the French are indeed capricious. But after all, Romanée-Conti is entitled to be capricious.

Fortunately, my friend was well-connected in Burgundy and took us to an estate next to Romanée-Conti's. When we entered the property, a medium-built man wearing a pair of jeans was cleaning the floor. He greeted us, then offered to take us to the cellar. I scanned the ordinary-looking, moustached man head to toe thinking, yes, labor costs in France are high, but tasking a cleaner to show us around is rather too casual.

"Where is the boss?" I asked my friend when we reached the cellar entrance. "He's the boss," was the answer. The appearance of the boss did not give me much confidence in their wine. But I thought since we are here, we may as well make the best of it. I entered the cellar.

The spacious underground cellar, built by priests, was lined with barrels. The boss explained the secrets of his barrels. For example, the plantation of oak used for barrels has to be carefully chosen. He only uses new tailor-made oak barrels and replaces them every two to three years. To express his sentiment for France, the wine barrel hoop bands are painted in red, white and blue – the colors of the

French Tricolor. His son bought him a pretty barrel bung in the United States, but he later discovered that it was made in China. He uses a special type of glass on the barrels to observe the progress of the white wine's fermentation ... He also showed the dust-covered barrels that stored aged wine, and the ones that store wines under one hundred years old. Pointing at the cellar lined with aged wine, he told us Romanée-Conti's cellar is just next door. I spotted a 1966 bottle and asked if I could buy it. Without hesitation, the gentleman offered to post it to my home address!

Words poured out. He knew all the details of winemaking like a truly knowledgeable vintner, and passionately shared interesting anecdotes about wine.

We eventually made it to the tasting room. It is underground but brightly lit. A grand piano graced the room. He told us about the four wine quality classifications in Burgundy. Regional appellations, village appellations, Premier crus and Grand crus. The smaller sites it refers to, for example Grand Cru wines (produced from the best vineyards), the better wine it is. The bigger the region it refers to, for example, Burgundy, the less prestige the wines have.

We tasted six of his wines. The last four were very good. He told us he does not like a tart taste which means the acidity of his wine has to be carefully controlled. He took delight in telling us that his son is also committed to winemaking, so the estate will continue to operate.

He also explained that the best wines in this region are produced on a short and narrow strip of land on geological faults with calcium-rich soils and good water retention. In his tasting room the original rock face is still extant. He sincerely attributed such beautiful wines he produced to the soil quality he is blessed with.

Perhaps because my first impression of him was still lingering, I asked, "How do you compare your wine to the more famous wines?" He seemed annoyed. "How do you compare Yan Peiming's paintings to Pablo Picasso's?"

he asked in response. Yan is a celebrated Chinese painter who lives and works in Dijon, France.

Like a man falling in love with a woman – there is no such thing as the most beautiful, only the dearest. Everyone's taste is different and that's equally true for artworks, love and red wine. Of course, he thinks his wines are by no means inferior to other famous wines. He has stopped adding sulphites (mainly used to kill unwanted yeasts and bacteria but which cause headaches) ever since 2016.

I felt bad for offending him, so I suggested we try a bottle of white wine we had not yet touched. It was beautiful! We were astonished. It was probably the best white wine I had ever tasted! And it cost no more than one hundred Euro a bottle!

We were elated and the mood must have been contagious – the boss went over to the piano and started to play a jubilant melody. It was probably local music and he played well.

I wanted to thank the boss for being so generous with his time and offered to buy two barrels worth of wine from him. One barrel of red wine and one barrel of white. But the boss declined. He explained that his wines have low yields and are not enough to be sold this way. I was again taken aback.

From the 'cleaner' at first sight, to the 'expert' and later an entrepreneur, then to the unyielding 'artist,' the fellow truly amazed me. Burgundy indeed is a land with understated brilliance. An ordinary-looking house is home to the famous Romanée-Conti and an ordinary-looking man is in fact an interesting, talented and passionate owner of a wine estate.

And up to this point, I still assumed his estate was an ordinary estate and his wines just ordinary brands. Upon returning, I did some research and was shocked to learn that the estate is very famous! Domaine Gros Frere et Soeur's Hautes-Côtes de Nuits, a hillside appellation, is very close to Vosne-Romanée's Grand Crus. The Gros family's winemaking history goes back to the 19th century.

Now there are four popular Gros estates and Domaine Gros Frere et Soeur, currently run by Bernard, is the most well-known. Wine lovers in China refer to the estate as the 'Golden Cup' because of the distinct golden cup on its label. The reputation of this estate is as good as the famous Romanée-Conti estate! The Burgundy trip taught me a painful lesson: I must not judge people by their appearances, and judge things on face value.

With the help of my friend, I later did buy some of Bernard's wines. Not because I wanted to thank him for his time but because I crave for his beautiful wines!

We finally left Bernard's estate. That evening, we attended a party hosted by Burgundy winemakers. I was even bestowed the Burgundy Fraternity of Knights of the Wine-Tasting Cup. Somehow, I have established a bond with Burgundy. What a rewarding trip! Secretly, my heart was filled with pleasant surprises.

30 November, 2016

NOTES ON SELECTING WINE

Everyone likes good wine. But everyone's definition of good wine is different. Sensory pleasure is a personal matter. If you think a wine is good, then it is good. Among the expensive First Growth Bordeaux Wines, the only one I like is Château Latour. I found Château Margaux and Château Lafite rather ordinary, so their price tags do not mean much to me. This approach will help us choose other products. You can also make decisions based on affordability to you.

When I choose wine for my guests, I try my best to choose one that is appropriate for the person, the occasion and the food. French people may not appreciate famous and expensive so-called 'good wines' – the wines for the nouveau riche.

If I invite guests to try seafood dishes of my hometown, I will choose wines from Montrachet in Burgundy. Styles of white wines can be very different. Some are tart, some are a little sweet. Some are full-bodied, some are not. White wines produced in Montrachet have fruity notes and are not overly tannic, which is what I like. But they are not cheap. I later found something similar but at a better price. It is from Domaine Gros Frere et Soeur, known in China as the 'Golden Cup.' The wine is just delicious, and it costs no more than 100 Euros a bottle.

To pair with meat dishes, such as braised pork in soy sauce, I will choose red wines from Pomerol within

Libournais in Bordeaux. Wines from this region are smooth, soft, full, not overly acidic or tannic. Many Chinese people like wines from this region. Their rich and full-bodied wines match well with strong-flavoured braised dishes with a slightly sweet flavour. Many red wines from Italy and Spain match well with braised dishes, too.

Guests appreciate my efforts. They know I truly care. My French guests appreciate my efforts, too. They will not think I am another nouveau riche who does not really know much about France. An ostentatious rich businessman may splurge RMB 200,000 to buy a bottle of wine, yet pay no attention to other factors. I choose wine with my heart and I win heartfelt friendships.

Once I told a French friend that I wished to see the Moon rise through the silhouette of the Eiffel Tower. He actually did find the right spot for me. There is a museum on the opposite bank of the River Seine. He took me to dinner at the museum café. Sitting there I really saw the Moon rising through the Eiffel Tower. It was a magical scene. That is a perfect spot to share with someone you love.

7 April, 2018

THE TASTE OF HOMETOWN

For many, childhood preferences for food never change. These days, even a frequent traveller like me rarely opts for foreign food. The food I always crave and like to eat is still the everyday dishes from my hometown Rudong.

In my childhood, I was constantly half-starved. A bowl of rice or some steamed buns were enough to make me thrilled. Even today, the taste of rice or steamed buns still delights me.

During the month of the Chinese New Year, families in the countryside steam many buns. I loved to watch adults make and steam buns. Since they were making so many, stealing one or two was tolerated. To prepare for the mid-autumn festival and Chinese New Year celebrations, batches of deep-fried dishes were made, such as deep-fried meatballs and deep-fried fish. The deep-fried fish is then braised in a wok in vinegar and soy sauce. The smell of this cooking is the smell of festivals, the aroma of luxury.

In those days, our family could not afford to buy red meat, so we ate fish caught in local rivers. My maternal grandfather was a famous chef in the region. When I visited my grandparents on school holidays, grandfather would carry a small basket to the local market every morning to buy fish. I would wait for him by the roadside for his return. Sometimes he came back with a sweet for me, sometimes he did not, but there was always a pile of food ingredients in the basket. I knew there would be a feast that day.

The time I spent with my maternal grandparents is a string of sweet memories.

Many of the dishes our chef cooks today are the same as my grandfather used to make. For example, wenge clam cakes – little cakes made by frying a mixture of fresh clam meat, shredded vegetables and flour – are a Rudong delicacy.

Meizi fish is another dish grandfather used to cook. In those days, we could not afford to buy Yellow Croaker fish, so the small local *meizi* fish was the alternative. Grandfather would use fish heads to make the soup. A *meizi* fish head does not have much meat, but they make delicious milky broth. Using simple ingredients to make tasty dishes is the wisdom of the poor. The taste of my hometown stays with me to this very day and is my unfading preference for food.

21 April, 2018

PILATES

I was coincidentally introduced to CK and started learning Pilates from him. Pilates is not as popular as yoga, so many are unfamiliar with it. However, it has helped me tremendously.

First, it helps shrink the belly.

Many middle-aged people do not exercise enough, eat too much and end up with a big belly. Pilates focuses on training core muscles, significantly reducing fat around the abdomen. Nowadays, almost everyone who sees me exclaims: "Wow, how did you get so slim?" My weight has not actually changed, just that muscles replaced fats and my metabolism has become more efficient and balanced.

Second, it improves body alignment.

I always thought that perfect balance was impossible – our feet have very slight differences in size, and both our shoulders will differ in height. In actuality, many imbalances and asymmetries in the body are caused by long-term bad habits. For example, when I was young, I used to splay my right foot outward while cycling, causing my right knee to shift off its natural vertical axis, leading to knee pain when running for extended periods. Pilates helps you correct these bodily imbalances, reducing risk of injury in daily life and exercise. This is why CK named his studio 'Body Concept.'

Third, it has inspired my personal philosophy.

For example, CK once told me: Use the least effort to make the best movement. Everything in nature is harmonious and perfect, so a good movement must require minimal effort.

If you exert too much force, your movements become distorted and other parts of your body will have to compensate. Is this not the case as well in both business management and daily life? This is the foundation of minimalist philosophy: using the fewest resources to achieve perfect functionality. It has become a key guiding principle in my aesthetics and work.

Hence, I highly recommend everyone practise Pilates. It might just be the start of your second spring. Refine your body, revitalize your spirit and embark on a more mature, more wonderful journey of life!

3 April, 2019

FROM DEPARTURE TO ENTRY

What kinds of things are worthy of
being luxury goods?
I think it should be something that
can hardly be bought with money.
What kinds of things can hardly
be bought with money?
The spiritual, the sincere, love –
these are the finest things in life.

LUXURY GOODS

It seems that Asians find it particularly difficult to resist the lure of luxury goods.

From time immemorial, the upper classes and the wealthy have deployed exorbitant products and brands to flaunt their status and differentiate themselves from the great unwashed – but not only do products draw the distinction, so too do spiritual and cultural aspects. As Japan, Korea, as well as the greater China sphere of Hong Kong (PRC) and Taiwan (PRC), experienced rapid economic development, they, with equal rapidity, became devotees of European and American luxury goods. In recent years in China, with the arrival of a wealthy class and the senior white-collar stratum, Chinese people have been scrambling madly like a gaggle of geese for luxury brands like Hermès, Chanel, Gucci and LV, as well as Rolls Royce, Mercedes Benz and Ferrari.

Mob godfathers in Hong Kong (PRC) resort to Hermès bags to hit on girls; middle-aged matronly plaza dancing enthusiasts will sling an LV bag (unconcerned if it is genuine or fake) over their shoulder to shop in the wet market. At one of our Hanting Hotels on Shimen Road in Shanghai you can often see young men who are staying in the hotel driving Ferraris or Porsches, and similar spectacles are also frequently seen in Hangzhou and Nanjing.

The frenzy for luxury goods in Japan has calmed somewhat as second-hand consignment shops in Tokyo and

Osaka display a lot of luxury goods in post-frenzy efforts at 'stock reduction.' With the fall of the price of oil, shopping sprees by Middle Easterners has gradually subsided. In future, the majority of today's luxury brands will be downgraded to middle-class brands – finally the nobility will disappear to be replaced by the new middle class. Only the far-sighted companies which truly understand the real meaning of luxury will persevere to launch products that will be the luxury goods of the new era.

I once witnessed a bunch of Russian tycoons flaunting their wealth in southern France, while the French people nearby did not show any signs of appreciation or envy. I couldn't help wondering why people in developed countries are rather more cool-headed in their attitude toward luxury goods.

Superior quality and beautiful things are good, and using them can be pleasurable but they do not necessarily bring happiness. I think this is the key.

What are the luxury goods of this era? Here's a popular meme about the world's latest top ten luxuries:

1. The awakening and enlightenment of life
2. An unrestrained heart filled with joy and love
3. The courage to explore the world
4. Return to nature
5. Peaceful sleep
6. To have space and time for ourselves
7. To be mutually loving soulmates
8. Someone in your life who truly understands you
9. Healthy body and healthy mind
10. Hope that can inspire ourselves and others

Not a single item on this list is material, they are all spiritual.

What sort of products can be luxury goods? My answer is, things that can't be bought with money. Spiritual things, dedication, love. These are the world's true first-class items.

Buddhism holds intent to be very important, that is to say the starting point, the motive for doing something, is important. When a master craftsman makes a leather suitcase, he fuses the best traditional workmanship into the suitcase because it gives him joy and happiness, and no matter what brand it carries, that suitcase will be a luxury good.

When our staff clean a guest room, they are in a happy place thinking about how their salary will pay for their child's school fees, or enable them to buy a present for their parents-in-law, so they will be diligent cleaning the room, making the bed, folding the quilt, placing the pillows. This room will be a luxury item far exceeding the luxury-level of the hotel's brand.

I've heard that in the old-school cigar rolling factories in Cuba, a person is allocated to read classics of world literature over the PA system, such as *The Hunchback of Notre Dame* by Victor Hugo and *The Count of Monte Cristo* by Alexandre Dumas. The cigars produced by these factories are mesmerizing.

From the point of view of commercial products, luxury products that bring happiness have the following characteristics: they are creative, compassionate and environmentally friendly, things that cannot be bought with money, but these characteristics are exactly the things we in this materially advanced era especially value.

Ji Hotels, mother's cooking and children of a couple who are in love, are my most treasured luxury items.

25 June, 2017

MY CIRCLE OF FRIENDS

Dunbar's number is based on the limited size of the cortex of the human brain, which means that people's cognitive ability can maintain at most 150 stable relationships. The number refers to the upper limit of friends with whom a person can have a personal friendship.

The British anthropologist Robin Dunbar researched primates and discovered that baboons became closer through mutual grooming. When humans developed the faculty of speech several hundred thousand years ago, the ability to socialize increased and the ability of the human brain to process thought also increased. This limit of 150 is derived from a calculation based on the complexity of the human brain.

In a group of five people, the members will have ten sets of bilateral relationships; in a group with 20 members the number of bilateral relationships grows to 190 sets; groups with 50 members have 1,225 bilateral relationships. These social relationships need a big brain. The larger the brain, the larger the social groupings humans can deal with. Because of biological limits, however, humans cannot have the ability to process communities of unlimited size.

Most people can only build substantial relationships with 150 people, and they cannot go very far beyond this figure. From a cognitive point of view, we are not born with brains equipped to do so. Once a group exceeds 150 people, the relationships between members begin to weaken.

Despite ever-advancing sophistication in modern societies and rising cultural levels, social interactions today are no different to those of the Stone Age. Dunbar says that 150 seems to be the upper limit of human social interactions, that is, relationships in which we know the people and know their relationship with us.

Dunbar's discovery can be seen in all sorts of groupings of 150 people.

Surveying Western military history, we can see that the smallest combat unit, the company, is usually 150 strong. The materials manufacturer GORE-TEX limits the number of employees at branches to 150. If the numbers increase, the company creates two branches and builds a new administrative office. A statistical analysis of the number of Christmas cards sent from London revealed an average number of 153.5 cards sent by each person. Of that number, about one quarter of the cards were sent to relatives, two thirds to friends and eight percent to colleagues.

In general, we have about five closest friends, including family and close female friends, as they are our most intimate friends. Next come 15 close friends. Within this circle you can reveal your true feelings or seek consolation. The sad news of the passing of one of these friends will inflict serious pain. Next come 50 people, which is the size of groups of hunter gatherers in Oceania and Africa who passed the night together. Maintaining stable relationships is limited to 150 people because a larger number is too complicated to manage. These numbers increase by about a factor of three.

Dunbar has other interesting discoveries: ordinary friendships can survive a lack of face-to-face communications for about 6 to 12 months; women can have two best friends (including their spouses) but men only have one.

Dunbar was asked whether digital technology can enable people to maintain friendships and also make new friends and expand their social networks. He decisively said,

"No!" He followed up with, "At least that's the way it looks at the present."

America's most famous social media platform is Facebook, but that was preceded by YouTube, Twitter and the job market social network platform LinkedIn. In China there's Sina weblog, Sina Weibo, WeChat and QQ, but WeChat is the most popular. When people meet, especially young people, they exchange their WeChat names first, and name cards not so much. We have many WeChat groups in our company for social contacts and sharing posts, far outnumbering email exchanges.

I have noticed that many people have been entrapped by social media. Digital social networking, like the WeChat moments function, for example. WeChat was originally an instant communications tool that was easy to use, in much the same way as WhatsApp functions outside China. It can send images, voice and text. The algorithm is very good, and the transmission is very fast. The social networking function on WeChat called Moments can help you know the latest developments with your friends, and we can send interesting things to the group.

Some people like to share pictures of their children, some love to share food porn, some people share their travel photos ... when a circle of friends is 15 you will enjoy looking because they are your close friends and you are happy to be in on their every trifle. But when the number grows to 50, 150 or even several hundred or several thousand, and it fills up with all sorts of these people's personal trivia, will you still feel happy? How much more so if the posts include feel-good motivational memes, fake pictures of beautiful faces, sensationalized clickbait, annoying advertisements, and a mixture of self-media from people with good or bad intentions?

There are the annoying monikers and handles that become so confusing you have no way of knowing, who is who. And then there's the overwhelming number of WeChat groups that you feel too embarrassed to leave ...

And because we carry our mobile phone with us wherever we go, when an instant message arrives from a social media platform like WeChat, the notification often interrupts us, fragmenting our time. It becomes difficult to have time to think or to stare into space or to just enjoy some quiet. The most irksome times are traditional Chinese festivals, as WeChat greetings, like an information bombardment, gradually supersede SMS text messages, making it impossible to hide.

Because of this, many people are trapped by this communication tool. Living in a mobile phone, wasting time, ignoring the real world and real feelings, diminishes the intellect. Mobile phones and social media are causing people to become lost.

I have come up with some methods to tackle this problem:

NO. 1

Set up a private WeChat account. I think dual function products like the iPod (which can act as both a desktop or a mobile computer) will gradually replace notebook computers, so bind the original WeChat account to an iPad to use for email and browsing the web for regular office use only, and no need to look at it unless there's a reason. IPads are sufficiently large to be inconvenient to carry around, so it won't disrupt your day. Sometimes, when I don't look at WeChat for half a day, or even a whole day, the sky doesn't fall. Especially urgent issues can be dealt with by phone or face-to-face, and nothing will be neglected. Particularly important matters can be handled by email which is safer and easier to file away. My private WeChat account has only 31 contacts, and adhering to the Dunbar Law, I will not allow it to exceed 50 people.

NO. 2

Withdraw from groups and dismantle groups. Some groups are too clamorous, so just withdraw. Some of the social media groups set up by my university classmates have over one hundred postings on some nights. I have turned on the 'do not disturb' function, but how can I possibly review that much news? There might be some useful information there somewhere, but it's hard to find. I decided to leave the WeChat group, yet the camaraderie with my classmates is unaffected – at least that's what I think.

I am obsessively tidy. I do not keep a single unnecessary item in my office and my study. My desk is always neat and clean. Although WeChat can be muted, I still feel it is disruptive. After reading or dealing with something, I delete it so that my WeChat screen is nice and clean. Either something is unread or waiting action, but all irrelevant items are deleted. I save important essays and news items.

It's the same with email; I only file important emails.

Over time I started quite a few groups which I am now making a conscious effort to dismantle. Apart from groups connected with work and close personal friends, only one group remains: Beautiful Life. This is comprised of close friends, all of whom are very interesting people who usually share things of interest, like food or fun places to visit. Many of these friends are artists who sometimes share things of beauty.

NO. 3

Close the Moments function on WeChat. I have gradually shut down most of the Moments groups to avoid being distracted by information not relevant to me. I keep Moments groups of some close friends who share high quality posts, as well as friends connected with work. I still skim friends' Moments and stop to read when I see something that looks interesting. I save good articles to read later. I print important articles with a high quality ink-jet printer on heavy 180-gram paper. It's not like I go through a cleansing and burn incense, but I am more conscientious when I read them.

NO. 4

Read the WeChat public platforms that you find interesting. Quite a few of these platforms are well done, like 'Read a Poem for You' and 'New Ways of the World' which are quite literary. Naturally, the H World public platform is essential reading because I often use it.

NO. 5

Resubscribe to magazines and maintain the reading habit. I have subscribed to magazines I like, such as *Chinese National Geography*, *Joint Publishers Life Weekly* and *Life*. Magazine editors ensure content is usually of a high standard and the writers possess the necessary skills. More importantly magazines are not a daily distraction, arriving weekly or monthly with content that is worth reading.

This is even more true for books. It is worth spending time to read carefully the works that have stood the test of time, and to learn from the experience of wise people to become exposed to the essential wisdom of humanity. As a rule, I do not read 'chicken soup for the soul' like the latest fashionable books or management canonical texts. I mainly read religious, philosophical and literary masterpieces.

I usually write to put my own thoughts in order, to record things I've seen or heard, or to explain my views.

Doing this, at the least I can avoid excessive fragmentation of ideas and steer clear of the fashionable and the tacky.

In this fragmented era, we should invest our time in things that are truly worthy – carefully choose things and then do your best. Give the people you care about as much of your time as possible to show genuine love to them.

The convenience of modern communication tools can lead to being inundated with information, and easily fragment our lives. This can be the beginning of mediocrity. In this age of fission, the most valuable things are to cultivate inner strength, hold fast to one's true self, and cherish the people and things you care about the most.

We must be calm to be able to hear our inner voice.

22 May, 2016

SOLITUDE

We usually do not get much time alone to ourselves. Most of it is spent among social groups: coworkers, family, friends, classmates ... Intentional or otherwise, humans are always involved in social settings and, because of this, have developed language, words and other communication methods. This, in turn, gave rise to clans, ethnic groups, nations, political parties and other human organizations.

Someone said this is the root reason that humans have surpassed other animals. Perhaps! The human obsession with socialization and group activities is an obvious phenomenon.

We came to this world alone and bawling. Unfamiliarity, confusion, and even some pain, are raw expressions of crying.

Our deep sense of loneliness may have stemmed from this moment. Because we hope to be accepted, to find companions, friends, integrate into society, join social groups and activities: meals, bars, tea ceremonies, outdoors trips, karaoke, clubs.

This impulse is particularly intense in younger people. They have just turned into adults, leaving their mother's embrace and family's warmth and security. Their self-awareness has truly awoken for the first time, that chilling loneliness stirring in their subconscious. They cannot wait to seek integration, find companionship, escape loneliness and keep solitude far away.

Even future heroes are no exception. In his dedication in the translated work of *Jean-Christophe*, Fu Lei said, "Warrior, when you know you are not the only one suffering in this world, your pain will surely lessen, and your hope will be forever reborn from the depths of despair!"

This innate loneliness is deeply buried in your subconscious and follows you throughout your life. We are afraid to sleep alone when we are young. We fear loneliness when we are adults. These are all tricks of the subconscious. Our fear of solitude far exceeds the pain of other matters and, most of the time, we can too easily avoid such situations. Especially in times of prolonged solitude – we will always find various ways to escape.

As an extreme example, the thing that prisoners fear most is not beatings, hunger or hard labor, but solitary confinement – prohibiting them from talking to anyone, completely and utterly alone trapped in a claustrophobic space. Even if they are allowed to eat and sleep normally, the prisoner will feel like they are going crazy and so usually cannot bear such punishment. Eventually they will all cooperate.

Because of particular reasons, some people cannot socialize for prolonged periods, having to stay home instead. Though they are with their families, their alone time is greatly extended – their experience with solitude becomes intimate, sometimes not in the best way. Many people struggle to adapt, becoming lethargic, anxious, irritated and depressed. In some cases, some even develop mental illnesses or suicidal thoughts.

In reality, being able to be alone, especially for long periods, is a skill and power in itself. Most people cannot do it. In fact, the vast majority cannot. It does not matter how strong or stubborn you are; these factors cannot resist the invasion of feelings of loneliness. You will finally succumb to that abyssal sense of loneliness devouring you.

Solitude is entirely a spiritual strength that has nothing to do with your magnitude of authority or wealth. Those who possess true and strong faith can be alone. Through philosophy, science and other recognized methods, those who have grasped eternity and meaning can be alone.

Through meditation, marathons, extreme sports or other methods to enter their flow state, those who have experienced the relativity of time, can be alone. Only those with immense spiritual strength are able to enjoy solitude without reason to escape it.

Schopenhauer was one such philosopher possessing resolute mental strength. He enjoyed being alone and thought that "a man can be himself only so long as he is alone."

To validate your own true strength, if you are the few who surpass the many, being alone for long periods of time is an evaluation method.

Of course, some will find it a piece of cake! When you watch shows and scroll short videos, time flies by fast. You will not be lonely or find it difficult to be.

When we are alone, we usually choose those easy shallow distractions to stimulate our senses and fill the void in our hearts. But, when your dopamine hit has passed, you are only left with an even bigger void of emptiness and loneliness!

We came to this world alone, and we will walk our final journey alone, leaving this world just as we came. Learning to be alone is an essential practice in our lives.

Of course, many will fail, and succumb to the indolence of human nature, going with the flow. Schopenhauer put it even more absolutely when he said that "In this world, with only a few exceptions, we really have only the choice between solitude and vulgarity." He also said, "Whoever does not love solitude does not love freedom either."

Born into this ever-changing world, this major turning point of human society, this era of unprecedented upheaval, the practice of being alone may be one of the most useful lessons of all. It can let us observe this world in silence, with a peace of mind, harmoniously blending into myriad possible changes, sparking vitality around us.

17 July, 2022

THE POWER OF QUIETUDE

Those who have read *Robinson Crusoe* will unfortunately remember that the most excruciating situation for a person stranded on a deserted island or drifting along the unfathomable sea, is having no one to talk to, or finding no one familiar. In such circumstances, the weak of mind might go mad or resort to irrational behaviour.

Young people are similar. They get bored easily, always needing to stay occupied to feel at ease. Simmer alone for too long, and they have to look for friends to meet for meals or other activities.

If a person can withstand solitude and boredom, is able to be alone for long periods and silently face their inner selves – that is a very impressive feat.

I have a belief that the less one needs external things, the more perfect this person is. The greater the difference between you and what you need externally, the more diminished you become.

Enjoying fine wine and dining, luxury goods, sports cars – these material pleasures that can bring you joy and happiness are at a lower state. When your happiness is not derived externally, but from within, that is a more perfect realm.

You not only know how to navigate the world, but you can also be at peace alone. You can move, and you can be still, weaving between states.

Imagine a still lake: When it rains, ripples form; when the wind blows, waves rise; when a stone is thrown, the surface is disturbed ... but slowly, everything returns to a calm, mirror-like state.

There are several ways to achieve this level of absolute inner peace (some call it the flow state).

Marathons are one. Hiking, long-distance cycling and other intense sports are also examples. Extreme physical activity lets you shed all the earthly bonds, leaving only the monotonous, mindless process of putting one foot in front of the other, to keep going ... Eventually, you might reach a realm where time and space vanish – that is the flow state. It is dynamic calmness.

Another method is meditation. Zen Buddhism, Taoist meditation, yogic mindfulness, as well as Christian and Islamic prayers, all fall into this category. Through breathing or repetitive chanting, or very devoted prayer, one can reach a state of selflessness, where the concept of time weakens. Often, it feels like time has shortened. An hour of silent sitting might feel like only 15 minutes, sometimes even as if space has disappeared. This is a relatively easy way to enter the flow state.

There are also other ways and methods, but some are not advisable, and others are unreliable or unpredictable, so are not worth recommending.

A mature person, someone who wants to elevate their soul, should find a method that best resonates with them in order to find that feeling of absolute peace within. Your life may yet change.

Technological progress, material abundance, more invented creations and even scientific advancements pale in comparison to the importance of humanity regaining inner peace. Humanity's next leap is not in technology or science, nor wealth and power, but in the elevation of human spirituality.

And having a peaceful heart, a state where one can calm down at any time, is the beginning of spiritual elevation. The strength imbued within will surprise you.

A true hero is someone who can be both still and dynamic, who can open and close, who can step up and let go. As the saying goes: "Openly lead like a general, with golden spear and iron steed; close threads like an embroiderer, with care as fine as a hair."

To be able to open and close in measure, to move and stop with order, is to be like the butcher who carves the ox with effortless skill, "it is done without effort!" Only then can we calmly "stand with the sword, survey our surroundings with determined pride" and "know how to hide a skilled blade."

28 August, 2020

BUSINESS AND FRIENDSHIP

I'm a sentimental person. And this dictates how I run a business. I have two principles: One, I work with people I know. Two, I work with people who share my values.

'Working with people I know' does not mean only doing business with close friends and associates. Instead, it refers to forming friendships with people I work with. We become friends through work and shared ideals. These people may not become personal friends but often they are more reliable than personal friends. A friendship that is built on shared ideals, shared goals and shared interests, is solid. For example, I have built a friendship with people who work for the publishing house that published the Chinese edition of this book. Our collaboration did not end with publishing my book. During the editing process, I invited the editing team to meals. Together, we tasted wine, we appreciated tea and delighted in flowers. Along the way, we got to know each other and exchanged ideas. I always hope to find more human connections and friendships in business collaborations, since we all live busy lives and do not have a lot of time to attend parties and go to bars to socialize.

Why do many people like to bring business negotiations to the dining table? This is because sensory pleasures make people happy. And a happy mood is good for business negotiations. Business deals that are mutually beneficial can also bring happiness and friendships.

I had thought foreigners are all business oriented. Later I realized it is not true at all, especially after I started doing business with French people. People in the West will not do business with you simply because the business deal is big. Instead, they do business with you because of friendship and trust.

The foundation of a friendship is shared values. There are some enterprises you should not work with despite lucrative return prospects because of vastly different moral values. The purpose of our company is to grow and make the world a better place, but not every company shares this virtuous goal.

How do we understand the values held by our business partners? We can have drinks together, we can have long conversations, we can go hiking together. I like to invite them to participate in my favourite activities. I like to hike. When Accor's co-founder Paul Dubrule visited me at home, I took him hiking. He suffers from acrophobia but still made it to the top of the mountain because he wanted to embrace what I like. He also shares with me what he likes. For example, Dubrule likes the work of a photographer, so he invited me to the exhibition and even gave me a work by the photographer as a present. Initially, the work did not excite me, but I tried to learn more about the photographer and later became more familiar with his work. Our mutual understanding deepened through this sharing.

Of course, once we know each other better, I no longer take him to climb high mountains. To requite his presents, I gave him an artwork that I like and told him what I like about it. This exchanging of presents is friendship. Of course, the small presents will not affect our business decisions, but through this interchange of views and presents, we understand each other better. Of course, we are very different, but we can overcome differences.

As time goes by, life brings me sedimentary accretion of old friends. Some friends have a profound influence on me. As a fresh university graduate from Jiao Tong University, a prestigious university in China, I once had a sense of superiority, believing I had figured out the most complex questions on Earth.

I had read many translated works by Western scholars, from Bertrand Russell's *A History of Western Philosophy*, to works by Immanuel Kant, Nietzsche, Arthur Schopenhauer and Freud. I was convinced that there was nothing I could not understand. As a science major, I thought I had successfully crossed the disciplinary boundary of knowledge. This attitude was common among university students in my generation. We felt on top of the world. This kind of superior attitude did help me with my career. Pride, assertiveness and confidence motivated me to chase commercial success.

Because of this pride, I once looked down on people with lower academic qualifications. Even people who graduated from a less prestigious university were not good enough for me. I thought I was another Nietzsche, a member of the philosophical elite.

But two people changed me. One is Zhang Yong, founder of Haidilao International, a chain of hot pot restaurants; the other is Wang Jianbin, chairman of the Chengdu Mingzhu Furniture Group, one of the largest furniture manufacturers in China. Zhang Yong only completed a junior high school education, but he has a profound grasp of business and human nature – an ability he developed by hanging out on the streets from a very young age. Wang Jianbin is also a good friend of mine. We have had many in-depth conversations. His empathy for people is superior to mine – he was born to have the heart of a Buddha. When he was only a child, his parents were not able to care for him and his younger brother and sister. Wang had to look after his siblings on his own. People in the village bullied him. One neighbor even threw faeces in their beds. In that bitterly cold winter, the siblings did not have a spare quilt, so they had to cuddle together and pile layers of clothes on themselves to keep warm. Years later, when Wang Jianbin learned that a neighbor was diagnosed with cancer, he donated thousands of yuan to the neighbor without hesitation. His actions had a profound impact on me. Both Zhang Yong and Wang Jianbin are successful entrepreneurs from Sichuan

Province who do not have high academic qualifications. They have made me realize that wisdom does not always come from knowledge taught in classrooms. Wisdom from the streets, an in-depth understanding of human nature, and compassion are far more important.

Human interaction is the most important aspect in all business and partnerships. In Chinese, the so-called *jiang hu*, literally 'rivers and lakes,' simply means society. The big society refers to the society we live in, the small society is the milieu we find ourselves in. Shared values are the most fundamental aspect of a society and human interaction. Nowadays, I only partner with people who share values with me. Otherwise, I can choose not to enter into a business deal. We can now afford to be selective in choosing business partners, including suppliers. We will not engage in bribery and other corrupt practices which are rampant in China. If a hotel guest does not respect our employees, for example, being verbally or physically abusive toward our employees, the guest will be blacklisted and will be denied service in the future.

It is often said that the customer is God, but I disagree. I believe customers should be our friends and relatives, and they should be equal. Who really is God? You are the master and you are even more superior than a master. You can punch me and swear at me and I must do nothing except say, "I am sorry." I believe this is wrong. We and our customers are equal, and the basis of equality is mutual respect. Only on such a foundation can a reliable cooperative relationship be established. Being equal partners is a healthy, win-win proposition, and it is also sustainable.

There is little common ground for understanding between persons of differing principles. For individuals and companies alike, the most important basis of cooperation is shared values. For this reason, I made a point of adding a line to the H World mission statement, "A group of like-minded friends happily working together to achieve something great."

1 April, 2018

FROM BUDDHIST RENUNCIATION TO SOCIAL ENGAGEMENT

If we look beyond the social level of human beings, looking at the human species from the spiritual perspective, all human behaviour, including love and religious practice, seems to be laughable. What is the point of pursuing it? Groups of different faiths are fighting with each other. This group builds a temple and another group builds a church. All of these activities are for what purpose? When we look down at the human species from outer space, we will perceive the insignificance of everything in our lives, be it languages, written texts, our behaviour or our faiths. The conflicts, wealth and fame, narcissistic thoughts and self-righteousness, are like passing clouds.

I am fond of the Song dynasty, for I think the aesthetics during that period were remarkably advanced. However, such an advanced culture was defeated by an unsophisticated culture, by war horses and swords. Alas! I used to grieve for the fate of the Song dynasty. But when I looked at the issue from the universe's perspective, my viewpoint changed. The fate of the Song, after all, is insignificant for the universe. The Tao models itself on nature. Renowned photographer Chen Man once shared a short movie with me: A small boy is playing soccer in a park while his parents dotingly watch him. It was perhaps in New York's Central Park. Then the camera zooms out, from Central Park to New York City, to America, to the Earth, then to the centre of the universe. From this perspective, what's the difference between Central Park and New York city? And what is the difference between a child and two adults? The boy looks adorable. It's a sunny day. Birds are flying across the park. Two squirrels are climbing a tree. Suddenly, the child falls to the ground and the parents rush over to help him get up. Everything looks perfect. Looking at the world close up after viewing it from afar is a good idea.

Zen Buddhism is in the same realm. Buddhist renunciation is not easy to achieve, and re-engagement is not easy either.

For a while I was reluctant to go to a temple in Hangzhou, the same temple where the Chinese scholar and artist Li Shutong (1880–1942) was ordained as a monk in 1918.

At that low point in my life, I could not see the meaning of my existence. I worried that I might decide to be ordained. After this period, I became more socially engaged. I embarked on another entrepreneurial adventure and started a family. Many years later, I returned to the story of Li Shutong and reread Buddhist works. I realized that religions provide shelter for people, and the act of Buddhist renunciation is a form of escape.

Now I think the best state of mind is to treat our world as both Heaven and Hell. And more importantly, treat it as a Bodhimaṇḍa, a place of enlightenment. In this life, I have come to this world for enlightenment. My actions in this process are to strive to be perfect, both physically and spiritually. I like good wine and good food, so I let myself enjoy them. I love my adorable children and my virtuous wife. I do my best to run a successful business and fulfil my social responsibilities. As for the spiritual aspect, occasionally I may look at this world through the eyes of Buddha for but an instant.

I think this is the best state of mind.

7 April, 2018

INFORMATION AND ENERGY

Many people do not trust Chinese medicine. I think the reason is the lack of genuinely good practitioners. Chinese medicine is an art form, an exquisite art form that is very different to Western medicine. Chinese medicine's predicament is that there are too many quacks and cheats who ruin the profession's reputation.

Chinese medicine, like Tibetan, Indian and Western medicine, is the result of people in a particular region drawing conclusions from natural information. There is some truth in these conclusions, as no one person possesses absolute truth, just as no one is absolutely in error. We cannot afford to hold absolutist attitudes. The Japanese operate Chinese medicine practices very well, which goes to show that we should use a scientific attitude and scientific methods to decide what to accept or reject.

I see the relationship of Western and Chinese medicine as being very similar to the relationship of Western realist art and the Chinese freehand style of painting. In Chinese medical practice it is all too easy to deceive people, but to do it well is no easy task. It is an art form that is an inheritance of traditions, including the use of traditional tools, to create a unique treatment plan for each patient.

This world is composed of information and energy, and the information that constitutes each person is different, and the distribution of energy is also different. People exchange information between each other. What I say may influence your life, and if the influence is sufficiently great, it might change your life. I believe that some of the therapeutic methods of Chinese medicine can create this kind of influence.

Take acupuncture and moxibustion, for example. What do they do? They change the way we process information. It's wrong to think that it's just as easy as sticking a needle wherever you don't feel comfortable.

I once went through a very anxious phase, complete with distressed dreams, like running late for an exam but being unable to find my bicycle. There are lots of bikes, but I can't find mine and I have to frantically go through the whole lot, one by one. Acupuncture and moxibustion can provide gradual relief for this kind of anxiety. In the past, when I was under stress, I would have similar dreams three or four times a month, but nowadays, hardly ever. When I meditate, I used to feel my thoughts were confused, I had too many ideas, and my brain felt like it was suffering from insomnia, but I became calmer after acupuncture and moxibustion treatment. Modern science currently cannot explain the mysterious information and energy of Chinese medicine, but scientific research will eventually uncover these mysteries.

As a science major at university, I did not comprehend these ideas until the last two or three years. What are scientific viewpoints? If something can't be measured, then it doesn't exist. In reality, our knowledge and experience are insufficient to understand these non-rational things. My approach is to open that window and have an open attitude to attain understanding. You may not necessarily believe in something, but you can open your mind.

I am not a believer in mysticism, but my attitude is open. At the very least, a world without a sense of mystery is boring.

22 April, 2018

METAPHYSICS AND PHYSICS

"Ji Qi, were you born to be in the hotel business?" Many people ask me that. I am not sure what I was born to do, and do not have a strong feeling about this matter. From the moment I was born, the universe added one more life, a life which is a combination of information and energy. In Buddhist terms, it was a creation of a union of causes and conditions. This new-born entity determines the rest of our life. An infant is in a state when the entropy is extremely low, and the entropy is even lower at the moment the sperm meets the egg. It was at an infinite smallness at the moment that determines the infinite greatness in the future.

I started to think about metaphysical issues in my university days. My subsequent experience in life is a physical reflection of my musing.

I vividly remember the day I was at the gate of Jiao Tong University on Huashan Road, in front of a statue engraved with a line that reads 'Gratitude and Responsibility.' Gazing at the nearby plane trees, I pondered the meaning of life. At the moment, when I was asking questions about metaphysical issues, I was enlightened with some answers that relate to the physical aspect of life: Life is a process. For the noumenon, there is no meaning. Meaning can only be defined by objects. For the noumenon, life is experience. My subsequent life experience – my business, my romantic loves, my family and everything else in my life – is the physical reflection of my musing of metaphysics in life.

Metaphysical matters relate to choices made by the noumenon. In this universe, when the metaphysics of the noumenon were decided at its initial moment, the noumenon does have possibilities and rights to choose. The possibilities at that moment are infinite. As the noumenon makes its choice, the noumenon's physical reflection begins and it is the only reflection.

Information and energy come from the cosmos. Though I do not know what this energy is, I firmly believe every single noumenon can choose. Otherwise, life would not have meanings. If our lives were truly ordained by God, then our existence will have no meaning other than being a circus. In fact, we can make decisions for our lives, by reading, thinking, experiencing and communicating with others, by drinking wine, sipping tea, by making friends, acquiring knowledge, collecting salaries, and by working with our bosses and colleagues.

From an infinite amount of possibilities, you made one unique choice. This choice comes with certainty and it is a source for both joy and sadness. It is a joyful matter because the choice makes you. It is a sad matter because by making this choice you have missed the other infinite number of possibilities.

26 April, 2018

OUR GREAT ERA

I often hear people say that anxiety is the epidemic of the times, because the youth of today is more plagued by anxiety than previous generations. I feel, on the contrary, that each and every generation is anxious, because everyone is situated in their 'own great era.'

So, there's no need to be conceited and think, "I'm different, I'm special," because it's not at all the case. When my generation was young, we also thought we were special. I was very egotistical after graduating from university, certain that the world was at my feet. I loved reading Nietzsche. I believed I was the Sun and the people around me were the stars. Youth are arrogant like that; it's human nature.

Is now a good era, or a bad one? I think the answer lies within us. When we regard the era to be a good one, we will perceive that everything is good, just as when we feel it's a bad era, everything before our eyes looks desolate. Our innermost thoughts are very important; though that may be idealistic, it certainly is true.

A great era implies there will be even more turmoil and more of the unknown. Youth these days indeed do experience anxiety because of their many desires, and the enticements and tensions of this era are indeed bigger than ever, but I believe the youth will find their own tempo and place in the world. Some will quietly live an ordinary life in a small town, while others will rush to the frontlines of the struggles of the day. But no matter what, they will realize life's wonders. My generation will age and not be able to take our riches and fame with us in our coffins. My once glorious generation will have to make way for the next generation. So, this will become 'their era.'

At the end of this book, I want to say to my readers, especially the young readers, don't be impatient, set your mind at ease. With your mind at ease you can concentrate on thriving and establishing yourselves. Otherwise, it will be all too easy to just blindly follow the crowd. In the past, I was far too impatient, and if I had been able to set my mind at ease earlier and not allowed my childhood experience of hardship to make me so anxious, I would be much more successful now. When you set your mind at ease, the pace at which you work, the way you treat people and the way you treat your business partners is different. I used to be hot tempered and I was known to scold people working in my companies. Later I realized there was no need to be like that and felt I should be more empathetic and tolerant.

A calm heart is very powerful and will ultimately lead you to the place where you want to be.

29 April, 2018

REALM OF THE HEART

BY JI QI